TRUTH, LIES, AND ADVERTISING

Adweek Books is designed to present interesting, insightful books for the general business reader and for professionals in the worlds of media, marketing, and advertising.

These are innovative, creative books that address the challenges and opportunities of these industries, written by leaders in the business. Some of our writers head their own companies, others have worked their way up to the top of their field in large multinationals. But they share a knowledge of their craft and a desire to enlighten others.

We hope readers will find these books as helpful and inspiring as *Adweek, Brandweek,* and *Mediaweek* magazines.

Published

Disruption: Overturning Conventions and Shaking up the Marketplace, Jean-Marie Dru

"Hey, Whipple, Squeeze This!": A Guide to Creating Great Ads, Luke Sullivan

Truth, Lies, and Advertising: The Art of Account Planning, Jon Steel

Under the Radar: Talking to Today's Cynical Consumer, Jonathan Bond & Richard Kirshenbaum

Forthcoming

Eating the Big Fish: How "Challenger Brands" Can Compete Against Brand Leaders, Adam Morgan

TRUTH, LIES, AND ADVERTISING

The Art
of Account Planning

by Jon Steel

John Wiley & Sons, Inc.

New York • Chichester • Weinheim • Brisbane • Singapore • Toronto

Library of Congress Cataloging-in-Publication Data:
Steel, Jon.
    Truth, Lies, and Advertising: The Art of Account Planning.
    Jon Steel.
      p.   cm. — (Adweek books)
    Includes bibliographical references and index.
    ISBN 0-471-18962-6 (cloth : alk. paper)
    1. Advertising campaigns—United States—Planning.
    2. Advertising—United States. 3. Advertising agencies—Customer services—United States. I. Title. II. Series.
    HF5837.S73   1998
    659.1'11—dc21   97-40334
                                            CIP

Printed in the United States of America.
10 9 8 7 6 5 4 3

This book is dedicated to
Ethel Alice Morris
1904–1993

Contents

Introduction
Firing Blanks

Is advertising worth saving? From an economic point of view I don't think that most of it is. From an aesthetic point of view I'm damn sure it's not; it is thoughtless, boring, and there is simply too much of it.

Howard Luck Gossage

More than 30 years ago, Howard Gossage, a legendary San Francisco advertising man, gave an interview to *Time* magazine in which he said of advertising, "I don't know a single first class brain in the business who has any respect for it." Afterward, he was appalled that none of his industry colleagues were upset by his remark and concluded that it was because they all agreed with him but were too lazy to do anything that might bring them some of that missing respect.

More recently, in 1992, a Gallup poll asked consumers across America to rate 26 different professions according to the degree to which they trusted them.

At the top of the list, with 65 percent of respondents giving them a "very high" or "high" ethical rating, were pharmacists, closely followed by the clergy, college teachers, medical doctors, and policemen. Farther down the list, journalists lay in eleventh place with an ethical rating of 26 percent, senators and lawyers were sixteenth and seventeenth respectively, and real estate agents and congressmen placed nineteenth and twentieth. Languishing in twenty-fifth place, with only an 8 percent ethical rating, just behind insurance salesmen, were advertising practitioners. Only one profession received a lower ethical rating, and I would thus like to suggest that all advertising people reading this should pause for a moment, raise their eyes to the heavens, and give thanks for the very existence of car salesmen.

In my first year working in the United States, I once naively suggested that a commercial my agency had produced might play well in movie theaters. Both my agency colleagues and clients looked at me aghast. "Oh God, no," I was told. "People would go nuts. The movies are the one place where they're not assaulted by advertising. They go there to escape, and we don't want to be the ones to piss them off."

In the eight years that have passed since then, I have come to understand why they felt that way. As I travel around the country conducting research for the agency, talking to people from all walks of life and economic strata, I hear consistent and heartfelt criticism of the way that advertising invades all parts of their lives. Their TV and radio programs are interrupted, their magazines are difficult to read because of all the ads that consume the features, their mailboxes are routinely jammed with unsolicited material, blimps and planes carry messages over their cities, moving images are projected onto the sides of buildings, and their dinnertime conversations are interrupted by telemarketers. The American public is surrounded, with the movie theater as its final line of defense.

In 1990, a study conducted by *The Economist* estimated that the average American is exposed to 3,000 commercial messages a day in "all media." Now I'm always suspicious of statistics, especially averages, because if you think about it, the "average American" has one breast and one testicle, but I wouldn't deny that we all see a lot of advertising. Maybe 3,000 messages is overstating it; other studies are more conservative, estimating anywhere between 150 and 300 exposures in just TV, radio, magazines, and newspapers.

Although I may really have seen or heard 300 messages yesterday, I can *remember* no more than about 10 of them. Of those, I liked and connected to maybe only two or three.

A host of other research suggests that I am not atypical. With remote control units permanently trained on every commercial break, radios on for background noise, and people flicking randomly through magazines, the majority of those 300 potential exposures just vaporize. People do not even need a remote control to successfully ignore advertisements—we have evolved to the point where we can recognize commercials that concern us or interest us and grant them at least a few seconds' attention, while ads that fall into neither of those categories are prevented from taking up valuable brain space by our newly developed mental deflector shields.

It's not that advertising is failing to present itself to its target. It appears in our homes with monotonous regularity, but when it gets there, it often fails to make the necessary connections. I suppose that if advertising were a person (to use a projective technique popular among moderators of qualitative research), it would be a person with a very low sperm count.

A GRENADE TO CATCH A TROUT

The purpose of this book is not to argue that advertising does not work at all, because there is a mountain of evidence to suggest that it does. Companies with higher advertising-to-sales ratios tend to dominate in their categories and on the whole are more profitable. Companies who have advertised during and after recessions have grown at the expense of competitors who have reduced their budgets. Advertising helps turn products into brands; and, in turn, brands build a company's value, sustain higher market share and higher margins, and provide a powerful barrier to competitive entry. All those things are true, and I could have filled this whole book with examples of advertising's effectiveness in building sales, share, and profitability.

Such a history of effective advertising would doubtless contain many examples of campaigns whose success was achieved more by sheer weight and presence than by smart strategic insights or distinctive creative executions. In these examples, audiences were bludgeoned into submission by large budgets and repetition, and I am certain that the advertisers concerned would say that it did not matter that people did not *like* their campaigns, or that some even found them insulting or offensive. As long as they met their objectives and got a return on investment, they were happy.

In an absolute sense, it is hard to argue that those companies are wrong. My argument, however, is more relative than absolute, and it touches on two main areas. First, the environment in which advertising operates has changed. Companies are under intense pressure to increase their earnings and profits year after year, quarter by quarter, month by month, and there is no category in American business where an extra point of market share comes easily. Companies have to fight for distribution, for sales, for margins, and for consumer share of mind, which, as the number of media choices and amount of advertising increases, becomes ever harder to capture. Moreover, as the pressure on the bottom line mounts, the amount of resources at most companies' disposal dwindles, so that every year they are being asked to achieve more, with less.

There are many ways to catch trout. One, which does not require either training or finesse, is to buy a hand grenade, remove the pin, throw the grenade into the pool, and, when it explodes, scoop out the bodies in a net. That is the way that many companies have traditionally advertised, but financial restrictions mean that they now have to find more skillful, intelligent ways of attracting and retaining customers.

While this may be new to some advertisers, others were smart enough to realize it years ago. They were not forced into it by the accountants, but came to it willingly, feeling that there was a better, more thoughtful, human way to advertise than that suggested by the industry rule book. That brings me to my second point. However effective advertising campaigns may have been using the blunt instruments of big budgets, Unique Selling Propositions and repetition, how much more effective might they have been if they had been distinctive and relevant to consumers, as well as omnipresent? How much *less* might they have been able to spend to achieve the same objectives?

BUILDING RELATIONSHIPS

In a speech to the American Association of Advertising Agencies in 1980, Bill Bernbach stated that "at the heart of an effective creative philosophy is the belief that nothing is so powerful as an insight into human nature, what compulsions drive a man, what instincts dominate his action, even though his language so often camouflages what really motivates him. For if you know these things about [a] man you can touch him at the core of his being."

That thought is central to the theme of this book: The best and most effective advertising is that which sets out to *involve* consumers, both in its communication and in the process of developing its message. That may sound obvious (it should), but I believe that very few advertisers and their agencies produce advertising whose message is involving in that way, and that their inability to engage consumers in a dialog or broader relationship is largely a reflection of an outdated, mechanistic philosophy on how advertising works, and a process that keeps consumers, at best, at arm's length. The result is, all too often, advertising that fails to recognize the truth of a consumer's relationship with a product or category, does not connect on a visceral level, and consequently does little or nothing to shift consumer perceptions or behavior. The truth is there to be found, but the client and agency between them either cannot, or will not, see it. The emperor is naked, and no one has noticed.

In Chapter 1, "No Room for the Mouse," I explore some philosophical and structural reasons many advertisers and their agencies find it hard to develop relationships with their consumers. It seems that for many advertisers, the inherent conflict between the forces of art and commerce in advertising is difficult to resolve. This ought not to be an issue, as the desired end result of advertising should be commercial, and art merely one of the means to that end (with different roles, there should thus be no reason to confuse the two). Unfortunately, not everyone in the business sees it that way. Those who regard advertising as an art form have a somewhat arrogant "if-I-create-it-they-will-come" attitude to consumers (and, for that matter, a somewhat naive view of what it's like being a "real" artist), and that is not always conducive to relationship building.

In the end, those who regard advertising as a pure art form are in a minority and rarely have the final say in what advertising finally runs. That responsibility tends to fall to a much larger and scarier group, whose definition of advertising more closely resembles that of a science. This view of advertising-as-science is counterproductive to the aim of embracing consumers, and it is also based on some erroneous assumptions about how *science* is actually practiced, because science itself has changed. The Newtonian approach of observation, measurement, and prediction that has characterized scientific exploration for the past 300 years has been abandoned by many scientists because they found that it was simply not capable of explaining everything. These "new scientists," the pioneers of quantum theory, have an approach to science that fits much more closely with the definition of effective advertising that I previously outlined, focusing on *relationships* as the basis for all definitions and embracing uncertainty and risk as positive forces, rather than trying to eliminate them.

In Chapter 2, "Silent Partners," I take a brief look across the Atlantic to Britain, where 30 or 40 years ago the public's feelings toward advertising were probably even more negative than the ones Howard Gossage described from the same period in the United States. In Britain, though, a remarkable transformation occurred in these attitudes toward advertising in a relatively short period of time, thanks largely to a creative revolution inspired by an American, Bill Bernbach, but also in part to the invention and widespread adoption of a new advertising discipline called *account planning.*

Account planning was conceived as a way for agencies to treat the very affliction that ails so many American advertisers and agencies today, by creating and maintaining meaningful relationships with consumers. The planner's role was basically to embrace consumers as partners in the process of developing advertising, to use their input at every stage of the process to inform and sometimes even inspire creative ideas, and to guide and validate the resulting advertising campaigns. I introduce the discipline and describe its founding principles as a foundation for the descriptions of the *application* of the planner's craft that will form the bulk of the remainder of the book.

One of the main objections to my central premise, that not enough advertisers and agencies truly embrace consumers in the process of developing advertising, comes from companies who protest that they *do* embrace consumers because they "do a lot of research." In Chapter 3, "The Blind Leading the Bland," I suggest that far from embracing consumers, much of the research these companies do has a distancing effect.

It is not my intention to condemn all advertising research, because I am a great believer in its value and power when it is done right. I do, however, point out some of the common abuses that tend to make research not only less useful, but often counterproductive. These range from outdated, Newtonian definitions of the role that research should play in advertising development, to ill-conceived and even shoddy research, and finally to the misinterpretation and incorrect application of research that is in itself very solid.

In Chapter 4, "Peeling the Onion," I present a planner's vision of advertising research, especially ways of thinking about and conducting research that can stimulate the kind of relationships between advertisers and their customers whose absence I have been lamenting. The vital bridge between such research and an advertising campaign—a mysterious form of advertising foreplay known as "creative briefing"—is discussed in Chapter 5, "The Fisherman's Guide." Chapter 6, "Ten Housewives in Des Moines," is devoted to the thorny subject of the research that is commonly done to "test" advertising ideas when they are still in an embryonic form. I prefer to call it "creative development research," for reasons that are explained.

Chapters 4, 5, and 6 are about planning in its broadest sense and focus on the parts of the advertising-development process where I believe the contribution of the planner is most critical: in finding a strategic solution to a problem, in translating that idea into a brief that stimulates creativity, and finally in finding ways to improve on raw creative ideas. I hope to make it clear, though, that the planner him- or herself does not and cannot bear sole responsibility for these tasks. The best advertising solutions, almost without exception, represent the combination of skills and ideas from clients, creative people, and consumers alike. A planner representing consumer opinions in the absence of an insightful client and talented creative people is unlikely to make any advertising any better.

The best advertising solutions also tend to demonstrate the application of common sense and creativity to research, the combination of rational analysis and lateral interpretation, the ascendancy of subjectivity over objectivity and simplicity over complexity, the positive energy that is created by combining several different perspectives, and the celebration of change, uncertainty, and risk as powerful, constructive forces. These are all discussed at various stages of campaign development.

In each of these chapters, my points are illustrated using examples from campaigns that have been developed by my agency, Goodby, Silverstein & Partners, in San Francisco. I chose to use our own advertising, not out of a myopic view of the industry or arrogance about the quality of our work, but rather because I am familiar with the thinking, the research, the creative development process, and the characters involved on both the agency and client sides, and all of that combined means I know in each case what really happened. If I had tried to comment on other agencies' work, I fear that I would have made some incorrect assumptions, and I did not want to make any such mistakes.

While Chapters 4, 5, and 6 feature several different campaigns at several different stages of development, Chapter 7, "Serendipity," focuses on a single campaign, the California Fluid Milk Processors Advisory Board's "got milk?" advertising, following it through *every* stage of development, from the initial client briefing through the first three years in market. I hope that it succeeds in pulling together many of the different themes that run throughout the book.

To pay the maximum possible attention to ways in which intimate relationships can be forged between advertisers and individuals in their target audience, I have chosen to focus this book on the parts of an agency's work that lead *up to* the production of advertising. This means that with the exception of the "got milk?" campaign, I have not discussed in any detail the important issue of campaign evaluation and results.

For the record, I have not included any campaign in these pages that has not worked for the client who paid for it. Each campaign has worked in different ways and to differing degrees, but all have succeeded in meeting, if not exceeding, the objectives set for them. And so far between them, these campaigns—for Bell Helmets, the California Milk Processors, Chevys Mexican Restaurants, Foster Farms, Isuzu, the Northern California Honda Dealers, Norwegian Cruise Line, The Partnership for a Drug Free America, Polaroid, Porsche, Sega, and UNUM—have accounted for one Grand Prix, and nine gold and four silver Effie™ awards from the American Marketing Association for advertising effectiveness.

When Andrew Jaffe of *Adweek* and Ruth Mills of John Wiley & Sons first approached me with the idea of writing this book, they asked me if I would write "a book about account planning." At first I was hesitant, because I had no desire to write a textbook or "how-to" book about planning, and also because I have always found it hard to talk about planning in isolation. The reason I do what I do is that I enjoy developing *advertising,* and planning is simply a means to that end.

As a result, this is at the same time a book about advertising, a book about planning, and also a book about the human relationships that are fundamental not only to successful advertising communication, but also to a happy and productive working relationship between agencies and their clients, and between different individuals and departments within the agency itself. At its best, advertising is simple and engaging, and almost always leaves something to the audience's imagination. The process of developing it should be fun. And in writing this book, I have attempted to reflect those characteristics.

I hope that it will be of interest to people in the industry (on both the agency and client sides) who want to know more about the role that planning plays in the process or how our particular agency operates, and to people outside the industry who are simply curious about the genesis of advertising ideas that they have seen only as consumers. Most of all, though, I hope that both groups will agree, if they succeed in reading beyond this introduction, that it is time for many advertisers to look at their advertising in a

new way, embrace change, and create and build relationships of honesty, affection, and trust with consumers as the
basis of their future campaigns. If so, perhaps we can take a
small step toward realizing Howard Gossage's dream: "I like
to imagine a better world where there will be less, and more
stimulating, advertising. I suppose all of us would like to see
this one come to pass."

If you share that hope, read on.

1

No Room for the Mouse
The Failure to Involve Consumers in Advertising Communication

The consumer isn't a moron. She's your wife.

David Ogilvy
Confessions of an Advertising Man

POINTS OF VIEW

This may seem like a strange way to start a book about advertising, but I have a degree in geography.

One of the few useful things I learned as a student of geography was a navigational technique called *triangulation*. The basic idea is that if you are lost (in my case a most frequent occurrence), it is possible to fix your position quite precisely on a map with the help of a compass, a pencil, and three landmarks that are visible to you in the surrounding countryside and that are also marked on your map. The compass is used to orient the map so that the landmarks on the map line up with the real landmarks, and pencil lines are drawn on the map as if to join the real landmarks and their representations on the map. The three lines should intersect, ideally at a single point, but most often they will form a small triangle. If it's a single point, that's exactly where you are on the map. If it's a triangle, you're somewhere inside it, and your problems are over, unless, of course, the triangle you have drawn appears on a part of the map marked "military firing range."

I should point out that this is a technique that works very well in an area where there are church steeples and easily identifiable hilltops as convenient landmarks, so it is tailor-made for English geography students. But it doesn't work too well in a desert, and the reason it does not is the point of this story. Triangulation needs three landmarks to work, and most deserts just don't have the landmarks. Maybe there's a far-off mountain, but if that's all you can see, it's useless. It allows you to know which direction to walk, but you have no idea how far. It could be 10 miles, or it could be 100. Two landmarks are better than one, but there is still a huge margin for error. Three are needed to work properly.

I mention that because in most fields of human endeavor, the chances of finding a solution or uncovering the truth are increased as more perspectives are taken into account. A commercial that was produced in Britain in the mid-1980s illustrates this point quite graphically (see Figure 1.1).

Produced by Boase Massimi Pollitt, a London advertising agency, for *The Guardian* newspaper, this commercial was shot in grainy black and white, more like a documentary than a commercial. With the exception of a simple voice-over, it is silent. It opens on a slow-motion scene of a rough-looking skinhead sprinting down the sidewalk of a dull terrace in an old industrial town. A car slows menacingly at the end of the street, perhaps in pursuit. A woman, standing on her doorstep, flinches as the skinhead runs past her, and a calm, matter-of-fact voice-over says, "An event, seen from one point of view, gives one impression."

We now see the same scene from a different angle. The skinhead darts past the woman, and this time we see that he's headed toward an old man, who is wearing a long overcoat and hat and carrying a briefcase. The old man raises his briefcase to defend himself as the thug makes a grab for him.

Figure 1.1 *The Guardian:* "Points of View."

The voice-over speaks again. "Seen from another point of view, it gives quite a different impression."

The commercial fades to a third scene, another replay of the same action, but this time shot from high up on a building across the street. We see that right above the old man, who is completely oblivious to the fact, a large tray of bricks is being hoisted up the side of a building. It is swaying dangerously, and the skinhead has spotted it. He races down the street. The voice-over continues, "but it's only when you get the whole picture that you truly understand what's going on." The skinhead grabs the old man and pushes him back against the wall to protect him as the bricks crash to the sidewalk. The commercial fades to black, and the name of the newspaper appears, still in silence. "*The Guardian*. The whole picture."

John Webster, the creative director of Boase Massimi Pollitt and writer of that commercial, told me that he once received a request from a teenage boy, who had been arrested for some petty crime, for a copy of the commercial to be shown in court in his defense. Sadly, John never heard if it helped secure an acquittal, but if so, it would have made for a very unusual advertising effectiveness paper.

That story is an interesting example of the broader applications of the idea that without perspective, nothing is certain. It's true in journalism, and if you read any good detective novel, watch a courtroom drama on the big screen, or take any interest in military history, you will see a similar process of triangulation being used by Pulitzer Prize-winning reporters, by detectives to solve their cases, by attorneys to get convictions, and by generals to win battles. It is the premise of this chapter, and indeed of the rest of the book, that the same methods of analysis are fundamental to success in advertising.

In simple terms, there are three important perspectives that advertising *should* embrace: the client's business perspective, the agency's creative perspective, and last but not least the opinions and prejudices of the people at whom the advertising will be aimed. The very best advertising represents a successful collaboration between all three of these parties and points of view, but, when any one of those perspectives is allowed to dominate at the expense of the others, the quality and effectiveness of the campaign will surely suffer.

JOINING THE DOTS

Jeff Goodby once told me that he does not think of his "product" as advertising. Not as a reel of commercials, or as beautifully framed magazine ads on a wall in the agency, but rather as a tiny reaction in someone's head after seeing, hearing, or reading that advertising. For him, advertising is merely a means to a desired end — a person thinking or behaving differently. Jeff believes that everything an agency does should be geared toward getting into people's heads to figure out what they currently think and understand how best to influence them.

I like this definition because it encapsulates all three of the perspectives I previously mentioned, giving each a clear role. The pivotal perspective is that of the consumers, in whose heads the real work of the advertising will be done. Their opinions have to be understood before they can be manipulated, and consumer research is meant to unlock the hidden truths that may define the nature and content of the message. As for the message itself, the role of creativity is to gain entry to consumers' minds and act as a catalyst for the desired thought process and change of opinion or behavior. And the client's business, or commercial, perspective defines the precise action that consumers are to be asked to take.

That process is seldom, however, as straightforward as it should be.

The most effective advertising involves consumers in two different, but equally critical, ways. First, it needs to involve them in the process of *developing* the communication. Their feelings, habits, motivations, insecurities, prejudices, and desires all have to be explored to understand both how the product fits into their lives and how they might respond to different advertising messages. This exploration of the consumer mind for information and inspiration will form the focus of the rest of the book, starting later in this chapter with some philosophical and methodological barriers to many agencies and clients making the necessary connections with consumers. Some agencies and individuals are arrogant enough to assume that they don't need to have a relationship with consumers or know anything about them before they talk to them. (I can only assume that these are the kind of people who, on a vacation in France, would converse with French people by speaking English, very slowly, and very loudly.) And some clients, while they agree that it is absolutely essential to "have a dialog" with consumers, are hung up on methodologies that make such a relationship impossible. More on that subject later.

The second way that consumers need to be involved in advertising is in the *communication* itself. In other words, advertising works better when it does not tell people what to think, but rather allows them to make up their own minds about its meaning. They participate by figuring it out for themselves. Rich Silverstein likes to use the analogy of those joining-the-dots games that we all played as children, where you draw a line from numbered dot to numbered dot, and when you've finished you have a picture of, say, a warthog. In Silverstein's view, it's not advertising's job to tell people it's a warthog. It should simply join up a few of the dots for its audience and leave the rest for them to join for themselves, thus allowing them to participate.

Leaving something to the audience's imagination is not a widely embraced concept in the advertising industry. Inspired by, among others, Claude Hopkins' *Advertising Science* and Rosser Reeves' *Reality in Advertising*, advertisers have for years been telling their audience what to think, then telling them again and again, each time louder than the last, all under the assumption that the target audience is so dumb that they need to be slapped in the face with the message if they're going to get it.

Howard Gossage was one of the first advertising men to make a stand against the one-way diatribes that formed the bulk of the industry's output. Four decades ago, he was espousing the principle of advertising as two-way communication and creating campaigns that were designed to engender relationships and interaction with his target consumers.

"Advertising is not a right, it is a privilege," he said, reflecting my own belief that an agency and client should consider themselves lucky for any attention that a person pays to their advertising. I have always regarded advertising as being like a person that you meet at a party. You meet, you decide very quickly whether you like him or her, and if you do, you stay and listen to what the individual has to say. If you don't, you spot a long-lost friend on the other side of the room and move on. Your new acquaintance could have given you the most important piece of information you ever heard, but if he or she had already bored you or insulted you, then you would not be around to hear it. So it is with advertising. Thirty seconds on television. A few seconds when a person is flicking through the magazine. That's all the time there is to create a connection and engage a person sufficiently for them to pay attention to the message.

How do you do that? By adopting the same human characteristics that make a stranger at a party seem attractive and interesting: attributes like respect, intelligence, wit, humility, and an interest in the other person. By asking questions instead of making statements.

Gossage wrote that "Our first duty is not to the old sales curve, it is to the audience," and recognized that many in the industry would regard these words as heretical. But as he rightly pointed out, "Any salesman will get it right off the bat. They are used to regarding their audience first and foremost, because if they don't please them, they won't get the order." In other words, if you have the audience's attention, then the sales curve will follow.

Gossage's advertising was ahead of its time, engaging, and effective. Three decades before the word *interactive* became hot, he was putting coupons in his ads, partly so that he could measure their effect, but primarily because he wanted to initiate a dialog between his customers and his clients. Perhaps the first to express the ideal of "consumer participation" in advertising, Gossage was fond of quoting from a short story of Saki's to make his point that too many advertisers told people what to think and left them no opportunity to form their own opinions:

> In baiting a trap with cheese, always leave
> room for the mouse.

Love, Money, Pigs, and Beer

The most important lessons of advertising are perhaps to be found all around us in our everyday lives and relationships, and the factors that lead to successful communication in that broader, human context are exactly the same as those that work in advertising across all types of media.

When I talk about advertising to groups of students, or even agency professionals, I often ask them to think about the times when, as kids, they wanted to ask their parents for money, or as adults, they wanted to ask someone out on a date (or something like that). Anyway, how did they approach the problem? What worked? What didn't?

Most people agree that a simple statement of one's intentions has the odds stacked against it, and a demand that your parents hand over the cash or that the lady or gentleman in question gives you his or her heart or body before even knowing your name is unlikely to yield either financial or romantic satisfaction. In the end, the majority agree that the only way to increase your chance of success is to mentally step out of your shoes and into theirs. I'm not talking about some kind of cross-dressing shoe fetish here, but rather about the ability to figure out the other person's hot buttons. What do they think of you? What is currently stopping them from writing you a check or falling into your arms? What could you do or say to remove those barriers? And most significant of all (everyone I have ever discussed this with agrees that this is a surefire winner), what could you do or say to make your parents decide *for themselves* that they want to give you a spot bonus, or cause the object of your wildest dreams to develop an uncontrollable crush on you?

Anyone who can figure out that kind of strategy will doubtless enjoy a phenomenally successful career in advertising. By the same logic, of course, as a complete loser in the dating department, I should probably resign my own position immediately.

Another story that illustrates the same point was related to me a few years ago by a man I met in Hawaii, whose idea of relaxation was to go out into the rain forest and hunt wild pigs, armed only with a knife.

"If you're going to learn to hunt wild pigs," he told me, assuming quite wrongly that I was remotely interested, "the first thing you've got to do is to learn *how to be a pig*. You've got to think like they think, move like they move, and have the same instincts for safety and danger." He went on to describe how he would stalk them, sometimes for hours and once even for two whole days, not looking, as I first thought, for the perfect moment to attack the pig, but rather for the perfect moment to provoke the pig into attacking *him*. That, he said, was altogether a much more difficult feat to pull off. I believed him.

Leo Burnett once said that "if you can't turn yourselves into a consumer, then you shouldn't be in the advertising business at all," and it is true that the best advertising people have the same instincts in relation to consumers that my pig-hunting acquaintance described, albeit without the violent fight at the end. In a later chapter I will make the point that at times it is very important to trust these instincts, but it is also important to realize that turning yourself into a consumer does *not* mean projecting your own tastes and opinions onto an unfamiliar consumer group.

A young creative team in London once told me, as I was briefing them for a beer advertising campaign, that they didn't need any help from me because they knew "everything there is to know about beer." I didn't doubt that they *drank* a lot of beer, but I feared that they might have a somewhat skewed view of beer brands and drinkers.

"Where did you drink your last beer?" I asked.

"It was Thursday night . . . in the Soho Brasserie," answered the writer.

"What were you drinking?"

"Kronenbourg 1664."

"Out of a glass or a bottle?"

"Bottle."

"How many did you have?"

"Oh, quite a lot. Three, four maybe."

Mmm. Just as I thought. Chic London restaurant/bar. Porsches parked outside. People dressed in black. Lots of kissing on the cheeks (once on the left, once on the right, and once more on the left to be properly European). High-octane, designer French premium lager, drunk slowly and decorously straight from the bottle, with label positioned for all to see and little finger outstretched.

Oh, they were right. It all sounded absolutely like Simonds bitter. Simonds was a cheap and relatively weak ale, drunk only in pints and sold almost exclusively in Welsh workingmen's clubs to guys who had just come off their shift in the coal mines or steel mills. It was hot, heavy work, and they needed a light, refreshing pint that they could drink in large volume. (I frequently came across people in focus groups and on pub-and-club visits who would quite happily consume 15 pints of the stuff after work. The size of their bellies corroborated their stories.) If the creative team had walked up to the bar in one of these places and asked for

"1664 . . . in the bottle, please, Antoine," they would have been torn limb from limb.

Okay, so they needed to be briefed, and thankfully, they obliged. And in the end, with the exception of a small hiccup over a radio script that seemed to many, including the network censors, to have connotations of bestiality (sheep jokes do not go over big in Wales), they hit the spot with the drinkers.

ART FOR ART'S SAKE

At about the same time, in London, I was present at a conference where John Webster, the executive creative director of Boase Massimi Pollitt (and creator of the commercial for *The Guardian*, mentioned earlier), was addressing an audience of young agency creatives. Preferring not to make a lengthy speech, he said only a few words before showing a reel of his work and inviting questions from the audience.

After a few innocuous comments and questions relating to techniques, directors, and the like, one young man spoke up. "John," he said, "some of those ads are among the best I've seen in my life, but there is something unusual about them. There's always a lot of product. The logo's big. Most of the creative people I know fight to cut down the amount of time given to the product and do everything to keep the logo small. Why is it different in your commercials? Do you do that of your own accord, or do your clients make you do it?"

John thought for a moment. "You know, I come across creative people all the time who complain that the client is making them put the logo in larger type, or that they have to mention the brand name and that by doing that, they are 'ruining the idea.' Well, we're not artists, as much as we might like to be. We are in the business of selling products. And that's my responsibility to my clients. I incorporate the product as artfully as I can, but if I don't center the ad on that product, however creative or entertaining it is, I'm wasting my time and their money.

"I don't know how many of you think you are in the entertainment business," he continued, with a wry smile, "but if you do, you should probably fuck off and get a job writing scripts for *The Two Ronnies*." (*The Two Ronnies*, for the sake of my American readers, was at the time one of Britain's top TV comedy programs.)

An agency's art has to be a means to an end, and that end, like it or not, is commercial in nature. Art is a vehicle that can make an ad more distinctive, more memorable, and at its best, carry a message in such a way that it will be more effective in influencing its audience. But that's only at its best, and it only happens when its creator, like Webster, knows that the artistic and commercial elements have to live together in an almost symbiotic relationship. If one starts to dominate at the expense of the other, the relationship becomes more parasitic than symbiotic, and its effectiveness, both in the short and long term, will be compromised.

In May 1985, Ronald Reagan delivered a speech to the recipients of the National Medal of Arts, in which he said that "in an atmosphere of liberty, artists and patrons are free to think the unthinkable and create the audacious; they are free to make both horrendous mistakes and glorious celebrations," and to those who see advertising as an art form, those words must seem like sweet music.

Some writers and art directors, and indeed some entire agencies, believe that the real power of advertising lies in their art, and that if they were truly free to create, they could break the rules, be audacious, and although they may strike out once in a while, they would hit some towering and memorable home runs. And sometimes they are successful.

There is, however, one substantial problem. The freedom of which Reagan spoke was not just celebrated by artists, but by patrons, too. Unfortunately, advertising's "patrons," better known as the clients who control multimillion-dollar advertising budgets, tend not to be too wild about swinging for the fences and are unlikely to risk their companies' marketing budgets, market share, profitability, stock price, and ultimately their own jobs, on the word of a twentysomething with tattoos and a nose ring, saying "trust me . . . it'll be cool." I must admit that if I were responsible for an advertising budget of $100 million, I'd probably feel the same way.

At times like this, names like Michelangelo, Stephen Spielberg, and John Lennon often get bandied around as evidence that art is a powerful force and that it is at its most powerful when the creator has total freedom. Would the roof on the Sistine Chapel be so glorious if Michelangelo had experienced the kind of interference that has characterized the development of this particular advertising campaign? Would *Schindler's List* have been three hours long if the marketing people had had their way? Would *Sergeant Pepper* have ever made it through copy testing?

I don't think we're really comparing apples to apples here. For a start, people *choose* to experience art, movies, and music, whereas advertising is forced on them. The audience for pure art is self-selecting, but advertising has to find them and draw them in. And when it does, it does not have time on its side to make its point. Spielberg has hours to draw his audience in. The Sistine Chapel can take as long as it likes. And is there really any such thing as "pure" art? Can you really imagine the Pope of the time giving Michelangelo an unlimited budget, no time constraints, and no idea of a theme? "No, Michelangelo, you're the creative genius. Surprise me." Just think about what studio executives at Universal must have said when Spielberg announced that he wanted to follow *Jurassic Park* with a three-hour movie about the Holocaust. Or when he casually added that he wanted to shoot entirely in black and white. The grass on the other side, where the true artists live, might not be as green as some of us would like to believe.

It's perhaps not surprising that some agency creatives prefer to think of themselves as artists rather than business people. Many of them have artistic backgrounds and interests, and if the truth is really known, they would probably prefer to spend the rest of their days painting, sculpting, or writing screenplays or the great American novel, rather than continue to work in the creative department of an advertising agency. Some have the nagging feeling that they have prostituted themselves by abandoning these worthier pursuits in favor of the security and salary that comes with a job in advertising. While the more realistic among them simply bite their lips and promise themselves that their advertising careers are just layovers on the way to these better things, others try and make the advertising the outlet for their artistic and literary ambitions.

In *Ogilvy on Advertising*, David Ogilvy denounced the "noisy lunatics on the fringes of the advertising business, [whose] stock-in-trade includes ethnic humor, eccentric art direction, and their self-proclaimed genius," and on many other occasions attacked those whose pursuit of advertising as a pure art form got in the way, as he saw it, of selling products. Having said that, he once admitted that he had to exorcise his own "pseudoliterary pretensions" in the early part of his career before finally realizing that he needed to focus on "the obligation of advertising to *sell*."

The system by which the advertising industry "grades" its creative people adds another dimension to the problem. Every year, there are numerous award shows that recognize the industry's most creative advertising; individuals and teams who create the most distinctive new campaigns are widely celebrated. Success in the award shows is translated into offers of better jobs and better money with better agencies, so it is hardly surprising that certain creative people struggle to maintain the "artistic integrity" of their ideas and regard the input of others, particularly consumers, as a surefire way of undermining that integrity. If they give in, they reason, their campaign will be compromised and with it, less directly, their own careers.

Unfortunately, many clients regard creative awards simply as an agency indulgence. Awards *do* benefit clients though, albeit indirectly, by ensuring that the top creative talent is able to work on their advertising. If the best creative people in the agency are winning awards for their work, then they will be less likely to want to work somewhere else where they might *not* win awards. If they do get poached away, then talented creatives on the outside will see the awards that the agency is winning and want to come and get some of the action. In short, awards keep an agency's creative gene pool healthy and productive.

Another important consideration is that there is no reason why the art or creativity that seems so distinctive to the Cannes or One Show judges should not be equally compelling to members of the target audience. Every year at the Cannes advertising festival, Donald Gunn of Leo Burnett makes a presentation of the top creative award-winning campaigns from around the world that have combined these creative awards with clearly demonstrable results in the marketplace, and many of the campaigns that are featured later in this book have achieved the same double.

I am not suggesting for one moment that art is not a vital component of advertising, for it is in the art that advertising's true magic lies. I am merely suggesting that art alone is not enough, and when it is allowed to overpower strategic and business considerations, it can be an obstacle rather than an aid to persuasion.

Rich Silverstein has said to me on many occasions that it is this juxtaposition of art and commerce that really interests him about advertising and keeps on challenging him. In his view, it is much easier to produce art than it is to produce art that *sells*, and the philosophy and process that are necessary to achieve the latter will be explored thoroughly in later chapters.

FIGHTING ART WITH SCIENCE

In advertising, perhaps in response to the excesses of the frustrated artists, or perhaps simply as a natural counterbalance to the uncertainties inherent in "ideas," writing, art direction, and human relationships, a doctrine has emerged that defines advertising not as a subjective, intuitive craft, but rather as a logical, rational discipline whose process and product can be defined, measured, predicted, and evaluated according to the same criteria and methodologies as those employed in the field of science.

In the first chapter of his famous book, *Advertising Science,* published in 1923, Claude Hopkins wrote, "The time has come when advertising has in some hands reached the status of a science. It is based on fixed principles and is reasonably exact. The causes and effects have been analyzed until they are well understood. The correct methods of procedure have been proved and established. We know what is most effective, and we act on its basic laws.

"Advertising, once a gamble, has thus become, under able direction, one of the safest business ventures. Certainly no other enterprise with comparable possibilities need involve so little risk."

Nearly three-quarters of a century later, this doctrine remains powerfully represented in the ranks of client marketing organizations, as well as in many agency account management and research departments, and in the host of independent research companies employed by both clients and agencies to assist in the development and evaluation of their campaigns.

These disciples of advertising-as-science consider that their raison d'être is to bring discipline, predictability, and accountability to advertising agencies in general, and to creative departments in particular. They bring with them powerful credentials (undergraduate and postgraduate degrees in marketing, advertising, statistics, and psychology, not to mention the potent Master of Business Administration, or MBA). Armed with impressively thick overhead decks, 95 percent confidence levels, advertising response models, brand recall and persuasion numbers, and normative data and correlations, they wield extraordinary influence at every stage of the process. Against this arsenal of facts, figures, and projections, creative "instinct" and phrases like "trust me" just don't have a chance.

In the course of the ensuing chapters, I will argue that there is a vital role to be played by research in advertising (when it is done right), but that to regard advertising as a science that can be built entirely on facts and measured, even predicted, is perilous indeed. It is perilous not only because advertising and the human mind by their very nature defy such scientific analysis, but also because those who adhere to these principles, like many of the "artists" I spoke of before, are basing their philosophy and process on an entirely erroneous view of how *scientists* practice science.

THE SCIENTIFIC METHOD

At the age of 11, in my first physics class, my teacher, Mr. Berry, spent the best part of an hour talking about the "scientific method." Later the same day, Mr. Ackroyd, in his inaugural address in the acrid environment of the chemistry lab, told us more, and Mr. Surl, the biology teacher, over the course of the next week, actually demonstrated it in action with the help of some fruit flies.

They all seemed pretty consistent in their definitions.

In this scientific method, as far as I understood the concept, the scientist was a person who was concerned only with facts and who collected and analyzed data with complete objectivity. Emotion played no part in the scientist's work; he or she merely observed, measured, drew conclusions, and formulated laws in a totally dispassionate way. This was, we learned, quite different from the minds and methods of those who taught and studied the arts, whom my science teachers condemned for their lack of discipline, precision, and rules. "In science," we were told, "we deal in the absolute, in irrefutable fact."

My experience of science at school suggested that they were correct. In physics, chemistry, and biology, it seemed that there was right or wrong, black or white, and I saw little or no evidence of any gray area in between. With no opportunity for interpretation, we simply learned the rules by rote and applied them to problems to which we were expected to supply the one, inarguable, correct solution.

(At this point, I should probably admit that of all the people who studied science in school, I am perhaps the least well qualified to criticize a philosophy and methodology that seems to have served mankind fairly well over the last 300 years. I left physics, chemistry, and biology behind at the earliest possible opportunity, so be warned that what follows is definitely a layman's, as opposed to a scientist's, perspective.)

This scientific method was based on a model of how the world works that was developed in the seventeenth century by Sir Isaac Newton, Descartes, and others. Their approach was based on the belief that any object of study, physical thing or system alike, can be stripped down to its component parts and reassembled, the underlying assumption being that the workings of the whole can be understood through comprehending the function and contribution of each individual piece. This is termed the *machine model*, which Margaret Wheatley, in her excellent book, *Leadership and the New Science*, describes as "characterized by materialism and reductionism—a focus on things rather than relationships and a search . . . for the basic building blocks of matter."

In this kind of science, everything has a place. Everything is separate from everything else. Everything obeys a law. And with knowledge of those laws, everything can be predicted. It's objective, it's simple, it's orderly, and constituent piece by constituent piece, it's easy to control. In the end, it is this illusion of control that makes the Newtonian universe such an attractive place and has led to the adoption of its principles way beyond the scientific community. Organizational charts divide and subdivide companies into their component parts and depict (and separate) people, knowledge, responsibilities, and problems as endless lines and boxes, all in the belief that if we succeed in dividing, we can truly conquer. Boundaries separate the "things" that comprise the machine, and in all parts of our lives there are boundaries that define the limits of roles, responsibility, authority, ownership, ability, safety, and acceptable risk.

Advertising is no exception. The scientific method of advertising development divides agencies into separate "disciplines" and puts consumers into neat little compartments where they can be targeted: nonusers, occasional users, heavy users, believers, nonbelievers, household income below $25,000, household income from $25,000 to $50,000, household income over $50,000, pioneers, early adopters, early mass-market, and mass-market targets. Advertising campaigns are analyzed execution by execution, each execution judged in terms of its impact, its recall, its brand linkage, and its communication and persuasion. What about the music? What about the pictures? What about the main character? What about the other characters? What about the words they spoke? What about the narrator's voice? What about the tagline? Opinions are given and reported as numbers, and these numbers wield absolute power.

Pretesting methodologies allow a rough commercial to be graded by captive consumers on a second-by-second basis. While watching the commercial, they turn a handheld dial up when they are interested and down when they are not, allowing the researchers to conclude that the first ten seconds work, the next five seconds need some attention, the next ten are very strong, and the final five come in "significantly below norm." Well done, creative department, 66.66 percent of your commercial is acceptable or better. As for the other 33.33 percent . . . In the scientific method, there is no place for art, inspiration, instinct, intuition, magic, or luck, because they cannot be measured, predicted, or easily repeated.

The kind of research just described, which is explored in greater depth in Chapter 3, seems to allow the industry to count the trees while remaining entirely oblivious to the presence of a forest. In their enthusiasm to put both people and ideas into those neat little boxes, researchers often forget about the connections between the two, and far from *involving* consumers, as many claim their research allows them to do, they succeed only in *distancing* or even *excluding* them.

In a paper delivered to the ADMAP/*Campaign* Seminar in London in 1990, the late Charles Channon, Director of Studies of the British I.P.A., drew a very important distinction between the concept of *effectiveness*, which is broadly defined as "doing the right thing," and *efficiency*, which is about "doing something the right way." In my own view, the advertising industry too often preaches effectiveness while actually pursuing efficiency, transforming, as Channon noted, "a real world of difficult decisions and uncertain evidence into a comfortingly simplified one where indices of performance are hard facts and acting on them will reduce risk as much as can ever be hoped for." We are not attempting to do things right. We're merely trying to avoid doing them wrong.

Here's an example of the damage that an efficiency mindset can wreak; it comes from the Soviet Union in the 1930s. Under Stalin's drive to increase industrial output, all factories were given production targets that they had to meet. The failure to meet these targets was punished very severely, by imprisonment and occasionally even death. One factory that produced nails was given an especially difficult target to reach, more than double the largest amount they had ever produced in the past; but, strangely, the required figure was expressed in terms of the *weight* of nails that it would have to produce, not the number of nails. The problem was solved by producing fewer, larger nails. In fact, nails more than three feet long. They were completely useless, but they were heavy, and they met the government's requirements. Efficient? Yes. Effective? No.

In *Zen and the Art of Motorcycle Maintenance*, Robert M. Pirsig wrote that "the traditional scientific method has always been at the very best, 20/20 hindsight. It's good for seeing where you've been." Even a cursory glance at the careers of those who have made the greatest breakthroughs in science will show that they made their discoveries precisely by *ignoring* the traditional method, even if their scientific papers later gave these discoveries a postrationalized sense of Newtonian order and decorum.

For example, James Watson, who with Francis Crick discovered the structure of DNA, for which they were awarded the Nobel Prize in 1962, wrote in *The Double Helix* that "Science seldom proceeds in the strait forward, logical manner imagined by outsiders. Instead, its steps forward (and sometimes backward) are often very human events in which personalities and cultural traditions play major roles." It was Albert Einstein who said that "the greatest scientists are always artists as well," noting that in his own work, fantasy and intuition had been more important to him than any talent for absorbing knowledge (which he regarded as limiting). And J. Robert Oppenheimer, the nuclear physicist, in a lecture delivered in 1954, also embraced the idea of a confluence between science and art at the outer limits of discovery: "Both the man of science and the man of art live always at the edge of mystery, surrounded by it. Both, as the measure of their creations, have always had to deal with the harmonization of what is new with what is familiar, with the balance between novelty and synthesis, with the struggle to make partial order in total chaos."

It seems remarkable that Watson, Einstein, Oppenheimer, and countless others that I could have mentioned, describe their work and their breakthroughs in terms that are so, well, *unscientific*. Watson's "human events," Einstein's "fantasy" and "intuition," and Oppenheimer's "harmonization," are all words that would send many advertising research directors into an advanced state of agitation. Why? Because these words imply the unpredictable, and most of advertising's pseudoscientists, despite much evidence that the truly great advances do, more often than not, emerge from a state of disorder, prefer to retain a state of total order at all times. To them, discovery and originality are fine, as long as they conform to historical precedent, meet normative standards, come in on time, and don't surprise anyone. We have all seen the advertising that results, so thank God that most of the proper scientists don't really work that way.

If they did, we'd all still be living in caves, and I'd be writing this on the wall with charcoal.

New Science, New Model, New Advertising

I am not trying to argue that the Newtonian model and its machine imagery is *wrong,* but rather that *it cannot adequately explain everything,* and that there are some applications to which it is unsuited.

In the early twentieth century, as scientists began to explore the world at the subatomic level, they found that Newtonian laws were not capable of explaining their strange discoveries, and that they needed a "new science" to explain them. From that grew the theory of quantum mechanics, which might sound very complicated and very scary (which it is even to those who are expert in it: Niels Bohr, one of the founders of quantum theory, once said that "Anyone who is not shocked by quantum theory has not understood it"), as well as wholly irrelevant to a book about advertising.

Many of the same circumstances that led to the birth of quantum theory, though, apply to the situation many advertisers and their agencies find themselves in today. The models and methods that have dictated the development of advertising campaigns for decades are clearly not working. Advertising in general is not liked or trusted. Research fails to make the connections that are necessary to *explain* the attitudes and behavior of target consumers, and advertising in turn fails to make the connections in its communication that are necessary to *change* them. Consumers are passive recipients of both research and advertising; both are done *to* them, as opposed to *with* them. Ideas are dissected until every component part is understood, but like a dissected rat, they are then very hard to put back together so that they work as a living, breathing whole.

A new model for advertising is necessary that is based on the understanding that consumers are *people* and recognizes that people are inherently complex, emotional, unpredictable creatures, whose relationships with each other and with the "things" (including brands, products, and advertising) around them are more important than the "things" themselves. This requires a change in both philosophy and methodology.

"In new science," writes Margaret Wheatley in *Leadership and the New Science,*

> the underlying currents are a movement toward holism, toward giving primary value to the relationships that exist among seemingly discrete parts. Donella Meadows, a systems thinker, quotes an ancient Sufi teaching that captures this shift in focus: "You think because you understand *one* you must understand *two*, because one and one makes two. But you must also understand *and*." When we view systems from this perspective, we enter an entirely new landscape of connections, of phenomena that cannot be reduced to simple cause and effect, and of the constant flux of dynamic processes.

I would prefer to leave the specific *scientific* discussion of the application of quantum theory to the scientists (some references are given at the end of this book) and instead focus on some direct parallels in the advertising philosophies and practices on which this book is based.

If quantum theory were to be applied directly to advertising, it would suggest that the way a member of the target audience will react to an advertising message is affected by many factors beyond what the advertising itself looks like and says. Where are they? Who are they with? What sort of mood does that put them in? All of those "relationships" will affect the person's receptivity to, and interpretation of, the message.

Environment matters, not only to advertising communication but also to research. Quantum physicists have proven that environment affects the outcome of research and that the simple act of conducting an experiment affects the situation that it is setting out to observe. In advertising, there can also be no such thing as purely objective research. I discuss this at greater length in later chapters, but isn't it strange to realize that the type of research that advertisers tend to regard as the most objective because of its quantitative, disciplined, easily replicable approach, is more likely to skew respondents *away* from the truth than toward it? And that *subjective,* unreliable, nonprojectable qualitative research, when done in the right way in the right environment, may actually provide a much closer representation of the truth?

The best advertising solutions often emerge out of a situation of apparent chaos. Many agencies would agree, I am sure, that they do their best work in the context of a new business pitch, when they are effectively working outside the system, under extreme time constraints and pressure, and with no time to engage in a logical, sequential process. People from different disciplines work in parallel, run into and bounce off each other, create energy, and out of that create ideas.

Quantum theory would support my earlier arguments that the best advertising is informed by as many points of view as possible, and that a campaign's (or an individual execution's) whole is greater than the sum of its parts. People do not see a typeface, a photograph, a logo, a tagline, x lines of copy, and a headline; they see an ad, and either they pay attention to it or they don't. It would also suggest that the risk and uncertainty that so many advertisers currently expend a great deal of energy trying to avoid, may actually be positive forces. Writing about the music business in

Rolling Stone in July 1997, Chris Heath observed that "it is not the plans you think up that make the difference, it is how well you use the accidents." Advertising is not a whole lot different.

Chance plays a critical role in the combination of people who are thrown together to create a campaign, the decisions of competitors, and environmental influences that affect consumer relationships with both brands and advertising. Some opportunities are one time only, and I am convinced that many of the campaign solutions described later in this book would not have been arrived at six months earlier, or six months later, and would probably have been incorrect if they had. Chance is not to be feared but encouraged, and the wider the perspective that is taken on a problem, the greater the opportunity for chance to reveal an unexpected solution.

In the course of this book, I explore all of these parallels and propose a new way of looking at, and developing, advertising that provides the kind of humanity, flexibility, and respect for relationships that were previously proposed. Although I at times draw direct links to new scientific thinking, I do not wish to belabor the point. Let it suffice to say that many of the themes that have been raised in this chapter will crop up again and again in the pages that follow.

"WILL WORK FOR FOOD"

At times, the principles and methodology of the new advertising model that I discuss may seem a little uncomfortable to client and agency alike, because they are different and unfamiliar. Believe me, at times I find it as scary as quantum physicists find their own discipline. While the process of solving advertising problems is never easy, the solutions themselves are often the epitome of simplicity, and this will also be a recurring theme.

George Orwell once defined advertising as "the rattling of a stick in a swill bucket," and I have tried to keep both my observations and examples to that level of complexity. Advertising is a simple form of communication, nothing more and nothing less, and to close this chapter I offer one final example, once again from the real world (as opposed to advertising itself), to illustrate that point.

Living in the San Francisco Bay Area, one of the most prevalent forms of communication is, unfortunately, that of signs held up by homeless people to attract donations from passers-by. There is one sign that I see perhaps more than any other: "Will Work for Food." Wherever you live, you have probably seen this sign, or one very much like it, and although it is by now so widely used as to be almost invisible, I think that at its heart, it is a very powerful piece of communication.

"Will Work for Food" works on a number of different levels, starting with the assumption that the passer-by knows that the holder of the sign is homeless. This credits the passer-by with some intelligence. It then addresses, head on, a popular prejudice, which is that all homeless people are lazy good-for-nothings who are on the streets simply because they can't be bothered to work for a living. "Will Work for Food" says, "Hey—I don't just want handouts. I'm willing to work to get out of this mess." And the nature of this mess isn't just being homeless. It's being hungry. That's why they're asking for help; they need to eat and they can't afford to buy food. The mention of food also deals with another prejudice, which is that any money given to a homeless person will simply be spent on cigarettes, alcohol, or drugs. It's amazing how so much meaning can be packed into four small words, and it's a great example of someone figuring out the hot buttons of the people they want to influence, rather than writing for themselves.

Now imagine for a moment the way a homeless person's sign might look if the writer belonged to the Newtonian school of advertising. In this school, remember, creativity is a needless distraction from the real work of selling, and the task of advertising is simply to tell people what you want them to think.

I'm homeless. I need money.

That's a good start, for a scientist. It clearly states the problem and the need, and passers-by should be very clear about what is expected of them. The Newtonian research director, though, may feel that it is not specific enough. People reading that sign on the street could sympathize with the sign holder's predicament but not be clear what was expected of them. That could be solved by the simple addition of one word that would give the communication some *focus:*

I'm homeless. I need *your* money.

The sign is still lacking, however. The copy test comes back, and while the communication is clear, the persuasion scores are dangerously low. Where's the call to action? Where's the sense of urgency? Perhaps the addition of another word would help:

I'm homeless. I need your money *now.*

Okay. So the passers-by are left in no doubt as to either the situation or the desired response. But it reads like a demand, there's no suggestion of anything being offered in return, and the suspicion may still linger that any money given will be spent on malt liquor, cheap cigarettes, or crack cocaine. This in turn raises the question of whether these prejudices can be addressed directly, which may require an approach that is more artistic in nature.

Nonsmoker. On the wagon. Faint at the sight of a needle.

Certainly it's charming, and the words portray a sense of the sign holder's character and personality, but it still doesn't overcome the perception that the person is "begging," when they should be working. And maybe it is trying a little too hard. By raising the issues of cigarettes, alcohol, and drugs directly, maybe it is concentrating too much on the negative and in some ways lacks confidence? A more direct, confident approach may be needed:

Just give it.

All of the above examples are feasible solutions, but none communicates on quite as many levels as "Will Work for Food." The problem for homeless people composing signs in San Francisco today, though, is that, while "Will Work for Food" is clearly a more interesting solution to their problem, it is widely used and has consequently lost much of its power. It's a problem faced by many advertisers: The solution seems clear, but it has already been appropriated by a competitor. (I return to that issue in Chapters 4 and 5, as part of a discussion about research that stimulates creative ideas, and the creative brief that provides the link between strategic and creative thinking.) Suddenly the *execution* itself may have to define the difference between competing products.

I want to finish with two more examples of signs that I have seen on the streets of San Francisco that certainly stand out for being different. It wouldn't be too much of a stretch to suggest that they are advertising in the Howard Gossage style, using honesty and humor to disarm, and at the very least, attempting to improve the environment of the street and its advertising by providing some entertainment. Both assume a level of intelligence and understanding on the part of passers-by. They know that we know they're homeless, and they assume we know what they want. They simply use a kind of reverse psychology to get there. One sign on Broadway proclaimed:

Why lie? I need a beer.

I was amused, but was passing in a car and would have been unable to stop, even if tempted. Bad media placement, that.

But only a week later, my eye was caught by a different man with a different sign in another part of town. This time I was on foot. The man holding the sign was clearly homeless, but his appearance did not suggest that his circumstances were any more or less fortunate than his fellow street dwellers. He was not playing a musical instrument or using a cat or dog to attract sympathy, as many do these days, but was simply standing on the sidewalk, holding a typical, roughly fashioned, brown cardboard sign. Only the words were unusual.

Need fuel for Lear Jet.

I have no idea why it affected me the way it did, but the human mind is an irrational thing that is sometimes affected in inexplicable ways. As soon as I smiled, a relationship was formed and from that point there was no going back.

I gave him five bucks and wished him a safe flight.

2

Silent Partners
Account Planning and the New Consumer Alliance

> *The best possible solutions come only from a combination of rational analysis based on the nature of things, and imaginative reintegration of all the different items into a new pattern, using non-linear brain power.*
>
> Kenichi Ohmae
> *The Mind of the Strategist*

BEATING BACK CALIBAN

On the morning of October 17, 1954, Lord Esher, a distinguished British political figure, spoke angrily about an appalling event he had witnessed on the previous evening. It had been, he fumed, "an unprecedented orgy of vulgarity." His fellow in the House of Lords, Lord Hailsham, agreed with that assessment, likening what both had seen to the specter of "Caliban, emerging from his slimy cavern," while the eminent author and playwright P.G. Wodehouse, never short of words, condemned the affair as "the foulest, ghastliest, loathsomest nightmare ever inflicted by science on a suffering human race."

This apparently apocalyptic incident had been witnessed by all three men, and a large proportion of the British population besides, from the comfort of their own living rooms. What was it? The launch, on October 16, 1954, of Britain's first commercial television station. So the object of their dismay, the episode that filled the pages of national newspapers and dominated discussions in the highest corridors of power, this "Caliban," was no more than the British public's first exposure to television advertising.

It took the British many years to learn to tolerate advertising. The commercial station, ITV, was regarded as lower class by comparison with the venerable BBC, which may suggest more about the British class system and attitudes to change than it does about advertising, but the British do have an innate aversion to being sold anything. To this day I know many people who would much rather stick hot needles in their eyes than open the door to a salesperson. Selling, to the reserved British sensibility, is "not quite nice," and door-to-door salespeople in particular are still regarded as one of the lowest forms of human life. As a result, mass-market advertising, which went a step further than showing up uninvited on the doorstep by appearing uninvited in one's living room, had a very steep hill to climb.

As steep as it was, advertising in Britain appears to have succeeded in making the ascent. Attitudinal data tracked over many years shows that the dislike and suspicion with which many Britons regarded advertising have been eroded, and far from achieving mere tolerance, as in the United States, advertising has taken its place in pop culture alongside (apparently with equal status to) top TV shows and movies. In Britain, advertisers don't just parody TV shows and movies; they parody other *advertising*, taking for granted a level of knowledge and interest among the viewing public that ensures they will not only get the joke, but enjoy it.

It would probably be shocking to most Americans to realize that in Britain today, most movie theaters are almost full 10 to 15 minutes before the scheduled time of the show, not because of some quaint British penchant for punctuality, but because British moviegoers actually want to see the advertising that customarily precedes the movie trailers and the main feature. Advertising is not just being passively consumed in Britain, it is actively sought out and enjoyed. Hell, if people are even paying for the privilege of seeing it on movie screens, they must like it.

So what happened?

It may sound strange, but I believe that Bill Bernbach is what happened. The creative revolution that he inspired in the United States in the 1950s and 1960s, for a while at least, challenged the long-held view that all advertising had to do to be successful was register a product message. That simple aim could usually be accomplished by a talking-head presenter, a side-by-side comparison, and enough money to repeat the message until people couldn't possibly forget it, but Bernbach and his agency eschewed these stereotypical, annoying tactics in favor of an altogether more humanistic approach. "Find the simple story in the product and present it in an articulate and intelligent persuasive way," he said, and in doing so, his campaigns succeeded in drawing his audience into the communication, not as passive subjects, but as active and willing participants. To Bernbach, an advertising execution was more than a vehicle to carry a product or brand message; in a way it *was* the message, and was meant to do more than grab people's attention. He believed that execution, just as much as a strategic idea, helped establish a brand's *relationship* with its users.

Bernbach's creative advertising was resisted by many in the research industry and feared by many clients, probably because it did not conform to any of their models of how advertising worked. While Bernbach talked of "the power of an idea," many in the industry remained fixated on measures of product message registration, branding, and persuasion, preferring to slice up advertising and evaluate it by each of its component parts rather than consider its strength as a whole. Some even dubbed DDB's famous campaigns for Volkswagen, Alka-Seltzer, and others "failures," presumably for their inability to meet norms on some spurious standard industry measures. The dimensions on which they would have scored very highly were presumably not considered important enough to bother evaluating.

Nonetheless, Bernbach was a powerful inspiration to many individuals and agencies who today are doing some of America's best advertising. The influence of the great DDB campaigns of the fifties and sixties was felt all over the world, and in Britain, a whole generation of creative people was inspired by his work to enter the advertising industry and apply the same kind of approach that had been so successful in the United States (research sour grapes notwithstanding).

The lessons they learned from Bernbach's success were about simplicity, honesty, style, intelligence, humor, respect, and consumer involvement, the lack of which in much British advertising before the mid-1960s had strengthened the public's general distaste for the industry and its product. And in the vanguard of this British creative movement, the creatives were joined by a fledgling discipline whose ideals and expertise made for a perfect partnership.

That discipline became known as *account planning.*

THE HIGH PRIEST

Twenty years had passed since the first stirrings of a creative and planning revolution when I first visited the London agency Boase Massimi Pollitt in the spring of 1984. I was still a student at Nottingham University and was searching for a job in an advertising agency, hoping to start work in the fall. I had applied to BMP for a place on their account management training program, and had been invited to an interview with one of the agency's group account directors, Michael Hockney. In the hour we spent together, we talked a little bit about advertising, but much to my surprise our conversation was mostly about antique maps, in which it turned out we shared a common interest. I was further confused when at the end of our chat, Michael asked me whether I had ever considered account planning as a possible career. (His question, he assured me, had nothing directly to do with my cartographic credentials or knowledge of Mercator projections; rather a hunch he had from the mix of experience and interests noted on my resume.)

I replied that I didn't really know enough about it to be able to answer his question. I had read in BMP's recruitment literature that the agency had pioneered the discipline when it opened its doors in 1968, and that it had given rise to a unique structure and way of working, but beyond the fact that planners did a lot of research to represent the consumer within the agency, I had to admit that I was rather ignorant. What I didn't tell him was that the word *research* at the end of the description's first paragraph had stopped me wanting to find out more, conjuring up images of the almost universally geeky research assistants who had populated the many laboratories of our university, all of whom appeared to lack both the social skills necessary for survival in the real world and the intellectual skills essential to a successful career in academia. I had pictured myself, albeit fleetingly, carrying a clipboard and wearing a pocket protector for my pens, and I have to admit that the image wasn't quite what I had in mind for the next 40 years of my life.

"Perhaps you would like to talk about it with one of our planning directors," Michael offered. I could hardly refuse, so a few minutes later I was in another office with Chris Cowpe, an engaging and brilliant man who was later to head the agency's planning department and is now its Managing Director. Through a thick cloud of cigarette smoke (it was London in the early 1980s), Chris answered my questions, and whenever the smoke rendered him invisible, the sound of his voice reassured me that he had not left the room.

He talked about the late Stanley Pollitt, one of the agency's founders and the "father" of account planning. Chris painted an almost paradoxical picture of, on the one hand, a highly intelligent, almost professorial Cambridge graduate, and on the other, a former University boxer who had apparently lost none of his pugilistic tendencies since joining the agency business. At BMP, Pollitt's sparring partners were the clients and research methodologies that in his view acted as barriers to effective advertising, and he was never one to back down from a dispute. Seldom seen after lunchtime without a glass of claret in one hand and a cigarette in the other, the ash always leaning precariously from the end as he searched for an ashtray, Pollitt could be so argumentative that legend has it that his partner, Martin Boase, once actually locked him in his office to prevent him from attending a particularly sensitive client meeting.

Pollitt had passed away a few years before, struck down by a fatal heart attack, and Cowpe spoke of him with both respect and affection. For BMP, he was clearly more than a founder and planning director; he was the agency's spiritual leader, revered in the same way as Leo Burnett and Bill Bernbach in their respective agencies. In the years that I later worked at BMP, I had a very strong feeling that whoever was the agency's Director of Planning had to be something of a high priest, responsible for encouraging us all to worship at the altar of Stanley Pollitt.

"So what exactly is account planning?" I asked through the pall of Dunhill smoke.

"Account planning is the discipline that brings the consumer into the process of developing advertising," Cowpe replied. "To be truly effective, advertising must be both distinctive *and* relevant, and planning helps on both counts." That surprised me. I could understand how the "relevant" part applied, but wasn't it the job of the creative department to make advertising distinctive? He agreed that it was, but pointed out that it was the planner's job to interrogate the data and consumers until they came up with an insight that helped the creative people on their way. He also added that when planners researched rough creative ideas (every single TV execution produced by the agency was pretested in animatic form in group discussions), they were charged with figuring out how to make an idea *better*, and thus even more distinctive.

Planners, he told me, were the architects and guardians of their clients' brands, the detectives who uncovered long-hidden clues in the data and gently coerced consumers into revealing their inner secrets, and the warriors who stood up and fought for the integrity of their strategic vision. They had the logical, analytical skills to consume and synthesize vast amounts of data, and the lateral and intuitive skills to interpret that data in an interesting and innovative way. Whereas traditional agency researchers tended to be more reactive and bound by the literal findings of their research, planners were by nature and decree proactive and imaginative, injecting their research-divined ideas into every stage of the advertising-development process.

What he was describing certainly sounded more interesting than I had imagined, but I was still curious about what planners actually *did* in the course of an average day.

Chris began by describing the in-person research conducted by planners to develop a relationship with members of their consumer constituency. In either group discussions or depth (one-on-one) interviews, planners would meet with target consumers and talk to them about both products and advertising, utilizing the learning to develop briefs for creative teams and to provide intelligence to clients on a number of nonadvertising issues.

Nonadvertising issues? Planners, it seemed, spent a large proportion of their time poring through Nielsen reports and sales figures, identifying the underlying reasons for distribution problems in a particular retail chain, or, say, the effect of competitive price reductions on a brand's rate of sale in the north of England. Virtually none of the agency's clients had their own research departments. As a result, BMP's planners did all of their research for them, not only on advertising-related matters, but also on general marketing issues. In fact, in many ways, they seemed to act more like members of their clients' marketing organizations than employees of the agency. It had not always been that way—only 20 years earlier, it had been the *lack* of qualified research professionals inside advertising agencies that had been one of the driving forces for setting up planning. Today in the United States the situation is also very different to the one that Cowpe described and I experienced in my years at BMP. The opportunities for most planning agencies to get directly involved in nonadvertising issues are few and far between.

As charming and intelligent as Cowpe was, and as interesting as the parts of the job that I understood from this largely abstract discussion seemed, I just couldn't shake off the image of clipboards and pocket protectors. That night, I wrote Michael Hockney a letter in which I thanked him for setting up the meeting with Chris Cowpe, but concluded, as diplomatically as I could, that planning was not for me. Privately, I was convinced that it was the last job I would want to do in an agency, which just goes to show how good *I* am at predicting the future.*

A PROFESSIONAL PAIN IN THE ASS

In 1979, shortly before he died, Stanley Pollitt wrote an article for the British advertising magazine *Campaign,* entitled "How I Started Account Planning in Agencies." (I should point out here that there remains some dispute in Britain to this day about exactly who *did* start it. The chronology seems to be that Stanley experimented with the idea at Pritchard Wood Partners, the agency from which he, Martin Boase, Gabe Massimi, John Webster, and others broke away to form BMP, as early as 1965, although the name *account planning* was coined by Stephen King—not *The Shining* Stephen

---

*My editor and everyone who read the manuscript asked, "So what happened? How did you end up as a planner?" A partial answer, in the unlikely event that anyone else is interested, lies in my "Acknowledgments" section at the end of the book.

King, in case you were wondering—at the London office of J. Walter Thompson in 1968. Later that year, when BMP was founded, Pollitt simply "borrowed" the name.)

He began his *Campaign* article with the observation that " 'Account Planning' and 'account planners' have become part of agency jargon over recent years. I've been able to track down about ten agencies currently using them. There's even a new pressure group called the Account Planning Group. Unfortunately there is considerable confusion over what the terms mean, making discussion of the subject frustrating."

This situation will sound eerily familiar to anyone connected to account planning in the United States today, and I suspect that if Stanley were still alive today, he would not have been any less frustrated. But in an attempt to clear up some of the confusion that existed in Britain in 1979, he outlined the original reasons that led him to create this new discipline, and the vision he had for the role that planners would play in the advertising-development process. Such a discussion is pertinent to the present-day American advertising business because, in my opinion, many of the U.S. agencies that have established planning in recent years have done so for rather different reasons from those for which it was originally conceived. That has serious implications for both the way that these planners work and the degree to which they are truly able to affect the outcome of their clients' advertising.

For Pollitt and King alike, the original impetus for establishing this new discipline was as much logistic as principled, a reaction to a very specific problem, which was, as Pollitt described it, "a considerable increase in the quality and quantity of data that was relevant to more professionally planned advertising-company statistics, available consumer and retailer panel data, etc. And facilities for analyzing data were becoming more sophisticated and more cheaply accessible." This was a problem because at the time there were few qualified people in British agencies to deal with that kind of data. There had been a time, before most consumer goods companies introduced marketing functions, when most general market research was conducted by advertising agencies, but with restructuring along marketing lines, most clients took market research in-house and left advertising agencies with responsibility for only advertising-specific research. As a result, most had pared their research departments to the bone. A small number of researchers remained but tended to be called in to advise on particular research problems on an ad hoc basis. As the new data began to flow, it was clear that there was too much information for too few researchers.

Thus it was in 1965 that Pollitt, an account person, found himself in charge of research at Pritchard Wood Partners. This seemed wrong to him, in part because he felt that few account people were qualified to decide what data should be applied to strategic and creative advertising issues and to know when a research specialist needed to be called in, but largely because he felt there was an inherent conflict of interests between an account person's job and the requirements of correct use and application of data. As an account person, the pressures of "clients on the one hand and creative direction on the other made one permanently tempted to be expedient," he admitted, whereas a research professional needed to remain independent.

"I decided, therefore," Pollitt wrote, "that a trained researcher should be put alongside the account man (that's what they called account people, male or female, in London in the 1960s; actually they still do) on every account. He should be there as of right, with equal status as a working partner. He was charged with ensuring that all the data relevant to key advertising decisions should be properly analyzed, complemented with new research, and brought to bear on judgments of the creative strategy and how the campaign should be appraised. Obviously all this was decided in close consultation with account man and client.

"This new researcher—or account man's 'conscience'— was to be called the 'planner.' "

A few years back, I remember Rich Silverstein introducing me to a client visiting the agency for the first time as *his* "conscience." My role in the agency, he explained, was to keep him true to the task of saying the right things to consumers. The next day, he introduced me to someone else as "a pain in the ass," and I suppose that if anyone is to successfully play the role of conscience, then they have to be a pain in the ass at times. A person's conscience doesn't always tell them what they want to hear, no matter how right they know it to be.

"Getting it right" is the issue, and both BMP and J. Walter Thompson, in establishing and growing their planning departments, charged their planners with adding the dimension of consumer response to the opinions and experience of clients and the intuition of creative people, in an effort to make their advertising more effective. Planners were thus involved not only in strategic development, where they would use research to figure out what the advertising should be saying, but also in creative development. Here there was a slight parting of the ways between the BMP and JWT "schools" of planning—BMP came to place much more emphasis on the role played by planners in working with creative teams and researching rough creative ideas, a role once rather unkindly dubbed "creative tweaker" by comparison to JWT's "grand strategists." Having never worked at JWT, I can't say how grand their planners' strategic insights may be, or how often they venture onto the creative floor, but I do know from experience that there were (and still are) some pretty terrific strategic thinkers among BMP's "tweakers." Ultimately I believe that any good planner has to be very strong both strategically *and* creatively.

"What we set out to do," explained Pollitt, "was to guide account planners to be able to be honest and clear about consumer response without stifling creativity," and in that aim BMP proved to be remarkably successful over the years. Whatever tweaking was being done, BMP consistently took top honors at creative award shows, but also, importantly, at effectiveness awards. And it was the same campaigns that were winning at both.

In the abstract, planning is a very attractive and compelling concept to most clients, and even to most creative people. Clients regard it as a tool that will help make their advertising more effective, which they obviously welcome, while most good creatives tend to like the idea of more information to help them get started on a campaign. (They remain, on the whole, very suspicious of research that is conducted with their rough ideas, but that is the subject of a later chapter.) Unfortunately, there is often a large gulf between the *theory* or promise of planning, as spouted at new business meetings, and the way that it works in practice in the agency.

"GETTING IT RIGHT"

"Planning," said Jay Chiat in a moment of reflection about his agency's success in the 1980s, "is the best new business tool ever invented." On the basis of Chiat/Day's continued new business record, and more recently that of agencies like Fallon McElligott and Goodby, Silverstein & Partners, it would be hard to disagree with his point of view. In July 1992, *Adweek* magazine published an article entitled "The Knights of New Business," which chronicled a number of recent high-profile pitch wins that had been attributed in large part, by both clients and agency insiders, to the influence of planning. My own agency's successful pitch for the Sega video game business was one of those featured, so I was not heard complaining at the time. But since then, whenever I have had the opportunity, I have begged to differ with both Mr. Chiat's now-famous statement and the message of the *Adweek* piece.

Jay is half right, in that the part of a pitch where a planner stands up and talks about the clients' business through the eyes of their consumers, hopefully revealing new insights and perspectives, can be the single most interesting part of the presentation. But that is relative to the inevitable hour of agency self-promotion, the agency's rehashing of the original client brief (to prove that the agency "gets it"), the media presentation (which is legendary for coming last, when all assembled hope that there will only be time for a brief summary), and the presentation of initial creative ideas, the majority of which are never likely to see the light of day again. If the individual planner making the presentation is compelling, and the agency tells a good story about how important effectiveness is in their philosophy, and how well integrated their planning department is compared to others, planning may very well appear to be a good new business tool.

In the end, though, clients tend to hire an agency based on their belief in what that agency can do for their brand and company. The whole agency, not just one part of it. That decision is not likely to be made based on what the agency *says* on the day of the presentation, but rather on the evidence of what it has done for other clients in the past and present. And while many agencies can talk a good game, not all can play one.

In my view, planning, when used properly, is the best *old* business tool ever invented. Because if the agency has a true planning philosophy, it is interested in only one thing, and that is getting the advertising right for its existing clients. Its planners are being smart about their strategic research; they have good working relationships with other departments, especially the creative department; and most important, when they take out rough advertising concepts and show them to target consumers, they are not only honest in their appraisal, but they are listened to. Not always necessarily agreed with, but at least their point of view is seriously considered. Under such circumstances, it is much more likely that the advertising will be effective, and that advertising will then become a powerful tool with which to attract new clients.

So if planning is a new business tool at all, I would argue that its greatest contribution is indirect, by helping the agency assemble a more impressive portfolio of results for its existing clients. And contrary to what some agencies appear to believe, simply hiring a planning department does not automatically open the gates to a flood of new business. If only it were that easy.

There are some agencies who use planners extensively at the front end of the process to gather intelligence, and then exclude them from the rest of the process, except perhaps to conduct some research to prove that a creative idea that seems to the client to be so off-target that it threatens his or her career is in fact enthusiastically endorsed by consumers and should run, "because the consumer opinion is the only one that matters." (This is a phrase that reappears in other places in the book, used alternately by agency people to prove their point and by clients to prove theirs. What both parties often mean is that "consumer opinion matters when it endorses my own.") Occasionally this kind of rearguard action may be legitimate, but in general a campaign that is sold over the dead body of a dissenting client doesn't have long to live itself. Using both consumer research and planners in this way is usually the fastest way to remove the trust that is the basis of the planner's power.

In truth, there is only so much a planner or planners can do to affect the outcome of their agency's advertising in the absence of a number of factors that Stanley Pollitt regarded as essential to the successful delivery of planning's promise to clients.

"First," Pollitt argued, "it means a total agency management commitment to getting the advertising content *right* at all costs. Getting it right being more important than maximizing agency profits, than keeping clients happy, or building an agency shop window for distinctive-looking advertising.

"It means a commitment and a belief that you can only make thoroughly professional judgments about advertising content with some early indication of consumer response."

These words would no doubt send cold chills through many agency presidents, client service and new business directors, and creative directors, but what Pollitt was advocating did not represent a *choice* between effectiveness and profits, stable client relationships, or outstanding creative work. The distinction, if one existed at all, was merely one of order, or priority. If you got the advertising right, Pollitt reasoned, the rest would follow naturally. It is worth noting that at the time he wrote this, almost all advertising agencies in London were compensated on the commission system, whereby media operators would return a percentage (between 15 and 20 percent) of the money a client paid for space or time to the agency that produced the advertising. This meant that until advertising actually ran, the agency did not make any money. I worked on a campaign at BMP where the process of getting the advertising right, from the client's initial briefing to the advertising appearing on-air, took more than a year. "Late, but great," account directors would joke, while figuring out how much money the agency had lost on the account. This may sound like very bad business, which in the short term I'm sure it was, but in the long term it provided an immovable foundation for some unusually long client relationships, which provided in turn a wonderful shop window of distinctive advertising and healthy profits besides. The client trusted the agency to do the right thing, however long it took.

The second prerequisite for successful planning is that the agency commits the resources to allow planners to be more than temporary role players. If they are going to have the necessary command of all the data relevant to a particular piece of business and be able to conduct their own research besides, they cannot work on more business than an agency would expect of an account director. My planners at GS&P work on an average of three clients each, which enables them to be equally and deeply involved in those clients' businesses (attending almost as many meetings as the account director), in the lives of their clients' customers, and also in the agency's internal process, working particularly closely with the account director in crafting strategy and creative briefs, and with creative teams in developing and honing the advertising itself.

If planners are stretched between too many accounts, the depth of their involvement will suffer, and with it their ability to contribute in a substantive way. If they are not attending client meetings, then they do not have the necessary understanding of business issues against which to balance consumer opinions. If they are not spending enough time with consumers, their opinions on the marketplace will be outdated, ill-informed, and inevitably come to reflect the agency or client point of view. And if they are not working with agency creatives, providing useful information and insight, then they might as well not be working in an advertising agency at all. Creatives will soon enough start to regard them as "internal clients," a hole that is very deep and difficult to climb out of.

The relationship between planner and account director is worthy of further comment. Pollitt regarded the two as equal partners, with equal status within the agency, and in some respects it is important that this equality be maintained. I have always thought of the ideal relationship between the two in the same way as the working relationship between a copywriter and art director. Both have a common aim, but bring different sets of skills to the table. The account director brings more of a business perspective, while the planner has more of a consumer orientation, yet between the two there is a considerable area of overlap. As previously noted, they work together on strategic positioning and share responsibility for working with creative teams to help the work along (some creatives may disagree with the word "help," but that's what they *should* be doing, at least). Ultimately, though, the account director is the one who runs the account, and whenever I work as a planner on a piece of agency business, I consider that I am working *for* the account director. The client also needs to regard the account director, in effect, as the president of his or her own small agency. This isn't my being charitable or overly democratic, merely selfish. I am certain that most planners prefer to fade into the background once in a while to do their thinking, and this is not possible if the client regards them as being in charge, even in a shared capacity. If the account director is truly running the show, he or she allows planners the luxury of distance from the client whenever they need it, and that is essential to balanced and insightful vision.

The final point that Pollitt made about the implications of planning for an agency is that, as he put it, "it means changing some of the basic ground rules. Once consumer response becomes the most important element in making final advertising judgments, it makes many of the more conventional means of judgment sound hollow." The "conventional means" he had in mind were the affection of a creative director for an idea, or a client prejudice that flies in the face of hard research evidence. In the face of such prejudice, I agree that consumer response is probably the most important element.

Having said that, not all clients or creative directors need to be regulated by consumer opinion, and in an ideal world, their points of view will complement and even enhance those of consumers. This is where I disagree with Pollitt's point. I believe very strongly that consumer opinion is sometimes *not* the most important element, because, for reasons that are explored shortly in greater depth, there are many ways in which those opinions can be misleading. Many consumers do not always say what they really feel; there are limits to their experience and imagination that make it difficult for them to imagine the way rough advertising ideas might be in finished form; and these factors combined, if taken literally, may well undermine the quality of the work.

I would like to add a final implication or prerequisite of my own, and that is that planning will only work in the presence of very strong and confident creative people. I have always thought that the reason it took hold and was so successful at agencies like BMP, Bartle Bogle Hegarty, Abbott Mead Vickers, Chiat/Day, Fallon McElligott, and GS&P had less to do with the quality of the planners at those agencies than with the presence of exceptional creative people (in John Webster, John Hegarty, David Abbott, Lee Clow, Pat Burnham and Bill Westbrook, and Jeff Goodby and Rich Silverstein), who embraced planning's contribution and were talented and confident enough not to be threatened by it. Their influence rubbed off on their respective departments, and the relationship between creatives and planners at all those agencies, while consistently evolving, is in large part both mutually challenging and constructive. There seems to be a very strong correlation between a creative person's level of talent and confidence, and his or her willingness to accept the input of anyone else to their work. That's not to say that the people named above and those who work in their creative departments never resist direction or argue with a planner's point of view (I have had lively arguments myself with three of the names on that list), but at least they are prepared to *listen* to it.

Stanley Pollitt said of his relationship with Webster, "John Webster and his creative people have grown up with the system. John would say that 'planning' is very far from perfect — but like 'democracy,' it's better than the alternatives."

TWO BOMBS ON THE SAME PLANE

In an article in *Adweek* in April 1995, entitled "Origin of the Species," Debra Goldman wrote that "thanks to planning's association with ads like [Chiat/Day's '1984' for Apple, Wieden and Kennedy's Nike campaign, and GS&P's Sega and Norwegian Cruise Line work], 'planning agency' is replacing 'creative agency' as the accolade of choice in the hot shop lexicon." As a planner reading that, I have very mixed feelings.

On the one hand it is gratifying to receive public recognition for one's role in the development of a famous and effective campaign, but on the other, such statements really exaggerate the true role of planners in the process. In the examples of my own agency's work that I cite in the following chapters (Sega and Norwegian Cruise Line included), it should be obvious in every case that planning was only one of a number of sources of inspiration.

The current "cult of the planner" in U.S. advertising makes me feel very uncomfortable, not only because it is largely based on a misperception of the contribution of planners, but also because it will create expectations of a consistent supply of brilliant ideas, which I know that most planners, myself included, are incapable of delivering.

In defining the skills and personality traits that are essential for successful planners, most people will talk about raw intellect, curiosity, the ability to think simultaneously with the left brain and right brain (so that they can be logical and disciplined, and at the same time creative, innovative and instinctual), and possessing excellent communication skills both verbally and in writing. All of those, I agree, are essential. But there are other attributes that, for my taste at least, are equally important.

The first is a blend of modesty and humility. In his introduction to *The Man in the Water,* a collection of short stories and essays, the journalist and author Roger Rosenblatt writes about the process of good journalism that it "requires a vanishing act on the part of the writer; the subject must appear to be exposing his soul to the reader directly, with no middle man intervening. The only two reasons for including oneself in a story are to make oneself an Everybody, or into a character who enhances the person who is the true center of attention. Otherwise, one ought to be as small as possible." So it is with the best planning. I have always thought of planners like the American Special Forces or British SAS— if they are doing their job properly, nobody knows they are there. The fact that the job gets done is all that is important, and none of them ever get publicly recognized for their work. Officially, they weren't even there.

A planner's job is to provide the key decision makers at both the agency and the client with all the information they require to make an intelligent decision. It's not up to the planner to *make* that decision for them. The aim, as far as the planner is concerned, is the production of the best possible advertising to fulfill the client's business objectives, advertising that will stand out from the crowd, say the right things to the right people, and cause them to take some action as a result of seeing or hearing the message. It's that little reaction in their heads that the planner is seeking, and all of my planners are evaluated according to their advertising's ability to do just that. Their performance in the agency, in other words, is evaluated in large part according to the effectiveness of campaigns that they have worked on, and it is therefore very much in their own interests for their advertising to work. (As indeed it is in the agency's interests, too. People often think we're being strangely philanthropic when we say that effectiveness is our number one priority, but they forget that if our advertising doesn't help the client's business we will probably get fired. That's bad for business.)

Planners may have to work very hard to influence the way that the advertising turns out, carefully laying out a strategic foundation with the client, handing over tidbits of information to creative people when, in their judgment, that information will have the greatest impact, giving feedback on ideas, and hopefully adding some ideas of their own. The kiss of death for any planner, however, is to claim credit for those ideas if they find their way into the advertising. Some of the most satisfying experiences I have ever had in my work were those few occasions when I subtly suggested something to creatives, and next day they told me that they'd had the idea I suggested to them the day before. Of course I would never let on. A planner's job is to make ideas happen, not necessarily to have those ideas themselves.

The second skill of the planner is to spend more time listening than talking, whether in conversation with consumers, clients, or other agency team members. A good way to think about this is that the ratio of speaking to listening time in a conversation should be the same ratio as the number of mouths to ears that we all possess.

It's remarkable how often people have, and express, good ideas without knowing it themselves. Unfortunately, nobody else in the room hears them because they are all too busy thinking about what they are going to say next, assessing which of their potential comments will sound most impressive to the assembled group. A good listener will recognize those good ideas and use them, thus allowing others to do their work for them.

The third attribute is a chameleonlike quality that allows the planner to develop relationships with an extraordinarily diverse range of people. In the space of 24 hours, a planner may be presenting a strategy to the chairman of a Fortune 500 company, moderating a focus group with single, low-income mothers, and briefing a creative team on a new project. It is important that he or she be able to relate to all of them, both to gain their trust and to understand their points of view. A planner once told me that he thought it was his job to act as a kind of interpreter between three alien species (i.e., creative people, clients, and consumers) who don't have any language in common. While planners don't necessarily have to be fluent in all of their languages, they should at least understand enough to be able to find a way for the different parties to communicate with each other.

Finally, and I know this will sound strange, *there has to be something a little weird about them*. Almost all of the good planners I have known are a little out of the ordinary. This manifests itself in two main ways: in a somewhat off-center perspective on situations and a rather eclectic mix of background and interests. I'm really not sure which of the two is the chicken, and which is the egg. In the end, I could argue that either one fuels the other, and perhaps the answer is that in the best planners the two are almost codependent. The quirky outlook draws them to some strange places and interests, which make them quirkier. Or is it the other way around?

When I was hired by BMP, with my degree in geography, two planning trainees were hired at the same time. One, an Oxford graduate, had been a professional chess player. The other had worked as a professional musician before applying to the agency. I was trained by a man whose degree was in aeronautical engineering, worked closely with a classics scholar (fluent in Greek and Latin, the ideal qualification for a planner on the agency's beer business), and now that I have my own department, I have hired, among others, a killer whale trainer from SeaWorld, a litigation attorney, a Stanford MBA, a senator's speech writer, and people who have worked in previous lives at places as diverse as Procter and Gamble, VH1, Power Bar, Silicon Valley start-ups, *Wired* magazine, the British Institute for Contemporary Arts, and even Saatchi and Saatchi. As far as I know, none of them has ever been in jail, although it would not surprise me if they had.

All these people have very different views on the world and different approaches to problem solving. In building a planning department in an agency, it is essential to recruit for such diversity. Without it, planners are likely to think and behave in the same way, and that in turn will lead to identical solutions and stagnation.

I once read an interesting perspective on this from the unlikely source of someone from the British Diplomatic Corps, writing in the early 1980s after the Falklands War (Margaret Thatcher's War of Re-Election, we call it). In his view, the Falklands war could have been averted, and the primary reason he cited for the failure to avoid conflict was, surprisingly, the policies of the Foreign Office when recruiting future diplomats into their ranks. Such recruits, he said, were almost universally from Oxford or Cambridge Universities. Before that, almost all had attended the same exclusive public schools (in Britain, "public" means "private," don't ask me to explain why); before that they had been pupils at the same exclusive preparatory schools, and a very high proportion had family connections "in the service" or in government. Add all that together, he concluded, and you have an entire diplomatic corps where everyone thinks the same as everyone else, and none of them even considered dissenting from the opinion that Argentina would not dare to attack the Falklands. Consequently, in the face of considerable evidence to the contrary, the islands were not adequately defended, the Argentinean government concluded that the British didn't really care about the islands, and several thousand lives were lost in the ensuing conflict. It was time, he said, to start recruiting people who would look at a situation like that and see something different.

In the context of an advertising agency, the ability of planners to look at the same information as everyone else and see something different is invaluable. They need to be able to take information of all sorts, shuffle it around, and rearrange it in new patterns until something interesting emerges. While this skill is certainly not the exclusive province of planners, there are few good planners who do not possess it. In Chapter 4, in a discussion of the need to take the wider view in analyzing and solving advertising problems, I offer some specific advertising and marketing examples. For now, here is my favorite example of the way that a planner's mind can work.

Years ago, when I worked at BMP in London, I had booked a vacation that required flying at a time of some terrorist activity in Europe. Airports and airlines were in a state of high security alert, and I, being a nervous flyer in the best of times, was very concerned. I happened to mention my fears to Ross Barr, who was at the time the agency's Director of Planning, and is one of the smartest, funniest men I have ever met. He stroked his chin, which for him always accompanied the process of deep thought, and after a moment's pause, asked, "So you're scared that your plane might be bombed?"

Yes, I was.

"Well, have you thought about taking your own bomb?"

I looked at him incredulously.

"Here's why," he said, very seriously. "Can you imagine the chances of there being two bombs on the same plane?"

I did say *weird*, didn't I?

Years later I discovered that I need not have feared at all. I flew to Greece on an airline of Mediterranean origin, which has never been bombed. Apparently, it's the commercial airline all the terrorists fly, and there's, shall we say, an "understanding."

PLANNING DOESN'T NEED PLANNERS

One of the consistent features of many of the planning gatherings that I have attended over the years is a burning desire on the part of many of the planners gathered there to be indispensable to their agencies. Many of them clearly believe that if they were not doing their jobs, the agency would not be doing good work.

That's horseshit.

Sorry, but it's the truth.

I often speak at conferences and teach student classes, and I am often asked to talk about the best examples of planning from my agency. One that I always include in my answer is a commercial that we made in 1992 for The Partnership for a Drug-Free America (see Figure 2.1).

In the commercial, a young African-American boy is seen running along the back of some houses, jumping fences. Faces peer out from behind drapes in the houses, watching him as he runs by.

We hear the boy's voice. "Our teacher tells us all we gotta do is 'just say no'." He keeps running and jumping more fences.

"And the other day a policeman came to our class talkin' 'bout 'Say No', too."

Figure 2.1   Partnership For A Drug-Free
America: "Long Way Home."

All the time he's running. "Well my teacher doesn't have to walk home through this neighborhood. And maybe the dealers are scared of the police. . . ." (he comes to an intersection where he has to cross the road. A gang of tough-looking young men are hanging outside a liquor store, and as he runs by, one turns and stares menacingly) ". . . but they're not scared of me, and they sure don't take 'no' for an answer."

As he continues on his way, a voice-over says, "To Kevin Scott, and all the other kids who take the long way home . . . we hear you. Don't give up."

And it's signed off by The Partnership for a Drug-Free America.

It's a very powerful piece of communication, based on a very insightful strategy. It was extremely effective in persuading inner-city kids that someone out there in adult-land did actually have an inkling of what it was like to live their lives and knew the pressures they were under to get involved with drugs. In that world, Nancy Reagan telling them to "Just Say No" didn't cut it. It won the American Marketing Association's Grand Effie™ award in 1994 for the most effective advertising campaign in America. And no account planner had ever been anywhere near it. Jeff Goodby and Jeremy Postaer, who between them wrote and directed this pro bono commercial, did their own planning in conjunction with the Partnership's own research people.

If I didn't believe that planning did help in some way to make advertising better and more effective, then I wouldn't be writing this book. But if all the planners disappeared tomorrow, the agencies who are doing good work in America now would still be doing good work in six months' time. It might not be as consistent, but it would still be good, because those agencies as a whole have the right instincts and sensibilities regarding the relationships between their advertising and target consumers, and they want their campaigns to be effective.

Several years ago, a cartoon strip created by Stan Mack ran in *Adweek*. In one of these "out-takes" cartoons, two advertising executives are walking in the snow on a street in Cleveland, and one mentions to the other that his agency "offers the account planning philosophy. It's the latest thing." He continues, "Y'see, the account people worry about market share; creative fights for ideals; marketing talks socio-economic strata; but account planners represent the consumer."

"But what do they do?" his friend asks.

"They look in the cracks, check relevance, persuade the strategic direction, glimpse the obvious . . ."

"But what do they do?"

". . . set up opportunities and challenges, get into people's heads, find out what makes them tick, find their real triggers . . ."

"B-but what . . ."

"On the other hand, some agencies do fine without account planners."

3

The Blind Leading the Bland
Advertising Follows Research . . . in the Wrong Direction

We are so busy measuring public opinion that we forget we can mold it. We are so busy listening to statistics we forget that we can create them.

Bill Bernbach

FEAR OF FLYING

"Without research," a client once told me, "we are flying in the dark. Not only are we in the dark, but we have no radio, no compass, and no fuel gauge. I don't know about you, but I sure would hate to fly on that plane."

I had to agree that I, too, would hate to fly on such a plane, but I am just plain scared of flying. To me even good weather, perfect navigation, the best equipment, and a skilled pilot at the controls have never been an absolute guarantee of safety. As far as I'm concerned, it's a miracle every time I land and the plane isn't in flames.

The client obviously had the same kind of fears about the process of creating advertising and used research not just as a navigational aid, but as a kind of talisman to protect both himself and his career from a fiery end. I imagined him sitting at his desk, running his hands fondly over a Nielsen report, examining topline copy-test data, making a call to the research company to ask for a particular type of cross tabulation, reading some focus group verbatim comments, and feeling *secure.*

He used research to inform and guide almost every decision he ever made, yet over the years an alarmingly high number of those decisions led to disappointing results. In some cases he was not exactly *wrong,* but neither was he exactly *right* in either his analysis or his recommendations. And while the precise reasons for his navigational errors tended to be different each time, their roots could almost all be traced back to the research that he had used to analyze his problem.

As a student at University, I used to derive considerable peace of mind and security from the presence of library textbooks on my bookshelves. Sometimes I didn't even open them, but as I stared at them from across the room, I felt that I was expanding my mind and moving another step closer to my degree. I imagine that my client felt the same way about research. For him, simply *doing* research, any research, brought him comfort and gave him the confidence to make decisions. The fact that often he was doing the wrong kind of research, or using its findings in the wrong way, never really seemed to occur to him.

If I had asked him the question that I posed in Chapter 1, whether he felt that he consistently and effectively involved consumers in the process of developing advertising, I am certain that his reply would have been an unequivocal "yes." Most marketing and advertising professionals in the United States would say the same and would probably be indignant that anyone would think for even a moment that they *did not* exercise due diligence on the research front. Unfortunately, many of them fall into the same traps as my aforementioned client, basing their decisions on research that is itself flawed.

It is flawed because in many instances the right questions are not asked—maybe out of laziness, or lack of thought, or force of habit—and as a result the research goes off in the wrong direction, leaving behind both the consumers it was meant to represent and the truths that they could have revealed. To compound the problem, such flawed research may be followed literally, without any kind of commonsense filter. The ensuing advertising, in the worst case, will not only reflect the mistakes of the research, but magnify them.

There are many ways in which research can lead advertising astray, and I explore some of them in this chapter.

Before I do, I should point out some of the areas that I do *not* cover. First, I can assure you that this is not a diatribe against quantitative research, which seems to be the normal refrain when anyone from a remotely creative agency is given a public platform to talk about research. I discuss the role of quantitative research, but only to suggest that, like every other source of information available to advertisers, quantitative research and the numbers it yields should not always be taken at face value. Numbers, just like focus group respondents, are capable of misleading, and even lying, and always require a commonsense filter before they can be used with confidence.

I also avoid a discussion of individual quantitative methodologies and measures, as it would be too lengthy, undoubtedly very boring, and to cap it all, if I started, I would probably end up getting sued by someone. Moreover, an extensive array of literature from academic, pseudoacademic, and industry sources already exists on the subject, and I feel no reason to replicate it. The bibliography at the end of this book does include some of those references, but not all, as I chose to include only those authors and titles that directly informed or influenced my own writing.

Finally, this is not a discussion of "research versus planning." A planner who worked with me years ago at GS&P, Dan Baxter, once silenced a conference of bickering planners with the observation that all the comparisons he had heard made between planning and research were between good planning and bad research. Wasn't it possible, he asked, that a good researcher might just be more useful than a bad planner? I agree with him. The best planners and researchers are fundamentally the same kind of people, the major difference being the environment in which they operate and the extent to which they are able to apply their craft to the creative process.

The purpose of the following pages is not to suggest that advertising agencies and their clients should stop doing research. Far from it. I merely want people to give it a bit more thought before they do it, make certain that they are doing the right *kind* of research, and exercise some judgment when they consider the results that emerge.

DOING RESEARCH WITHOUT ANYONE KNOWING WHY

The first reaction of many advertising and marketing professionals on being asked a difficult question is to say, "let's do some research." I know, because I have been guilty of it myself on more than one occasion. It's a knee-jerk reaction, for we know that at some point we will have to conduct research of some sort, and in our enthusiasm to make some early progress, we commission a quantitative survey or recruit some focus groups, all before we have asked ourselves some rather important questions.

The first is, do we really need to do research at all?

There are two possible reasons the answer may be no.

The first is that the agency and client might be able to answer it themselves, without recourse to research, using some combination of their own experience, intellect or instinct. It's strange how often the answer that immediately springs to mind on hearing the question is the right answer. While some people may enjoy having their instincts confirmed by a 50,000-dollar research study, others, with the benefit of hindsight, may well wish that they had trusted their instincts and saved the money.

Unfortunately, many people are afraid of following their instincts, and in particular are afraid of making decisions without any backup. Because they *can* do research, they defer to it every time, even when it is not really necessary.

A few years ago, in the National Football League's first experiment with instant replay (whereby the officials on the field could request a TV replay as a second opinion on a close call), the intent was to use the replay to make calls that were too close to make on the field, in situations that would have a profound impact on the game's outcome. In many such circumstances, it was a great success. However, officials gradually came to request the replay in situations that were far from pivotal, and for calls that were patently clear to 80,000 fans in the stadium and millions at home watching on television *without* the benefit of slow motion, and the experiment was dropped. Simply because they *could* ask for another opinion, the officials were absolving themselves of their responsibility to have opinions and make decisions themselves.

Perhaps the first question that should be asked by people with very large research budgets at their fingertips is, what decision would I make if I could not do any research at all? They should imagine themselves without that crutch and spend some time considering the merits of the answer that comes up without any outside help. For many people, the first answer that springs to mind may seem too *obvious*, and it may seem obvious because it is actually right. I never cease to be amazed at the fear with which most people regard such obvious answers. Perhaps they feel that a complex problem deserves a complex answer, and that somehow if they choose the solution that has 100 people in a room nodding their heads and saying, "Duh! Of course!" then they are not doing their jobs properly. I return to this point in later chapters, but almost all of the best advertising campaigns with which I have been associated are based on ideas so obvious that it's almost embarrassing to be paid for coming up with them (I said *almost*).

In many categories, there is a "high ground" positioning based on a simple truth about the reason people buy a product or the way that they use it, and it is often there for the taking. Why? I'm sure that it was once owned by someone, but over time, competitors probably succeeded in making other criteria important, and the original leader moved out of its stronghold to fight for control of those new dimensions. As more time passes, all of the competing companies spend their time scanning the horizon for a clever, previously undiscovered point of difference, when that powerful, simple truth is laying right under their noses. The Norwegian Cruise Line and "got milk?" campaigns, featured in Chapters 6 and 7 respectively, are good examples of solutions of the "under-the-nose" variety.

I am not advocating making all decisions on the basis of either experience or guesswork (even though both have played a significant role in the genesis and development of many of the best ideas that I have ever seen in the industry). But at the very least, using them as a starting point should be possible, or using them to generate hypotheses, which can then be tested through research. If nothing else, that will give the research a clear focus. The more that goes into it, in terms of ideas and hypotheses, the more useful the information that will emerge at the other end.

The second reason that research may not be needed is that previous research may have already answered the question. I won't dwell on this point, but any research-dependent company will already have vaults stacked high with old data and analysis that can perhaps be utilized to help solve a problem without spending more time and money on new research. Even though previous studies will not necessarily answer the specific question that is being posed now, they may have touched on it from a number of different angles and can be used to great effect, even if only in a supporting role, as a kind of sounding board for new hypotheses.

When I mention existing research, I am not merely referring to thick, dusty documents, or to videotapes of focus groups. One of the advantages of the system of account planning envisioned by Stanley Pollitt was that, unlike traditional agency researchers who tended to be called in on an ad hoc basis to answer specific questions on any one of a number of clients' businesses, account planners would work full-time on the same piece of business, and over time would build up a valuable reservoir of knowledge that could be applied to future problems.

Such knowledge, though useful on occasion, should also be treated with some caution: As valuable as it is to have a true feel for the way that a particular audience might react to a certain message, with *too much* knowledge it is possible to lose sight of subtle changes in the outlook of that audience, under the complacent assumption that you have "seen it all before."

When I worked as a planner in Britain, I must have conducted more than 300 focus groups on the subject of beer alone, over a period of four or five years. I felt, probably rightly, that at the time I knew British beer drinkers' habits and motivations inside out, but I also know that the more times I asked why they drank beer in general, or an individual brand in particular, the less I listened. It wasn't that I didn't want to listen, but rather that I thought I knew the answer before I had even asked the question. And consequently, I suspect, the more detached I became over time from the truth.

Anyone who flies regularly will have experienced this phenomenon. Every time you fly, before you take off, the flight attendants recite the list of safety instructions, telling you where the exits are located, how to open the doors, where the flotation device is located and how to inflate it. I must have heard those instructions 400 times, and because I have heard them so often, even though I imagine every take-off and landing as a possible Armageddon, I assume I know them, and no longer listen. I know I'm not alone, because almost every other seasoned traveler talks or reads through the presentation, too. But I swear that if ever I were unlucky enough to be in a plane that made a water landing, I wouldn't be able to find my flotation device; and even if I could find it, I'd find myself blowing in the wrong hole and strapping it on so that I floated face downward.

Simply considering the question, "do we really need to do research at all?" will have a positive effect on any research that *is* conducted, because it at least focuses attention on the key issues that need to be addressed and begins the process of figuring out the most appropriate methodologies.

THE WRONG QUESTIONS ARE OFTEN ASKED

The quality of information that results from any research project, whether quantitative or qualitative, is directly proportional to the quality of the information and thought that went *into* the research. That means it's important to apply the kind of thinking just described, as well as have a clear idea of the target that the research is supposed to address, the key issues that need to be explored, and some preliminary hypotheses that can be examined. Most important of all, the use, or uses, to which the research findings will be put need to be clearly defined.

The most common mistake that emanates from lack of clarity (or complete lack of attention) at the planning or preparatory stage is that the wrong questions are often asked. These wrong questions are in turn often asked of the wrong people, in the wrong places, at the wrong time, by the wrong interviewers, which in combination tend to produce some less-than-accurate answers. But even if these subsequent, more methodological, issues were handled properly, the initial strategic problem of asking incorrect questions creates an almost insurmountable obstacle.

One of my agency's clients is UNUM, the world's leader in disability insurance. While I don't know how much you know about disability insurance, I would hazard a guess that it is not very much. Most companies who provide health insurance for employees also provide some kind of disability insurance, but many of the employees don't know it. And if they do, they tend not to understand why they have the coverage, don't know how it works, and are not particularly inclined to think about it. Disability in general is something that few of us really want to think or talk about, and the whole area of insurance is regarded at best as a necessary evil. The two in combination don't generally make for sparkling conversation. In fact, even the brokers who *sell* disability insurance policies tend to find such a conversation difficult, because people's low interest levels make them harder to sell than, say, medical or life insurance.

With that in mind, imagine for a moment a focus group comprising brokers, corporate benefits managers, or holders of disability insurance policies. Now imagine that the first statement from the moderator is, "We're here tonight to talk about disability insurance. What is the most important feature you look for in a disability insurance policy?" It's a legitimate question in the abstract; but coming right at the start of the discussion, it will take the research in completely the wrong direction. People will talk, as requested, about the stuff that's important, no doubt creating the impression to all those assembled to observe the research that disability insurance is truly a very important issue in these respondents' lives. The problem is that no context has been established for the questions that the client wants to ask about their policies. Consequently, what is said about those policies, and indeed about disability insurance in general, will be more likely to reflect the client's view of the world than that of the respondents whose opinions are ostensibly being sought.

Without a broader perspective to understand where a product or category fits in the context of people's lives, and not the other way round, answers that may imply a company's or product's *absolute* strength are in reality no more than *relative* measures, and as a consequence may well be worthless.

It's perhaps not surprising that so much research starts from this somewhat myopic position. After all, if you work in a toilet paper company, you spend every waking hour, and probably a considerable proportion of your dreamtime besides, thinking about things like softness, absorbency, and number of squares per roll, and they take on a disproportionate importance in your life. It's perhaps only natural that you assume a similar level of knowledge, interest, and enthusiasm in the outside world and take *that* as your starting point for research.

In my old agency in London, there was a famous story (which I believe to be true) about a client from Nabisco, who was responsible for a chocolate-covered biscuit (cookie) called *Club*. He briefed the agency one day on a product improvement, the result of new technology that allowed an extra half-millimeter of chocolate to be added all around the biscuit. To say he was flushed with excitement would be an understatement. He waxed lyrical about the technology that was making it all possible and talked of a response from the British public to this great advance that would be little short of life changing. Housewives would be beating down the doors of the grocery stores once they realized that Club's chocolate was layered thicker than they had ever dreamed possible. He was abruptly pulled out of his fantasy by one of the agency planners, who said, "John, excuse me for saying this, but . . . but . . . it's only a fucking chocolate biscuit."

It's a sobering discovery for many of those who live, eat, and sleep their products that their customers do not feel the same way, but many do not make that discovery until it is too late.

When GS&P was first awarded the California Fluid Milk Processors Advisory Board account, we were given access to a vast amount of historic research that had been commissioned over the years by various groups within the dairy industry. One particular question appeared in the questionnaire of a number of studies that purported to be exploring people's milk consumption and habits: "How much milk do you drink?" or words to that effect.

On the surface, it seems a reasonable enough question, but if answered literally, it can tell a lie about how much milk people consume and about how they consume it. The reason is that "how much milk do you drink?" implies glasses of milk, yet people could, in all honesty, reply that they do not drink milk, when every day they eat 17 bowls of cereal. Cereal, in fact, accounts for more than half of the occasions on which people use milk. I personally blame the years of advertising where people drained glasses of milk and slurped direct from milk cartons, at least in part, on the way the industry asked this question in its research and on the distorted picture of consumption that emerged as a result.

Beyond the potential of individual questions to lead research astray, the wider role of quantitative questionnaires or qualitative discussion guides (the list of questions and topics that a focus group moderator or in-depth interviewer uses to guide discussion over the session) can be called into question for the way that they guide, or sometimes pervert, both the process of research and the validity of the responses extracted from it.

Both questionnaires and discussion guides are used in the interests of consistency and efficiency to ensure that all respondents are asked the same questions in the same way. Thus their responses can be analyzed and compared in an apples-to-apples way. The order of discussion or questioning is determined according to what makes for the most logical flow (from the perspective of the client or researcher) and allows for the most efficient exploration of the key issues.

I have seen both questionnaires and discussion guides that are so long they put some reports to shame, and whose structure depends not only on a particular line of questioning, but also a particular line of *answers*. In other words, whether consciously or not (and in all fairness I think that it is usually not) researchers are supposing in advance what the answers will be, and by the order and manner in which the questions are posed, they become almost self-fulfilling.

Research conducted in this way works in a completely different manner from the human mind, which tends not to be logical or linear, and for which both thought and conversation are on the whole a series of random events. I have always felt that there's an inverse relationship between the degree of order and control that one might have over any research project and the quality of the information that it yields.

The final point to make about asking the wrong questions is that by extension, the *right questions are too often missed*. This is largely the result of not enough thought up front, and in particular an avoidance (some may say fear) of the commonsense, obvious, dumb questions of which I am so fond. What anyone who resists asking the obvious questions should consider, though, is that failure to ask them may avoid a certain level of embarrassment at the time of the research, but when things go wrong as a result of ignoring them, there can be no greater embarrassment. Consider the following example, from outside the world of either advertising or marketing, as a warning of how bad this can be.

For reasons best kept to myself, I recently purchased a book about the flora and fauna of the Hawaiian islands. On reading it, I was surprised to discover that Hawaii is home to a large population of the Indian mongoose, a mammal that looks like a large weasel or a small otter and is famous for its ferocity, especially its ability to kill large, poisonous snakes.

The mongoose hadn't always been resident in Hawaii. In fact, there is only one endemic species of mammal on any of the islands, a bat, which is sadly irrelevant to this story. But many other species have been introduced over the years, either by design (the pigs I mentioned in Chapter 1 were originally brought in as domestic animals), or by accident, as stowaways on ships arriving from the Americas or Polynesia.

Among these unwelcome immigrants were rats, which quickly colonized every island in the chain, and with no natural predators to control their population, became so numerous that they wrought havoc on the islands' sugar plantations. The plantation owners, frustrated by the failure of their efforts to control the rats' numbers by other means, and desperate to save their crops, turned to nature for a solution. If the rats had no natural predators on the islands, they reasoned, they would introduce one from elsewhere, and research to find a suitable animal was immediately launched.

The predator they sought would need to be resilient enough to adapt to a new environment, with the strength and aggression necessary to overpower the none-too-timid rat, and the ability to breed sufficiently fast that only a limited number would have to be introduced at once.

Their research quickly revealed the perfect candidate. The Indian mongoose—legendary for its bravery, speed, and strength—could kill a cobra, the most dangerous of snakes, and also had a taste for rodents. That these tastes extended to rats was proven in laboratory experiments where mongooses and rats were put into cages together to see what would happen. In every instance, the mongoose killed, and sometimes ate, the rat.

On the basis of this research, large numbers of mongooses were captured, transported to Hawaii, and released on all the islands except for Kauai. (Their absence on Kauai is explained by the coincidence of Kauai's native chief traveling on the same boat as the caged animals. Concluding that the snarling, vicious creatures just "didn't feel right" for his island, he threw the cages overboard and the mongooses drowned.) Unfortunately, the plantation owners soon realized that their rat problem was not going away. In fact, on the big island of Hawaii, where most mongooses had been released, the damage continued at the same level as on Kauai, where none had been released. The reason? Despite all the research, the mongoose's killing credentials, and the successful laboratory tests, one important fact had been overlooked.

The mongoose is diurnal, while the rat is nocturnal. And no one had thought to ask.

So while rats were out gnawing on sugar cane, their fearsome "predators" were fast asleep. Once the rats retreated to their nests, mongooses would emerge to feast on domestic chickens and the young and eggs of endemic, ground-dwelling (and now often-endangered) wild bird species. All things considered, the whole experiment was a disaster.

The research that was conducted was clearly not wrong in terms of the validity of the answers it had derived from the questions asked. It had set out to identify a fearsome preda-tor, and the mongoose seemed to be exactly what the brief described. The tests that measured the mongoose's rat-killing potential were perfectly legitimate, and the data on its rate of reproduction and expected population growth unerr-ingly accurate. But it was guilty by omission. One important question had never been asked, and as a result, all the time and money devoted to solving the rat problem was com-pletely wasted. Even worse, in addition to the rat problem, Hawaiians now had a mongoose problem to deal with.

So what do mongooses and rats have to do with adver-tising and marketing? Ask the Coca-Cola corporation. I won't go into this in depth, because it is an example that has already been written and talked about so many times, but in launching New Coke in 1985, despite all the research that showed it was a good idea and the taste tests that demon-strated New Coke's superiority over the old, Coca-Cola missed one important fact. They ignored the power of the emotional attachment that people had toward Coke and their unwillingness to part with a product that was so much a part of their lives in favor of a supposedly better-tasting but unfamiliar newcomer.

"All of the time and money and skill that we poured into consumer research could not reveal the depth of feeling for the original taste of Coca-Cola," said Donald Keough, presi-dent of the soft drink giant, in an interview in the *New York Times*, after consumer outcry caused the company to reintro-duce its original formula.

Could not? Blind taste tests had shown that consumers preferred the new taste over the old by 55 to 45 percent. When the trademark Coca-Cola was identified, the new taste was preferred over the old by 61 to 39 percent, but the consumers expressing that preference were not told that the original Coca-Cola might be scrapped. They thought the new formula would be available alongside the original. Oops.

The most important question, "How would you feel if the original formula was no longer available?" was never asked, so they never heard the answer. Until it was too late.

THOSE QUESTIONS ARE ASKED IN THE WRONG WAY

A large, middle-aged woman, holding a clipboard, blocked my path into the mall.

"Sir, I'm from ____ market research, and I wonder whether you have a few minutes to answer some questions."

"I'd love to help," I replied, "but I'm a guest of the company that's sponsoring the research. I'm here to observe. Can you direct me to the facility?"

She pointed to some trash cans, which marked the entrance to a narrow alley. A rough cardboard sign with an arrow announced the presence of the research facility, and as I entered the alley I was joined by another, even larger, clipboard lady, leading a young, male respondent to his fate.

It was ten o'clock in the morning, and I was in this mall in San Diego to observe some research, commissioned by one of my clients, to test an advertising campaign that we had developed on some "target consumers" and quantify their response. We had played no part in the study design, but had at least been invited to observe its execution.

Research respondents were stopped as I had been. If they were willing to spend a few minutes and conformed to the recruitment specifications, they were promised a small financial incentive for their time and led back to the facility. There they spent 15 minutes in a small, dark room answering questions from a questionnaire, before being taken into another room, seated in front of a screen in what resembled a dentist's chair, and wired up to a strange headset. Images that attempted to replicate the pages of a magazine were then projected onto the screen. An ad here, an editorial there, and at some point our agency's ad was shown. The headset, which covered the eyes, was designed to track the motion of respondents' pupils, and a beam, invisible to the respondents themselves, danced across the screen to show where they were looking and how long they spent there. After that exercise was completed, they filled out a questionnaire, and finally, almost an hour after entering the facility, they were released.

The most interesting thing I learned from the exercise was that when shown an ad with a photograph of a beautiful female model, most men will look at her breasts before they read the headline. That wasn't the purpose of the research, but it proved to be an unexpected and exciting bonus.

But I also saw very clearly that *the way that the research was conducted* could exert a dramatic influence over its outcome. On this particular occasion, a number of factors were in play that I believe made a positive response to the advertising less likely.

At this point, I should reveal that the campaign in question was for Cuervo Gold tequila. It was based on the idea that Cuervo is a kind of catalyst that takes a party to a different level, a premise with which anyone who has ever had any experience with the brand would find it hard to disagree. The ads themselves featured close-up pictures of people in an advanced state of excitement, or shot glass and margarita paraphernalia (salt shakers, limes), covered by type that filled the entire page. In each execution, one word or phrase was highlighted in larger type. In one, GET NAKED, in another ROCKIN', and in a third, LICK.

Now back to the research. It's ten o'clock on a Wednesday morning in a mall in San Diego. Now what kind of people do you suppose were in that mall at 10 A.M.? I seriously doubt that even if they were under 35 and said that they drank Cuervo on a regular basis, they were the young *opinion leaders* that the campaign was setting out to address. Those people would have been somewhere else, doing something much more interesting. Even if they *were* the right people, it's not hard to imagine that their minds, at ten in the morning on a Wednesday, differed in some important ways from their condition on a Friday night. It is thus extremely unlikely that an image of someone standing on a table in the wee small hours, screaming "Get naked," is going to turn them on. An emotional campaign was being tested according to rational criteria, in a sterile environment, at the wrong time, with the wrong people (as I said, large, crabby, middle-aged women) asking the questions. The campaign was far from perfect, but under those circumstances, it didn't have a chance.

It doesn't seem to occur to many researchers who spend their lives in the pursuit of objectivity that the simple act of doing research changes the situation that they are attempting to observe or measure. This is Heisenberg's uncertainty principle applied to advertising research, and in advertising research, as well as in quantum theory, it is possible that there is no such thing as scientific objectivity.

The people who make up our research samples may seem on the surface to be representative of a particular target or population, but in reality what they represent is a subset of that sample—a subset of individuals willing to interrupt their shopping and answer a long list of questions for a few dollars, or a subset of individuals who are willing to give up a whole evening to attend a focus group. These people may be doing it because they need the money, or because they have an unnatural interest in advertising or marketing, either of which could, in the worst case, make the carefully selected sample more *un*representative of the broader population whose characteristics they are supposed to reflect.

THE HUMAN ZOO

The environment in which much research is conducted also has a profound effect on people's responses. It's impossible to tell *how much* of an effect it has, but I know that it is substantial.

When I worked in England, the way that focus groups were conducted differed from the way they happen in the United States in one very important respect. In the United States the vast majority of focus groups take place in custom-built research facilities, usually in downtown locations. In the United Kingdom there were hardly any such facilities, and almost every group I ever moderated was located in a private home.*

Boase Massimi Pollitt had an extensive network of recruiters in every major town, who would recruit respondents to come to their homes for the session. On the lunchtime or evening in question, the respondents would come to the house (which was usually in their own neighborhood—for blue-collar projects we would use blue-collar locations and go to the other side of town for white-collar studies), have a glass of wine or beer in the kitchen while they were waiting for the group to start, and finally come into the living room for the session itself. There they would sit in armchairs and sofas, have another drink, and chat. And under such circumstances, even the famously reserved English would have quite a lot to say.

The picture in the United States is very different. Respondents who have been recruited for a focus group arrive, typically, at a downtown high-rise, where they take the elevator to the 24th floor. There they take a seat in a reception area filled with respondents for four different focus groups that are scheduled to take place simultaneously. Perhaps there's a group of African-American teens who are there to talk about basketball with a sneaker company. A group of women who have brought their nine-year-olds to a discussion about chocolate milk. Maybe a group of affluent (mostly white) males who have recently purchased Porsches. And the respondents' own

---

*Eight years after leaving the United Kingdom, I am dismayed to learn that there are now many more custom-built facilities and that research in people's homes is now a much less common occurrence.

group, a mixture of men and women aged 25 to 45 who have been invited to talk about telephone companies. So there they sit, often in silence, among total strangers, concentrating on the deli sandwich that is the dinner they were promised.

When the time comes, they enter the research room. A moderator, perhaps with a British accent, asks them to sit down at a long, boardroomlike table and put their name cards in front of them. On a first-come-first-served basis, if not directed otherwise, the respondents manage to seat themselves so that all four women are sitting next to each other and all six men form a separate alliance. The two Hispanic respondents are sitting next to one another, as are the two African Americans. In one corner of the room, a large man with red hair tied back in a ponytail is operating a video camera on a tall tripod, surrounded by professional video decks and a monitor. Microphones dangle from the ceiling above the table. Behind the moderator, who is seated teacherlike at the head of the table, there is a wall-to-wall and floor-to-ceiling mirror. Behind that mirror, which is of course not a mirror at all, but a viewing window, an assortment of agency and client staff are eating M&Ms, making telephone calls, and making fun of the ugly respondents. From time to time, these jokes result in uproarious laughter that, believe me, can be heard through the glass by the respondents. (One time when I was moderating a group, one respondent was a little slow in understanding a particular piece of advertising, and was rather negative in her comments about it. As she finished her sentence, the other respondents were silent, and a muffled voice from behind the glass could be heard exclaiming, "For God's sake, Margaret, get a life!" Margaret didn't talk much after that.)

Add all of that together, and imagine how the respondents feel when the moderator tells them that "the most important thing tonight is for you all to relax, be natural, and be *yourselves*."

There is a chance, in the hands of a skilled moderator, that at least some of the respondents will be themselves and say what they really think about the issues under discussion, but the odds are often stacked against that outcome. The strange surroundings, the boardroom table, the surveillance equipment, all affect the respondents in subtle and not-so-subtle ways. Some are intimidated into silence, and their opinions are never heard. Others perform for the cameras and cannot be silenced. Some regard their entire reason for being, in that apparently corporate environment, as that of a critic, whose job is to spot the mistakes that the advertisers and marketers are making. I will repeat the point that I made previously—that a skilled moderator can reduce or even overcome such problems. But anyone reading this book who has ever witnessed one or more focus groups will recognize that such moderators are a rare breed, and that even the best of them are often defeated, or at least bruised, by their surroundings.

I have a keen interest in primates (the ape, as opposed to the ecclesiastical variety) and have been lucky enough to observe both gorillas and chimpanzees not only in captivity, but also in the wild. A chimpanzee in the Gombe forest of Tanzania looks pretty much the same as a chimpanzee at San Francisco zoo, and they share many common traits in terms of gestures, vocalizations, and other types of behavior. But in many more ways than that, they are different from one another. The behavior of a captive chimpanzee is modified by its surroundings, and any observations of a captive group's behavior cannot be reliably projected to the wild population.

When Jane Goodall first observed chimpanzees at Gombe fishing for termites with tools that they had fashioned from twigs, she was able to challenge the long-standing definition of what separates humans from the animal kingdom — that humans create and use tools, and animals do not. Her evidence suggested that either we should consider chimpanzees as humans, or find a new definition.

Both Jane Goodall, with her continuing chimpanzee studies, and Dian Fossey, who spent many years observing mountain gorillas in Rwanda, opened the eyes of the world to the proximity of both species to humans, not only in terms of their genetic makeup, but in their family bonds, their power struggles, and their emotions. None of this would have been possible without going into the wild and observing the animals in their natural habitat.

I believe that the thoughts and behavior of a human focus group respondent are as representative of the broader population as the thoughts and behavior of a chimpanzee in San Francisco zoo are of chimps in the east African forests. Which is to say, not very representative at all.

In later chapters, and particularly in Chapter 4, I explore ways in which research can create a relationship with people outside traditional facilities, in surroundings that are more representative of their "natural habitat," and thus more conducive to natural, relaxed behavior. This, in turn, makes it more likely that the respondents will actually tell the truth about their experiences or feelings.

"We Have Ways of Making You Talk"

The last point to make about the way that research questions are put to people is that even in qualitative research, whose purpose is to gather opinions in a very relaxed, informal and nonprojectable way, many of the interviews that are conducted, whether in groups or one-on-one, bear more resemblance to an interrogation than a discussion. The problems inherent in lengthy discussion guides and questionnaires, where the obsession with asking the right questions, in the right order, relegates the right *answers* to a secondary role, make me feel that much research is done *to* people as opposed to done *with* them. If all they are doing is responding to an interminable list of questions, they will remain in a reactive mode, and it is unlikely that their answers will go beyond the superficial. To get the best out of focus group respondents in particular, it is important that they be given time to think. It's no coincidence that most of the best insights that I have ever extracted from a focus group have come at the end of relatively long (and some would say uncomfortable) silences, silences that allowed respondents to give an issue some thought before they offered an opinion. Those insights may well have been lost had I simply filled the silence with yet another in a long list of questions.

In these interrogations, it is surprising how often the language that is used in asking the questions is that of the interviewer or their sponsor, rather than that of the respondent, or "detainee." Perhaps the problem exhibited by much advertising, that it talks in the language of the company rather than the consumer, actually starts at the research stage, where moderators use inside jargon to describe products and assume that respondents understand them. Geoffrey Frost, who is the global advertising director at Nike, has a good phrase to describe this habit: He calls it "them-r-us marketing," where on the inside of a company everyone assumes without question that their customers are exactly like them. In reality, that is almost never the case.

This is a particular issue where marketers and their agencies use different words to describe products than the words of people who actually buy and use the products. For example, "sport utility vehicle" is an often-used phrase in the corridors of automobile company marketing departments, while in the outside world, drivers will be just as likely to describe their Isuzu Trooper, Ford Explorer, Jeep Cherokee, or Toyota 4Runner as a "truck," a "four-wheel drive," or even (to the chagrin of all other manufacturers) a "Jeep." If respondents in a focus group are asked for their opinions of "sport utility vehicles," some, even owners, do not understand the question. I have made the mistake of asking it myself, and for some reason one or two respondents have looked puzzled, not joined in the conversation for a while, and finally said, "Oh, you mean *trucks*. Yeah, my Explorer . . ."

It's not just a question of product names. Many companies expect their customers to think and behave in the way that their company is *organized,* and very often the way that they conduct their research tends to compound that belief. For example, many technology and telecommunications companies divide their businesses along "business" and "consumer" lines, with different executives responsible for each, and often different advertising campaigns for the two sides. The assumption guiding all of this is that a person using a telephone for business is a different species from a person using one at home. In many respects, especially where telecommunications products beyond the telephone itself are concerned, this argument has some validity. However, even the most technical of business people have home lives, and if they see advertising from a telephone company, it is usually when they are sitting in front of the television with their families. So simply talking to them as a businessperson, especially on issues related to overall brand perceptions, may be limiting or even misleading. Their whole life has to be considered, not just one neat little compartment that mirrors the marketing department's organization chart.

PEOPLE DON'T ALWAYS MEAN WHAT THEY SAY

The wrong questions being asked in the wrong way have an alarming habit of eliciting the wrong answers. Those answers are not necessarily wrong because people deliberately go out of their way to give false information, but because the research leads them down a path from which it is difficult to stray. It's like falling into a river that moves through a steep-walled gorge—there's only one way out, and that's downstream.

Without a broader context for the discussion, as previously described, it would be very easy to conclude that disability insurance is really a very interesting topic of conversation, or that the world cannot wait for the next 15¢-a-minute long-distance telephone calling plan, or that all milk advertising should refute peoples' concerns about its fat content. I know that with the right discussion guide and an unwavering commitment to the order of my questions, I could find out all of those things, and in good faith report them as key findings from my research. They would be wrong, but they would still be key findings.

As already noted, some respondents will take positions on issues that reflect their perception of what the moderator really wants to hear ("if he wants me to be a critic, then I'll criticize"), while others will be deliberately contrarian. But beyond simple group dynamics, which again can be controlled up to a point by a skilled moderator, there is another reason respondents may not be saying exactly what they mean. The problem is, in this particular case, they may actually *believe* that they mean it. It's a weird gray area, falling somewhere between truth and fiction, where respondents have become almost conditioned to say certain things because that's what decent, or intelligent, or informed people are *supposed* to say. Political correctness is a phenomenon that I have observed muddying the waters of research all over the United States, but especially in California. In San Francisco, it is rampant. It affects a whole host of issues, from the general ("I am not affected by advertising"), to the specific ("I think the person should get the milk at the end of the commercial, because there's too much unhappiness in the world already"), to the extreme ("I think it's wrong to advertise milk because people in some religions regard cows as sacred and they might be offended").

I once had to abandon a focus group in England after one of the respondents rushed from the room in tears after receiving a lecture from one of the others on how she should be feeding her child, whatever her financial restrictions. "If *I* were you," the antagonist stated, "however little money I had, *I* would focus on fruit and vegetables." In all likelihood, the woman didn't even feed her own child that way, but there was an opportunity to take the moral high ground, and she grabbed it gleefully. Unfortunately, in the process, she accused the other woman of failing in her responsibilities as a mother.

To hear people talk in focus groups, and indeed to believe the answers they give in larger, more reliable quantitative surveys, one would think that Americans are the cleanest living, healthiest race on the planet. They all eat well, they work out, and cholesterol levels are universally low.

For example, in a recent survey, American businesspeople were asked which hotel facilities were most influential in their choice of one hotel over another. At the top of the list came the presence of a hotel gym, with 70 percent of respondents indicating that it was a very important factor in their decisions. On the basis of such a finding, it would be easy to imagine hotel owners rushing to expand their gym facilities. If 70 percent of guests are going to use them, then two treadmills and a stationary bicycle are probably not enough. The reality, though, is that 17 percent actually use the gym. The rest settle in for the evening with a handful of gin bottles from the minibar and the soft porn channel on Spectravision.

Similarly, in a recent five-year period, the number of Americans expressing concern over their intake of french fries rose by 39 percent. Over the same time period, actual consumption of french fries fell by a mere seven percent. And for all the protestations of cutting down on red meat, beef remains America's favorite meat, and steak restaurants from coast to coast are doing record business.

Why is there such a gap between what people say and what they actually do? In research, many people tend to present the personalities and habits they would like to have, rather than the ones they really have. Sometimes they do it to impress other participants in the research, but sometimes I truly believe they do it to impress themselves, to convince themselves that they are more discerning, and live for a moment at least in the body and mind of the person they always wanted to be. After all, they are among strangers, none of whom know the truth.

In the days when I was traveling around Britain talking to people about beer, I would always ask at the start of a session what beers they consumed on a regular basis. Each respondent would name his beer (we rarely talked to women because at the time they accounted for such a small percentage of total beer volume), often citing small, regional brands of ale, like Theakston's Old Peculiar, Marston's Pedigree, Old Sweatysocks, or whatever, implying that he drank little else and displaying his credentials as a beer connoisseur for all to see. Later on in the conversation, though, it would somehow quite frequently emerge that for every pint of this illustrious brew that he consumed, he was throwing back 15 pints of cheap lager. Respondents' claims should always be compared with hard market share data as a reality check.

In case that example is viewed as too British, or even too male, I ask all my readers to remember the times that they have completed those questionnaires on the back of warranty cards. You know, the ones that ask you questions about your recreational activities and your media habits. Have you always told the truth?

I admit, right here, that in the world of those questionnaires, I say that I watch a lot of PBS, spend a great deal of time reading, run marathons, and scuba dive. Well, I do watch *Barney* with my son; I did run several marathons (ten years ago) and scuba dive, on average, say, once a year. So I'm not exactly *lying*, am I? Go on, tell me that you've never even stretched the truth on one of those forms. And then spare a thought for the person whose job it is to analyze the responses and make recommendations based on them to his or her Board.

"POP" RESEARCH

Many of the untruths, or half-truths, or half-lies that we hear in research are the result of a basic human desire for a better life, but others seem to be influenced by outside forces. A powerful industry has grown up in the United States that identifies "social trends," fundamental shifts in the attitudes of the American public that affect the way they think about their lives, and most important, the way they vote and buy products. That last part is most important because this trend spotting is not an academic or philanthropic exercise, but big business. Books are published, seminars are run and presentations are made to Fortune 500 companies on the rewards of riding new consumer waves, and perhaps most significant of all, a lot of interviews are given to the media.

Hardly a day goes by when we do not read in a newspaper or magazine, or see on a TV "news" program, something about a new trend that will be shaping all of our lives. The reason, it seems to me, is that there is too much time to fill on television, and too much space to fill in print, and not enough news to fill it. Social trends are great for journalists, because someone else has already done the work of identifying them, and that person simply needs to be interviewed and edited to fit the required format. So what happens is that the media runs a story about, say, people eating less red meat these days, along with footage of clogged arteries and cows being electrocuted, and people in the world at large see the story. Researchers then ask how people feel about red meat and they in turn play back what they saw on TV. The researchers report the responses to the Pork Council, or whomever; the council runs an advertising campaign positioning pork as white meat; and the media then run a story on the advertising, citing it as evidence of a social trend.

Tom Wolfe, who coined the phrase "the me decade" to describe the 1970s, has little patience with the soothsayers' attempts to label the 1990s as "the caring 90s," or "the decency decade," which they started to do as early as the late 1980s. He points out that he waited until the end of the seventies to coin his phrase, thus basing his insight on observation of what had actually happened, rather than on guesswork about what might.

Those who had the audacity to label the nineties in advance predicted a fundamental shift in American values, away from the "conspicuous consumption" of the 1980s, toward a deeper appreciation of the truly important things in life. The home would be the new place of choice, family the number one priority, with time a more valuable commodity than money. The effect on many companies would be immediate, and for some who represented status, like certain German automobile manufacturers, perhaps devastating. Yet so far in the 1990s, business for BMW, Mercedes, and Porsche has been booming. And in 1997, the bonuses given out for another record year on Wall Street in 1996, were almost double what they were in the biggest year of the previous decade.

Wolfe describes the whole thing as a "media construction," saying that "all that happened in the nineties is that the money stopped flowing." Indeed it did, if only for a year or two at the end of the eighties and the start of the nineties. For a while, many people couldn't afford expensive German sports cars, but it didn't stop them wanting them. Rather than admit they couldn't afford them, though, they justified their lack of action on the grounds of newly found principles and values. "It's much more satisfying," Wolfe says, "to think in cosmic terms, that God had something to do with it." And presumably, "cosmic" and "God" also make for better television.

In the elections of 1992 and 1996, family values played a prominent role in the debate between both parties and individual candidates, and countless advertising campaigns have either explicitly or implicitly paid homage to that particular social trend. Arnold Brown, a futurist with New York consulting firm Weiner Edrich Brown, was quoted in *Fortune* magazine, saying that in this era of family values, "rock climbing and rafting have replaced love affairs as society's pulse-quickeners." What a load of baloney. Maybe if Dick Morris had been sticking his toes into crevices on a rock face instead of having them sucked by a hooker he'd still have a job now, and he'd still be the one whispering to Bill Clinton that there are votes in family values. And as for nurturing families, it is now sadly true that any woman under 30 years of age in the United States is likely to have more husbands than children in her lifetime.

We have also heard a great deal over recent years about the emergence of a new social group, first labeled by Douglas Coupland as "Generation X" in his novel of the same name. I've heard "Gen.X" music, seen "Gen.X" fashions, watched "Gen.X" movies, and, because I probably did something very bad in a previous life, I have read "Gen.X" research reports. Research directors have told me that our advertising has to "talk to Xers, because they represent a significant opportunity," and the mere presence of a goateed actor has led more than one earnest brand manager to proclaim that a certain piece of advertising has "X-appeal." I would say something about this whole "X" thing myself, because I have a strong opinion about it, but I'll defer to Douglas Coupland, because as he had the first word on the subject, he deserves the last. In an article in *Esquire* magazine in 1995, Coupland wrote that "Now I'm here to say that 'X' is over. Kurt Cobain's in heaven, *Slackers* is at Blockbuster, and the media refers to anyone aged thirteen to thirty as Xers. Which only proves that marketers and advertisers never understood that X is not a chronological age, but a way of looking at the world."

Many marketers spend much more time than is healthy trying to avoid *missing* opportunities than they do taking advantage of the ones that already exist and that make the most sense for them. Thus they fragment their attention, their time, their research, and their media dollars, chasing after trends or people that they don't necessarily understand, and which don't necessarily even exist. Many an agency has been told to "make sure we're not missing Xers with the campaign," or produce a campaign that conforms to George Bush's vision of a "kinder, gentler America," without the person issuing the instructions pausing for even a moment to consider that not everything they hear on the ten o'clock news, or from a focus group in San Francisco, is necessarily true.

NUMBERS, CONTRARY TO POPULAR OPINION, ARE NOT INFALLIBLE

Every day, the research industry in the United States spews out billions of numbers that track the performance of both products and advertising, both in reality (that is, in-market) and in the abstract (projecting how they *would* perform if they ever *did* go to market). Those numbers wield extraordinary power within many organizations. Executives in fast food companies rush to their desks in the morning to see the columns of figures that say whether the launch of their new sandwich the day before was a success or a bust; research directors demand top-line results from their suppliers to see whether their company's commercial scored above or below norm on brand recall and persuasion; and even in qualitative research, brand managers ask whether the show of hands from respondents had scored eight out of ten or higher (without which the idea being tested obviously sucked). It's all pretty cut and dried. A number above a certain preset threshold is good; a number below that threshold is bad. And on the basis of such Newtonian methods and measures, multimillion-dollar decisions are being made every minute in American business.

In *Thriving on Chaos*, the management guru Tom Peters wrote that "Inspiring visions rarely (I'm tempted to say never) include numbers," and I am inclined to agree. Unlike many account planners, I am a great believer in the use of numbers to analyze and define the extent of a problem. I always use numbers to corroborate findings from qualitative research, but I have yet to experience a situation where numbers actually provided the inspiration for a great advertising campaign. I'm sure that there are some examples out there and would love to hear about them, but I am equally certain that they are the exception rather than the rule.

The only time that I have ever had to work with a *strategy* that was "inspired" by numbers, it was a disaster. When

GS&P started to work on the Cuervo brand in 1989, we were asked to work to a strategy that had been defined by a very expensive and impressive multivariate statistical analysis. (I think that's the right description.) People had rated tequila in general, and Cuervo and its competitors in particular, on a number of different attributes, and their responses had then been "mapped," I know not how, to see if Cuervo represented anything that other brands, and other types of liquor, did not. And there on the map, in a little area all on its own, had popped out three phrases:

"Good Drinks."
"Fun Times."
"Real People."

The three were rolled together, and the Cuervo that we were to portray in advertising was "Good drinks, fun times, real people." I used to get them mixed up and think that the drinks were fun, the people real, and the times good, but that was the least of our problems. The process of averaging people's responses had created a personality for Cuervo that was essentially benign, and which could have fitted any one of a host of other beverages, from Budweiser to Coke, from wine coolers to Sunny Delight.

The quantification did not stop there. Many of the campaigns that were developed (and there were a lot—we estimate about 30 by the end of the relationship) were quantitatively copy tested, and each time the campaign was graded according to three key dimensions. These were its ability to communicate good drinks, fun times, and real people. Unfortunately, we could never get it to do all three at the same time. The "Get Naked" campaign mentioned earlier scored very high, as one might expect, on "fun times" and "real people," but disappointingly low on "good drinks." Others had "good drinks" up the wazoo, but no "real people." It was deeply depressing.

It was all the more depressing given the unique character of Cuervo as a brand. I don't think I have ever worked on another brand where the mere mention of its name would create such an immediate, visceral reaction. In qualitative research, people would laugh, shoot sideways glances at others, shake their heads, and even bury their faces in their hands as the memories came back. Everyone had a story. And most of them were unprintable. We asked people to imagine a party where they were answering the door to arriving guests, each of whom was toting a six-pack of beer. Imagine also that one guest then arrived carrying a bottle of Cuervo Gold. What did that signify? The response was unanimous. They said it with words, facial expressions, and body language. It was going to be one hell of a party. They did not, and never would, say that it suggested "good drinks, fun times, and real people." But numbers had said that they should, and numbers dictated that if they did not, then the campaign was wrong. No one ever thought to question the validity of the numbers themselves.

There's something about such reverence for numbers that is peculiarly American. Americans love numbers, and indeed have a number to describe almost everything. Nowhere is that more apparent than in sports, and a glance at the sports pages of any American newspaper, or even five minutes of TV commentary, will demonstrate that very clearly. Players don't just have batting averages, they have batting averages while batting left-handed against right-handed pitchers in night games on the road in June after eating lasagna. Players' stats define their ability, which in turn define their salaries, which in turn are made public so that we can all share the numbers. Somehow, without a number there is something missing, and that something is probably the truth.

Here's an example, which I selected at random from the *San Francisco Chronicle* on June 2, 1994, to illustrate a lecture I was giving about the extreme quantification of American society:

TIGERS WIN, ESCAPE CELLAR

The Orioles have lost five of six, including three straight to the Tigers. Mike Mussina (7-3) gave up four runs and ten hits in six innings. He entered with a 5-0 record and a 1.57 ERA in eight lifetime starts against Detroit.

Belcher (3-8) gave up four hits, walked three and struck out three. He is 3-1 since losing his first seven decisions.

"He didn't look like a 2-8 pitcher out there. He looked like an 8-2 pitcher," Mussina said.

Detroit took a 10-0 lead with a six run seventh inning. The outburst was fueled by an error by first baseman Rafael Palmeiro, ending his string of 161 straight error-less games.

I'm sure you'll agree that it's quite typical of its genre. Now compare it with an article from the British *Sunday Times* from three days earlier, May 29, 1994.

ROSEBERRY FLOWERS IN THE HARDEST TOIL

This was a day of chilled winds and pocketed fingers, a day of grit and gruel, of edges to third man and thudded pads, a very English sort of day. Dour struggles between county teams on grudging pitches and under resentful clouds have always been part of English cricket, shattering the dreams of our youth and correcting the memories of our ineptitude . . .

. . . His life in cricket has been one of bluff commonsense interspersed with occasional shafts of stroppiness, although he remains a fine batsman. As he walked off it was hard to say if he were fed up with himself, the umpire or life. But he was fed up about something, a not unusual circumstance.

I'm not sure whether those two examples say more about Americans or Brits, but a similar comparison between the two cultures is also apparent in the somewhat distant field of professional wine tasting. I recently read an article in the British *Daily Telegraph* about Robert Parker, Jr., the wine critic and publisher of *The Wine Advocate.* When you shop for wine in the United States, you will find his "Parker scores" on wine racks in many outlets. Parker developed a system for scoring wines based on the way that he was graded in a previous life as a law student, with a wine scoring 50 just for showing up, and 100 for perfection. These Parker scores are very potent, and when a wine scores 85 or more, it walks off the shelves. Less, and it's bad news for both the winery and the retailer. "Every time he sips," the writer of the article observed, "the wine world shudders."

His British counterparts, however, are skeptical of his system and fear that his scores "take the poetry out of wine." But more than that, they fear that the "Parkerization" of wine causes wineries to produce a wine just to suit the palate of the great man. The same can happen in advertising. It would have been comparatively easy to produce a Cuervo campaign that scored high on the communication of "good drinks, fun times, and real people," (a headline that said exactly that, above a large group of real-looking people smiling, slapping each other's shoulders, and sniffing their shot glasses appreciatively would probably have done the trick) but while it would have checked off the relevant boxes, it would probably have made for a lousy piece of communication. We were unwilling to let the research tail wag the advertising dog, and consequently we were never able to run a campaign.

Some advertisers, unfortunately, are more concerned with checking the boxes and running a campaign than they are with actually getting it right. Every day I see campaigns where I am convinced the writer and art director were thinking less about what people wanted to hear than about what they needed to do to beat the quantitative test.

One problem is that numbers have such potency, they take on a life way beyond their true application. A case in point is the *USA Today* Adtrack survey, which features a well-known campaign every week and asks a reasonably robust sample how much they like it and whether they think it is effective. Back in 1996, the Isuzu Rodeo campaign was featured, and it scored particularly badly on the effectiveness measure. No doubt Isuzu's marketing department got a lot of calls from dealers telling them they should change their campaign as a result. In fact, Isuzu chose to ignore the story, and particularly the effectiveness measure, because they rightly concluded that the sample did not reflect their own target audience for the Rodeo and was therefore irrelevant, and that someone *thinking* a campaign is effective or ineffective means absolutely nothing. Especially when they are not the target of the advertising. And to prove that point, in the same month as the article was published, the Isuzu Rodeo broke its previous best sales figure.

The *USA Today* poll is fielded by Louis Harris & Associates, a highly reputable and competent research company, and although I take issue with one part of their methodology—namely, asking people what they *think* about a campaign's effectiveness—the research is undoubtedly well executed. The problem lies more in the way it is reported, and subsequently in the way it is consumed, especially because people tend to concentrate on the raw answers without paying any attention to the exact way the questions were asked. It is thus dangerously tempting to use the answers in imagined responses to questions that were not exactly asked, and to project the answers to populations of whom the sample was not in the slightest way representative.

In a recent (July 6, 1997) *New York Times* article entitled "It's Awful! It's Terrible! It's . . . Never Mind," Stephen A. Holmes wrote that the reports from several research organizations in 1995 indicated "a hefty percentage—in one study 65 percent—of teenage mothers had babies by adult men." In response to this shocking information, several states stepped up enforcement of statutory rape laws to protect the young girls and to reduce the number of out-of-wedlock births. The problem was, this information was not what it seemed.

To quote the *Times* piece, "What many news reports on the studies neglected to mention was that 62 percent of the teenage mothers were 18 or 19 years old and, therefore, like the fathers of their babies, adults. Also ignored was the fact that the researchers did not differentiate between married and single teenagers. Subsequent studies have determined that of all those aged 15 to 17 who gave birth, only 8 percent were unmarried girls made pregnant by men at least five years older." Holmes called this the "whoops factor, a phenomenon that starts with shoddy research or the misinterpretation of solid research, moves on quickly to public outcry, segues swiftly into the enactment of new laws or regulations," and ends with embarrassment all round.

It's all around us, so be careful what you believe.

IN THE WRONG HANDS, EVEN THE BEST RESEARCH IS DANGEROUS

The aforementioned examples represent many (but certainly not all) of the pitfalls of research, and the opportunities to be led astray by its findings. Of course, there is also a lot of smartly conceived, well-planned, and smoothly executed research out there, but it too can run into problems if it is handled in the wrong way. I have often heard it said in debates over gun control that it is not the guns themselves that are the problem, but the people using them. In the context of gun control, it is a completely spurious argument, but it does have some relevance in a discussion of advertising research. Advertising research, for reasons that I have already stated and expand on in subsequent chapters, is not in itself a bad thing, but I have come across many people in positions of authority in both agencies and client companies whose *handling* of even the best advertising research is as desirable and constructive as putting chemical weapons in the hands of Saddam Hussein.

I have always regarded research as a means to an end, and in that sense I probably differ from many who make their living entirely from the execution or administration of research. Research provides some guidance, but in my view seldom provides the answer (if indeed the answer ever really exists). Much of it, however, is taken literally, or if interpreted at all, done so very selectively. That's a big problem even when the research is good. When it's bad, as described in previous sections, it's a disaster.

Anyone who has ever sat in the viewing room at a focus group facility will have observed the random and partisan attention often given to research proceedings by clients (both marketing and research executives) and creative people. Many of them arrive at the facility with their own preconceptions, which often mean that the clients have concerns and issues and are waiting for consumers to echo their fears, while the creative people think those fears are groundless and are looking for endorsement of their ideas. A comical situation ensues whereby every time a respondent says something positive, the creatives will write furious notes, cast knowing glances in the clients' direction, and on occasion rise from their chairs and high-five anyone within reach. When the comments are negative, it's the client's turn to write notes and shoot knowing glances. Regarding themselves as more rational, sensible, and mature, they tend to stay seated and do not engage in overt celebrations of bad news.

As a moderator, I am always terrified of what may be going on in the viewing room while I conduct the group, because I have virtually no control over it. Aside from the M&M feeding frenzies and sporadic attention paid to what people are saying, the two sides of the backroom "house" are drawing their own conclusions from what they are hearing, even though this may be the only evening of groups that they are attending out of a project that may encompass five nights and five cities. Whatever the balance of opinion from the other nights, the comments of that one night in Seattle will come back to haunt me again and again.

"What do you mean, the ad needs changes? Remember that guy in Seattle who said that it would make him buy one on his way home? Man, he really *got it.*"

"From what I saw in Seattle, I really can't recommend that spot to my boss."

The example previously given reflects the deliberate interpretation of research to suit one's own purposes, and while it is more common than I would like, there is a certain inevitability about it. It is, however, easier to persuade a partisan client or creative that they are letting their own opinions get in the way of the truth than it is to persuade someone of my next point, which relates to a much more subtle kind of misinterpretation.

Sometimes, people interpret research in different ways according to the different perspective afforded by being an active participant in the research as opposed to an outside observer. A person viewing a focus group from the apparent proximity of the viewing room will almost certainly miss a lot that I, as the moderator, am able to sense from inside the research room itself, and this is not just because of the inevitable behind-the-mirror distractions.

Experienced moderators will have an appreciation for the subtleties of body language that cannot be spotted from the viewing room or from a videotaped version of events. They will have an instinctive feel for the chemistry that exists between the respondents and the ideas, products, and advertising being discussed, and they will know how a session "feels" compared with previous sessions on the same subject. These moods, feelings, and delicate differences might be subtle in their expression, but quite profound in their meaning.

All of this may be lost on the observers, and it can result, as I have seen happen on many occasions, in the moderator and the observers drawing quite different conclusions about what the research is suggesting, not only in matters of degree, but on substantive, important issues.

I have worked with several clients who do not like to attend focus groups, preferring to watch the entire project on videotape before we deliver our debrief. Almost inevitably, their distance from the project causes them to draw different conclusions from those who were more intimately involved, and that distance is amplified by the way some of them use the video medium to watch the groups. They admit that they make generous use of the fast-forward button on their VCRs, which not only makes them miss certain parts of the conversation, but, most important, precludes them from observing the ebb and flow, the *momentum*, of the discussion. As a sports fan, I have experienced this many times when I have attended a game live and later discussed it with someone who taped it and watched it by skipping from one piece of action to the next. It's as if we watched entirely different games.

On the day the verdict in the O.J. Simpson criminal trial was announced, I was watching a news program where the studio anchor was expressing her surprise at the jury's decision. She had watched most of the proceedings and could not imagine how, on the basis of all the evidence she had seen, O.J. was walking free. The reporter on the scene had been in the courtroom on every day of the trial, and he asked her whether she had been in the courtroom at all or had watched on television. Her answer, of course, was that she had seen it only on television. "Well, I'm not surprised at all," the reporter said. "If you had been in the courtroom, you would have had a completely different impression. You would have sensed the way the jurors reacted to Johnny Cochrane. You would have sensed that they didn't really like Marcia Clark. How bored they were by the DNA evidence. At times you could almost *smell* the way they were feeling. And you wouldn't have got that from television." What he was describing was the moderator's sixth sense, which evaporates once glass or a television screen comes between the observers and the respondents.

The examples just given at least involve observers and decision makers bringing some opinions and making some judgments about the research. But it is also very easy, much too easy in fact, for research to become a substitute for judgment. If the number comes in above the norm, then let's run the commercial; if it trails, let's kill it. If the groups think it's a good idea, we'll proceed. If they don't, we'll simply start over.

The prejudice that the British wine experts have toward Parker scores represents exactly the same concern. The *Daily Telegraph* article referred to earlier included a typically snotty British prejudice that Parker scores provide a good excuse to avoid forming one's own opinion about a wine: "Americans are particularly fond of being told what they should like, and Parker's scores remove the necessity to do any thinking." As evidence, the article cited the recent example of a man in Washington, D.C., who bought a case of chardonnay, only to return it because he didn't like the first bottle. Next day, Parker gave the wine a high score, and the customer repurchased the remaining 11 bottles. So he tasted it; he didn't like it; someone else told him it was good; and he liked it after all.

Far too many people in advertising and marketing shrug their shoulders when asked a question and say, "Let's see what the research says," without considering that what the research says may not necessarily be correct, or that their own prejudices may make them believe it to be saying something it is not, or that their distance from the research prevents them from hearing everything it says or means. Yet they blindly follow what they think it is telling them.

Using (or abusing) research to make decisions without recourse to common sense and one's personal opinions is, as Tim Delaney once stated so succinctly, "not a job for grown-ups."

FOLLOWING THE "RULES"

The final point that needs to be addressed is *why* companies persist in adhering to methodologies that are at best not helpful in making better advertising, and at worst downright destructive. I have asked that question on many occasions, and oftentimes the best answer I have received is "because we have always done it that way." In other words, to be consistent with previously established procedure, and to allow comparison to normative data that stretches back over *x* number of years, we are going to do more bad research.

"The reason that men oppose progress," wrote Elbert Hubbard, "is not that they oppose progress, but that they love inertia," and in advertising research, inertia is a very powerful force. A culture develops in a company whereby research results have an impact way beyond the future (or otherwise) of an advertising idea; executives' performance evaluations become linked to gains on key research measures, and in turn agency compensation becomes dependent on certain awareness gains, distribution targets, or market share thresholds. When those measures and methodologies become so ingrained, it is extremely hard to change them.

Equally persistent and virulent are the "rules" that represent the collected wisdom of research studies and both category and industry experience. In *Ogilvy on Advertising,* David Ogilvy had quite a few rules to share; for example, reverse type doesn't work as well as black type on a white background, opening paragraphs should be limited to "a maximum of eleven words," and "when you put your headline in *quotes* you increase recall by an average of 28%." They are all presented in a pretty black-and-white fashion, as irrefutable fact.

In a similar vein, I frequently receive mailings from research companies who claim to have made breakthrough research discoveries of some kind or another that should forever change the way we go about producing our advertising.

The rules they lay down, like Ogilvy's, issue commandments from the page as if they were carved in tablets of stone.

"Busy layouts often pull better than neat ones," a recent mailer informed me. "One recent split-run test showed busy layouts outpulling neat layouts by 14%." The same research study also concluded that "putting something odd into a picture will attract attention," citing the famous eye patch in David Ogilvy's Hathaway shirt campaign as evidence. It tempts me to use my Indonesian tribal penis gourd as an "odd little detail" in a campaign to test that theory for myself, but I have yet to find a client who shares my enthusiasm for the idea.

Such rules tell us how many times to mention the brand name in a 30-second commercial, how many words are ideal on a billboard, how large the font size in body copy needs to be. The only thing I can say is that if all these rules were followed literally (and many companies have guidelines that insist on exactly that), all advertising would be the same.

Those are just the general industry rules. Then there are the category rules, representing the collective wisdom of the "car guys," the "beer guys," and the "fast food guys," the experts, the kind of people who preface every sentence with phrases like, "In my 23 years in this business," or, "When I was at (admired company name here), we found that it worked better if . . ." (In other words, I'm right and you're not.)

Theirs are the rules that give us the bite and smile in every burger (and dog food) commercial; people dancing and jogging with milk cartons in milk commercials; car commercials where leaves blow out from under the car as it sweeps around a bend on the Pacific Coast Highway; cruise ship commercials with white ships, blue seas, buffet tables, unfeasibly large lobsters, and women with big hair and glittery dresses sipping cocktails at sundown; and antidrug commercials where we tell kids to "just say no." At a certain point in time, for a certain brand, they might have made sense, but the only effect they have when projected to the category at large is to replicate what others have already done, make the messages less interesting or distinctive, and thus blur the lines between brands.

These rules are a constant reminder of the reductionist, Newtonian model on which so much of our marketing, and even our management, systems are based. They represent the industry's never-ending battle to understand and predict cause and effect in advertising and to isolate the variables and "things" that affect the outcome of a given situation. Even more than that, they are a way for us to feel *in control*. Rules give us security. They give us the guarantee that we will not do anything wrong. But do they provide any guarantee that we will do anything *right?* I don't think so.

BREAKING OUT

If an agency and client are to be successful in establishing a relationship with their customers, they simply cannot adhere to a 300-year-old model of how things work. Their research has to embrace the inherent unpredictability of people. It has to recognize that the whole (of a brand, of a target audience, of an advertising campaign) is greater than the sum of its parts. It should also not ignore the wider context in which all of these brands, people, and advertising campaigns operate and live, and the influence that external factors beyond our control exert on the relationships between them. In this "new scientific" way of looking at the world, risk and uncertainty should be regarded as more powerful allies than control, because with risk and uncertainty come energy, disruption, ideas, and breakthroughs.

The point of the research methodologies outlined in the next chapter is not to make anyone feel comfortable, but rather to make a difference. Making a difference means doing it differently, and I suggest a number of ways by which advertisers and their agencies can avoid the pitfalls of the type of research described earlier in this chapter, and instead forge relationships, gain unexpected insights, and achieve genuine breakthroughs. At times it might be scary. It may seem undisciplined. But to quote a guy who predated even Newton — the Italian politician, schemer, and writer Machiavelli — "the end justifies the means."

4

Peeling the Onion
Uncovering the Truth and Stimulating Creative Ideas through Research

The real giants have always been poets, men who jumped from facts into the realm of imagination and ideas.

Bill Bernbach

INTRODUCTION

The first company president I met when I moved to the United States, Bill Johnson of Heinz Pet Products, had a sign above his desk that read, GUTS IS CHEAPER THAN RESEARCH. I have to admit that the first time I saw it, I was worried. After all, my only reason for being in his office was to talk about some research, and here was this sign, suggesting before either of us had opened our mouths, that he didn't really give a rat's ass what I was going to say.

Fortunately, however, my initial fears were groundless. He was not antiresearch. In fact, his company did a lot of research, and I later discovered that it was this research that had indirectly led to my working in the United States in the first place. Heinz Pet Products had hired a qualitative research company called QRC to do some new product work, and they in turn had worked closely with Goodby, Berlin & Silverstein in naming, positioning, packaging, and developing advertising for Reward dog food. Through working with Vicky Johns and Arnie Jacobsen of QRC, Rich Silverstein told me that for the first time he saw research acting as something other than a barrier to good advertising. Quite the opposite—it was helpful. Vicky and Arnie were interesting people; they had good ideas, their criticism was constructive, and they understood the delicate balance between business and creative considerations. Overall, Silverstein said, they "got it," which is the highest praise anyone outside the creative department can expect from a creative director. It made him want to hire someone like them to work in the agency full-time.

Bill Johnson was happy to commission research where he thought it might help solve problems, but he was not a slave to it, preferring to regard it as just one of a number of sources of information from which he would make his decision. He simply considered that his own gut instincts, based on years of experience of marketing, advertising, and life, were as valid as an expensive research project in making such decisions. As such, he was one of a very rare breed.

I have not come across too many clients over the years who are truly masters of their own decisions, but I have enormous respect for the ones who are. I know that not every decision they make is correct, and sometimes that is frustrating. But over a reasonable time period, I believe their average to be much higher as a result of such a balanced decision-making process than if they were to blindly follow the recommendations of research alone.

I remember many occasions when, as a child, I couldn't figure something out, and my mother would tell me, "use your common sense." Maybe I was overcomplicating things; maybe I was trying too hard to impress someone else; or maybe I was just being plain dumb. Whatever the case, she would try to get me to wipe my brain clean for a moment, look at the situation as if for the first time, and start over. And funnily enough, it sometimes worked.

At the height of the space race in the 1960s, NASA scientists were perplexed by a problem their astronauts faced in the recording of data and experiences while in orbit. The problem was that they were unable to write anything down, because they could not get a pen to work at zero gravity. To crack this difficult nut, NASA embarked on an expensive research and development program. Some time and a million dollars later (quite a lot of money at that time), they proudly presented their "astronaut pen," which immediately went into service. Happy astronauts were able to record data to their hearts' content, commit their most profound thoughts to paper while viewing the world from outer space, and no doubt write mankind's first "space postcards" to their families. This astronaut pen also achieved some success as a novelty item, sold at great expense to earthlings as a genuine NASA souvenir.

Meanwhile, the Soviet space agency had solved its own pens-not-working-at-zero-gravity problem. They used pencils.

I think that's what Bill Johnson's sign was really all about. Keeping it simple. And using *common sense*.

This chapter is devoted to the principles of simplicity, common sense, and also *creativity*, as applied to advertising research. These three principles are, for the account planner, a kind of Holy Trinity, although there is really no reason they could not be practiced by other types of agency researchers, if they were so inclined and if their agency's structure and process allowed them the latitude to operate in the ways that I will suggest.

The aim of the best advertising research is to embrace consumers; reach a deeper level of understanding of the way they think, feel, and behave; and then use those observations and discoveries to kick start the creative process and begin to build a relationship with them through the advertising itself.

The initial process of discovery, as reflected in the title of this chapter, has often been likened to the way one peels an onion, removing layer upon layer until the core is reached, although in many ways that is not a satisfactory analogy, as the core of an onion isn't a whole lot different from the layers that enclose it (they all make your eyes run, and your breath will smell no matter which part you eat). It also implies a logical, sequential process, not unlike the Newtonian scientific method that I described in Chapter 1. The latter need not be a problem, as peeling off layer after layer is not the only way to get to the heart of an onion. You can simply take a large knife and chop it in halves.

Some of the ideas that follow do reflect a careful prizing away of the insecurities, prejudices, and other barriers that stand in the way of a person revealing an important truth. Others reflect the approach of a sharp blow with a knife.

Many people assume that the planner talks to consumers, figures out what they are really thinking, then (and only then) uses his or her intuition and imagination to interpret and mold those findings, and finally briefs the creative team on a direction. In fact, that is rarely the case. Imagination and intuition should be at work at every stage of the research, not just in interpreting findings, but also in the process of their extraction. If harnessed early enough in the process, imagination, intuition, and creativity can dramatically reduce the distance between an apparently innocuous consumer point of view and a potentially powerful advertising idea.

It would have been easy to write this chapter as a list of antitheses to the problems I described in Chapter 3 ("How to Ask the Right Questions," "Smart Use of Numbers," and "Trust Your Gut," for example), but I concluded that in general the antidote to the problem was probably obvious enough without my spelling it out. The only substantial exception is the influence of environment, or habitat, on research findings. As part of a discussion about encouraging the people we talk to in research to be themselves, I share several examples of projects where environment was used successfully both to put respondents at ease and to act as a catalyst for creative ideas.

I have also chosen not to present a lengthy how-to of either qualitative or quantitative methodologies. That subject alone could fill several books, and I have little interest in writing about how to prepare a focus group room, write a discussion guide, design a questionnaire, or analyze a Nielsen report. I'm not suggesting that such things are unimportant and do not require some skill (although there is much in the preparation and even execution of some research that could be handled by a computer or a trained monkey), but in the grander scheme of things, they are mere details. Even if all those details are attended to perfectly, a research project may still be useless if they are being used in the wrong context or for the wrong reasons. Knowing how to set up a focus group room is certainly less important than knowing whether to use a focus group room at all, and it is on such macrolevel issues that I will concentrate.

I want to suggest some ways of looking at research, some *approaches,* that may make it possible to take a step back and see the problem through fresh eyes before trying to understand or solve it. These approaches are as much philosophical as methodological, and, although most of the examples I offer are qualitative in nature, the general ideas are equally applicable to quantitative research. In this chapter I focus almost exclusively on the strategic development phase, where I believe the ideas will be most useful, though they do clearly have some application at other points in the process. In no way do I mean the following sections to be a prescription for success: The ideas are neither all-inclusive nor infallible, although all have helped me greatly over the years.

I have tried, where possible, to illustrate each one with an example from a campaign that I have worked on at Goodby, Silverstein & Partners, but I should point out that each of those examples has been selected as a demonstration of the singular dimension under discussion, and should not be regarded in any way as a full case history. In many instances, it would have been possible to say something about a particular campaign's development under almost all of the following headings, which are not arranged in any specific order of either chronology or priority.

Finally, I do not want the following to be interpreted as "rules" to be followed at all costs. Having previously criticized the blind obedience to rules exhibited by many in the industry, I certainly don't want to try and impose any of my own. I prefer to regard them as suggestions at most; I offer no hard evidence to back them up, beyond some positive personal experiences and the feeling that they "make sense."

BE SUBJECTIVE

Objectivity, I have heard many times, is a critical element in the personality and working method of a planner. Without objectivity, planners are not able to truly understand target consumers, because their own preconceptions and prejudices may get in the way, and without it they may also lose the trust of both creative people and clients, arguably their most valuable commodities.

That argument has a certain validity at the strategic development stage, when planners need to put a stake in the ground to record how people feel about a particular company or product, and to understand their attitudes and behavior in their purest form before the agency attempts to change or influence them. It is also valid at the creative development and evaluation stages of the process, because there planners need to be dispassionate about a commercial idea's potential to involve and move target consumers. Whether the planners have any attachment to the idea themselves should not be allowed to influence that analysis.

Sadly for those proponents of the scientific method, I question whether true objectivity *ever* exists in advertising research, whoever conducts it (it's less an issue of interviewer prejudice than the influence of the very act of doing research, as described in Chapter 3), and if it does, whether it helps in any way.

In creative development, it is rare for an idea to be so cut and dried that it is either "perfect" and needs no tweaking, or such a disaster that it should never again see the light of day. Much more often, ideas have potential but need to be simplified or clarified, or have serious problems and require some degree of surgery to put them back on the right track. In both such cases, the planner needs to figure out what needs to be done, occasionally even suggesting possible improvements or deletions on the spot. Such improvements are more likely to be achieved through the use of subjectivity and creativity than by objectivity.

The application of subjectivity is not confined to the interpretation of research data. It is equally essential when planning a research project, designing a discussion guide, and asking questions. Knowing who to ask is not always best accomplished objectively. Sometimes a hunch that leads the researcher to a different and unexpected place, or to an apparently strange person or group of individuals, will provide the most revealing and rewarding information. Starting a conversation in a place that surprises even the respondents will almost always ensure that it ends in a place that even you, as the researcher, could not have predicted. Moreover, research respondents have to be encouraged to use *their own* imagination and creativity, and anything that can be done to make the research feel less like a dry, scientific experiment will inevitably reap great dividends.

Take the Wider View

The best place to start this process is in the definition of both the scope of the research project and the role of the client's product. As noted in Chapter 3, a very strong and understandable urge is exhibited by people on the inside of any company to assume that all those on the outside share their own level of knowledge of, and enthusiasm for, the company's products. It often falls to the planner to break that illusion.

Remember that in any research, the subjects, or respondents, are not really subjects or respondents at all, but *people.* People who happen to buy products from a certain store, or who drive a particular car, or who have switched between long-distance telephone providers in the last month. This is why they were asked to participate in the research, but they also have lives, relationships, pets, children, problems, hobbies, idiosyncrasies, and prejudices beyond that fact.

One example I cited earlier to illustrate the problem, as opposed to the solution, was that of an imaginary focus group of insurance agents, corporate benefits managers, and holders of disability insurance policies where, right off the bat, they were asked to discuss features of disability insurance policies. Such a situation isn't really that unusual, because many clients and researchers consider that they are paying good money for the research facility rental, and for the respondents' incentives, and they had better get to the point fast. But what is the point? If it is to produce advertising that helps sell more disability insurance policies, then it is of course important to understand the way that insurance brokers sell those policies, and the way that they feel about specific policy features, as well as the way that their customers (both direct and indirect) feel about those policies and features. Such a direct, focused question, however, may not reveal the most important information.

One aspect of any qualitative research project that is rarely spoken about is the need to experiment in the first one or two groups. No one really has any idea how much there is to say about a particular topic, or which lines of questioning or techniques might reveal the most useful information. It is thus important that a moderator has the latitude to deviate from a discussion guide, to reverse a sequence of topics, or to introduce a completely new idea if it seems that any of those actions may stimulate a more interesting conversation. (It's almost worth officially designating the first two groups of any study as "test" groups, for that reason.)

A case in point was the UNUM insurance research. We quickly realized that among brokers, company benefits managers, and holders of disability insurance policies alike, interest levels in disability insurance were universally very low. Benefits managers bought them to round out their companies' employee benefits packages, but only after they had sorted out the medical plan, the dental plan, the 401k program, gym memberships, and the company's policy on bringing pets into the office. People who work for those companies then look at their conditions of employment, read the words "disability insurance," either shudder at the thought or dismiss it as irrelevant, then never think about it again (they hope). Brokers thus found themselves in the position of selling a product whose very name caused people's eyes to glaze over. If the words *disability insurance* caused people to switch off, we had to find another way to begin a dialogue, both in advertising and subsequently for the brokers' sales pitches.

So in our exploratory focus groups we decided to spend the first half of each session not talking about insurance at all. Instead, we began the conversation by asking our respondents to talk about themselves and their lives. Their families, their jobs, what they did on the weekend, whether they might have predicted their current situations 10 or 20 years before, and where they saw themselves in another 10 years' time. We asked the same questions of brokers, benefits managers, and end users, and it was fascinating to see the similarities between the responses of these different groups. People spoke of their kids, and their hopes and fears for them, of the need to pay for their educations (or, for the older ones, the relief that at last that was over and done), and the intimidating responsibilities of parenthood; they talked of retirement, the dreams of which they had carried for years, and now the uncertainties of their financial security if they lived for 30 years beyond the time they retired. Some people had elderly parents who needed both their care and financial support, and others were fearful that one day they too would be in that position—trying to put their kids through college, saving for their own retirements, yet having to pay for parents who had not saved enough to pay for theirs. Their own health was a major concern, which led to a discussion about health insurance, then social security, and the question of whether, having paid in for all these years, they were ever likely to get anything back.

The dominant theme running throughout was *uncertainty*. Much of what had already happened to them had come as a surprise, and few had any doubt that the future held more such surprises.

At this point, we asked them to talk about financial planning and security. How were they taking care of themselves and their children financially? Their answers covered owning property, mutual funds, stocks and bonds, 401k plans, and insurance of various kinds. "Okay," we said, "tell us about insurance. Don't think about individual policies when you answer this, just think about insurance *overall*. What does it do? What is it for?"

Insurance, it seemed, was regarded as a necessary evil. Something you had to buy to drive a car (unless you're a recent immigrant to California), or to protect your investment if you owned a house, or in the case of life insurance, to protect your family in case you weren't around to provide for them. "Why is that a necessary *evil?*" we were curious to know. "Well, insurance companies make their money out of other people's misfortune," one person replied, and the others nodded their agreement. Silence for a moment.

"Well, I don't know about that," said one benefits manager. "It seems to me they don't make money out of misfortune—quite the opposite. When something goes wrong it's them who have to pay. I think insurance, for me, is to protect me against uncertainty. Like the stuff we were talking about. I can even get insurance to pay for my parents to be taken care of if they can't take care of themselves."

"The thing is," a broker in another group explained, "a lot of people are in denial about stuff that is pretty likely to happen to them. Chances are a lot of us are going to have to take care of parents when we're older, but it sure as hell is hard to get someone to see why a long-term care policy is a good idea. The statistics say that one in four of us is going to have some time off work disabled at some time in our lives." He looked around the room. "That's three of us in this room, if you believe the numbers. Yet people just don't wanna know. It's never gonna happen to them."

> Insurance makes it easier to deal with unpleasant surprises.
> It's in an insurance company's interests for nothing to go wrong.
> People need to be made aware that they are not invincible.

All of these ideas came out of a conversation that turned to the subject of insurance, and even disability insurance, without any prompting from us. Because they were allowed to emerge naturally out of the respondents' own concerns, their importance relative to other issues was much easier to gauge. And many of the ideas fit very closely with what we knew to be at the core of UNUM's own philosophy and practices.

UNUM, as a company, is active in reducing causes of disability at work and in the home through education programs, helping to rehabilitate and return disabled employees to the workforce, and its research attempts to identify and avoid possible future causes of disability, before they become problems. This research benefits both UNUM and the population at large: The impact on UNUM of new forms of disability (in terms of claims against existing policies) is reduced, and the general population is protected from suffering the disability in the first place.

The combination of these company philosophies and practices, together with the ideas expressed by the focus groups, led quickly to a campaign idea, tone, and theme.

The advertising strategy was to communicate UNUM's grasp of these issues in human, individual terms, to overcome the barriers of low interest and distrust which plagued the industry. To use understandable, everyday language that would demonstrate the importance of the company's products, and position UNUM as a company that had a vision of the future and was best able to help its customers prepare for that future. They take a larger view of things. They see further ahead. And while they recognize that insurance does have a dark side, it can also suggest security, health, good fortune, and long life. Which, surprisingly enough, is in the interest of both the insured and the insurer.

"You probably feel like the bear," proclaimed one headline, over the picture of a bear in an Alaskan river, mouth open, with a salmon about to jump into its open jaws. "We'd like to suggest you're the salmon." Then, in smaller type, "Now, let's talk disability insurance" (see Figure 4.1). Another was about UNUM's commitment to getting people back into the workforce and used the device of the dreadful topics discussed on daytime TV chat shows as an incentive to get out of the home and back to work: "Left-handed twin non-smokers, and the men who love them. Sagittarians who like to dress up as Aquarians. Women who marry their mother's ex-husbands. Pets who steal. (Who wouldn't want to get back to work fast?)" In a third, a man is photographed holding an infant, with a headline that says, "In fifty years, it's quite possible this scenario will be reversed" (see Figure 4.2). On all of the ads, the copy ends with the cheerful line, "Here's to a long life."

The UNUM solution came out of a very general conversation, which it was hoped would somehow find its way to the subject of insurance. No one really knew where it might lead, and as such it was unpredictable and not a little scary. In other instances, though, it might be possible to *lead* people to the wider picture, as opposed to having them do the leading.

An example is the campaign that Goodby, Berlin & Silverstein produced for the Northern California Honda Dealers Advertising Association (NCHDAA) in 1989. Rather than conform to the stereotypical dealer group advertising ("one of a kind, never to be repeated deals, this weekend

Figure 4.1   UNUM: "Bear and Salmon."

Figure 4.2   UNUM: "Father and Child."

only, the Honda-thon, fifteen hundred dollars cash back . . ." shouted over cheesy running footage), it was decided that the campaign should reflect the tone of the national campaign that it ran alongside. After all, we reasoned, the only people who know that one spot is from the national campaign and another from a regional dealer group are industry insiders. In the real world, all people see is the name "Honda" at the end. It's dumb having one of (Los Angeles agency) Rubin Postaer's intelligent, stylish commercials for Honda in one break, and then in the next, 30 seconds of car salesman hell, also apparently from Honda. All the good work done by the first ad would be undone by the second.

What if, we asked ourselves, we could in some way *regionalize* the national message? In other words, take the tone and quality of Rubin Postaer's campaign and make it unique to Northern California? All of the regional dealer groups signed off as the Northern California Chevy/Ford/ Toyota Dealers, yet none of the ads would have seemed out of place in Florida or Wisconsin. In fact, that's probably where they got them from.

In our research, we began not by asking people about cars, or car dealers, but about living in Northern California. What's it like? What does it mean? How would you describe it to an alien? (There are times when my British accent comes in very useful.) How does it compare to Southern California?

"Oh, North and South are very different," a man in a focus group told me.

"How so?"

"Well, let me put it this way. There's a great rivalry between the (San Francisco) Giants and the (L.A.) Dodgers," he said. "But the Dodgers' fans don't know about it."

Everyone laughed. People in the "Southland" were on a different planet. All they cared about was their suntans and flashy cars. Northern Californians, by comparison, were more modest, discerning, less likely to buy things to "make statements," interested in how products performed as opposed to what they looked like, more environmentally conscious, and concerned with the quality of life.

We already knew from American Honda–supplied research what Northern Californians thought of Honda's cars. They were perceived as stylish without being ostentatious, reliable, understated, good value for the money . . . the parallels were remarkable.

The creative brief asked the team to consider placing Honda in the unique context of Northern California, and to imagine that "Hondas are designed with Northern Californians in mind." Dave O'Hare, who always swore that he hated advertising taglines and had no talent for writing them, came back immediately with a line to which he wanted to write a campaign: "Is Honda the Perfect Car for Northern California, or What?"

The launch commercial took advantage of the rivalry between Northern and Southern California. Set in the state senate chamber in Sacramento, it opens on the Speaker trying to hush the house. "Please, please," he admonishes, "the gentleman from Northern California has the floor."

"What my Southern Californian colleague proposes is a moral outrage," the senator splutters, waving a sheaf of papers at the other side of the floor. "Widening the Pacific Coast Highway . . . to ten lanes!"

A Southern Californian senator with bouffant hair and a pink tie shrugs his shoulders. "It's too windy," he whines (note: windy as in curves, not weather), and his fellow Southern Californians high-five and murmur their assent. The Northern Californians go nuts, and the Speaker struggles in vain to call everyone to order. The camera goes outside as the noise reaches a crescendo, and we see the parking lot. In the Southern Californian section, all the cars are huge, gas-guzzling land yachts. In the Northern Californian lot, everyone has a Honda. The commercial finishes with the line, "Is Honda the Perfect Car for Northern California, or What?"

It is far too easy to take products at face value and think "this is a car," or "this is an insurance policy," but it is often possible to find a way of talking about them that raises them onto a higher plane, and most important, out of the morass of competitive activity. It's an interesting exercise with any product. Just imagine a scenario where some new law has been enacted that prevents you from calling your product, say, a "car" or a "camera." What else could you call it that would have some credibility? In the case of UNUM, or the Northern California Honda Dealers, or the campaigns for Polaroid or Norwegian Cruise Line referred to in later chapters, defining the product outside traditional category boundaries changed the rules of engagement and allowed the companies to compete on what *they* did best, avoiding areas of potential weakness or competitive activity. This doesn't work for everyone, but when it does, it can be very potent.

Be Out of It

In the introduction to *The Man in the Water,* Roger Rosenblatt describes a series of "perverse sounding rules" that he asks his students at Columbia's Graduate School of Journalism to try. His main aim in doing this, he says, is "to tell students how to enjoy journalism." Many of his rules resonate with me as a planner and go way beyond matters of personal enjoyment, seeming to hold the key, if applied correctly, to unique perspective and insight. Most important, they are the kind of rules that liberate, as opposed to restrict.

"Be out of it," he wrote.

> That is almost an unnatural rule for jour-
> nalists to follow because journalists strive to
> be frantically "in it," that is, on top of the
> world's events. Yet I believe it is more useful

> to one's work to be out of it, aggressively out
> of it, when it comes to the news. Instead of
> urging students to read ten accounts of a
> story, I urge them to read one account and to
> do nine unrelated things while brooding
> about the story. Read history, fiction,
> poetry—especially poetry, as the similarities
> of structure, voice, and intent between
> poetry and journalism can be striking.
> Instead of busying oneself with the daily
> papers, journey into the past. Or take a long,
> meandering walk, or do anything that keeps
> the mind dealing with other knowledge.

When I am flying across the United States on my way to a meeting on the east coast, I am certain that I get as many ideas from magazines and books that I am reading as from consumer research that I have conducted. That reading material, incidentally, almost never includes business publications. When young planners ask me for lists of books they should read, I have never recommended a book about advertising (although I suspect that with the publication of this book, I might be tempted to modify my position), preferring that they draw their ideas from outside sources. Some of the books I recommend I quote in these pages and include in my bibliography. But generally I prefer people to just open their minds, draw from as wide a range of stimuli as possible, and be sure to let me know when they have found something interesting.

Of course, a delicate balance exists between the degree to which a planner is involved with his or her business or consumers, which is necessary if truly informed judgments are to be made, and the level of detachment that is necessary to see things clearly. Howard Gossage had a phrase to describe this detachment: "extra-environmental man," the person who was able to stay just far enough from the fray to see things that others cannot. As an Englishman living in the United States, I can relate to that.

Oscar Wilde once said that "we [the British] have really much in common with America nowadays, except, of course, language." I found that out to my cost in my first week in San Francisco, when, having failed to locate the agency's office supplies, I asked my new assistant if she had a pencil eraser that I could borrow. At least, that's what I thought I had asked. I used the English term for a pencil eraser, and she kindly explained to me that in the United States a "rubber" was not used for erasing unwanted pencil marks.

Apart from that early embarrassing incident, I have found my alien upbringing to be quite useful, mainly because I can plead ignorance everywhere I go to do consumer research, and can get away with asking really dumb questions that might seem strange coming from the mouth of an American. I can also look at a situation and see it completely differently from the way an American would view the same situation, because I have not grown up with it and have not been taught how to interpret it.

In that sense, being out of it has two main advantages. It allows me to see things that may be so familiar to a native that they have become invisible. It also allows others to see me as someone who needs to be educated, which in turn may lead them to offer observations and opinions that they would not otherwise have considered relevant or useful to the conversation.

The ability to detach oneself from a situation or even from previous knowledge does not, of course, necessitate moving to a different continent to work. My British accent is a helpful tool, but it is not essential to my work. I was able to be out of it when I worked in Britain and had the same accent as everyone else, and I know many American planners who do it very successfully in the United States today. The key is to train yourself to keep one foot outside the conversation, and also how to force others, namely research respondents, to do the same.

LOOK THROUGH THE EYES OF A CHILD

In the same way that it is important for a planner to take the bird's-eye view of a situation, research respondents often need to be drawn out of themselves for them to reveal the really interesting perspectives that we seek, and to be creative themselves. Somehow, many people, when playing the role of themselves, are incapable of articulating what they really think and feel. But once asked to put themselves into the shoes of another person, or even to think as they might have done at a different time of their lives, their minds can open up.

Roger von Oech, who runs workshops on creativity and is the author of a book on that theme entitled *A Whack on the Side of the Head,* suggests that as people get older, their minds close and they become less creative. This decline is not only apparent from childhood to adulthood. Research studies have shown a precipitous decline in levels of creativity even before a child reaches second grade. Von Oech blames this rapid decline on a school system that "insists there's just one right answer, when often there are many. If you believe that there's only one answer, you'll stop looking — and thinking — as soon as you come up with your first answer."

Many British planners working in the United States have argued that the reason Brits tend to make "the best planners" is that by contrast, the British school system tends to reward students' approaches to, and discussions of, a problem, as much, if not more, than the final answer they come up with. I agree with their analysis of the difference between the education systems, but have worked with enough excellent American-born and -educated strategic and creative thinkers to know that Americans *can* develop open and inquiring minds, and debating skills that would not be out of place in the British House of Commons.

It is also clear that the education system alone cannot be blamed for the rapid decline in people's levels of openness and creativity. The pressures not to rock the boat are very strong in most social groups at any age, and that prevents people from taking points of view that are different. Being an adult means living under all sorts or rules and restrictions, many of which are self-imposed. People with good ideas keep quiet because they are afraid of looking silly in front of others. They won't take risks, and without risk, they cannot be creative.

This raises the question of why I would want people in research to be creative in the first place. Isn't that what the creative department back in my agency is for? Yes, but it's a different type of creativity I'm looking for from the people I talk to in my research. *Webster's* defines *creativity* as

> 1. the state or quality of being creative. 2. the ability to create meaningful new forms, interpretations, etc.

And it is meaning and interpretation I seek. I don't want them to solve problems for me or write advertising, but rather to tell me the truth from as many different angles as possible until I start to understand it. I stress, *the truth.* I don't want people making stuff up; I simply want to find ways to unlock truths that they have maybe never acknowledged themselves. And because I want to use those truths later to inform and hopefully inspire creative people, I want them to be pithy and in a form that I can show to creatives without boring them to death.

When I am asked to help develop a communications strategy for a client, I first like to talk to as many people as possible *inside* the organization, to understand how the company defines itself before I seek opinions on the outside. Almost every time I have done this kind of internal company audit, in a wide variety of sizes and types of companies, I have been struck by two things. First, it is amazing to me how often a large number of senior people in the same company will hold completely different perspectives from one another on their company's reason for being. On more than one occasion, I have interviewed more than 20 of the most senior people in an organization, and having asked them the simple question, "What is the purpose of (company name)?" have received more than 20 different answers. When I ask them about their own reasons for being, I get similar responses, as they tend to talk about *what they do* rather than *what it is for.* Second, there is a common tendency for many of these executives (who are extremely successful individuals in highly successful companies) to describe the preceding in almost incomprehensible industry jargon.

As part of a consulting project for a specialist practice of a leading accounting firm a few years ago, I needed to find a clear, simple way of expressing the purpose and ideals of the practice, both to communicate with potential clients on the outside who spoke a different language, and also to my own creative people so that they would understand what to say in the first place. But the more interviews I conducted, the more complicated the problem seemed to become, as one partner after another gave me a different perspective based on what he or she *did* as opposed to how that might be useful to a client. Finally, I asked one of the partners if he had any children. Yes, he told me, a little puzzled by my question, he had two kids. I asked him how old they were.

"A boy of six and a girl of four."

"So when they ask you what you do at work, what do you tell them?"

His eyes lit up. He had, he said, tried to explain it to them only the other day. Something like, "Daddy helps make other people's businesses more efficient . . . er . . . run better. Like the coach on your Little League team tells you how to hit better, or catch better, or throw better, that's what Daddy does for people who want to make more money." He then went on to tell me that the real *art* of accounting was not in the audit of what a company had done in the previous year, but in interpreting those numbers and using them to define future strategies.

That was interesting, and it had the added advantage of describing what he did in terms of its *benefit* to a client. If I had continued having an "adult" conversation with him, I am certain he would never have said anything of the sort.

In the same vein, in focus groups for a variety of clients, we frequently ask people to express themselves using drawings, which usually has two effects. First, it scares them.

"Oh my God, I can't draw . . ." they protest.

Then they start to enjoy themselves.

I give three examples of variations on this technique in action, all in the context of developing a new campaign for Porsche in 1993, which helped not only to extract some very important information, but also to open up creative opportunities.

By way of brief background, Porsche had seen a precipitous decline in sales in the United States over the previous few years. In 1986, the company had sold over 30,000 cars in the United States, but by 1993 that figure had dropped below 4,000. The decline was in part due to a change in model lineup (Porsche had discontinued the cheaper 924 model that had been part of the mix in the record year in 1986), but also to a combination of price increases (an average increase of 117 percent between 1989 and 1993) and recession that had put a Porsche beyond the reach of many who might otherwise have bought one. In addition, Porsche had also done a lot of research that suggested their brand had lost some of its appeal. It was an eighties car, a symbol of greed and conspicuous consumption that time had simply passed by.

In focus groups of non-Porsche owners, we asked people to imagine that they were sitting at a stoplight, when a Porsche pulled up next to them. We gave them cartoon drawings with empty thought bubbles emanating from their vehicles. What crossed their minds when they looked at the Porsche and its driver? The response was fairly consistent and was summed up by one respondent in one word (see Figure 4.3): "Asshole!"

Figure 4.3   Porsche research drawing: "Thoughts at a Stoplight."

Mmmm. We were beginning to get worried. A specially commissioned quantitative study confirmed that the "asshole factor," as it came to be known, was a fairly widespread phenomenon. Out of 1,000 people we interviewed, 200 had bad things to say about Porsches and Porsche drivers. One in five. That's a lot of people to drive past on your way to work who don't like you. No wonder a lot of previously loyal Porsche owners were starting to think again about buying another one. So what had happened to the dream car status we all remembered from when we were kids? Where had it gone?

In an elementary school in San Francisco, we conducted an experiment with the help of a friendly teacher who agreed to let us lead her kids' next art project. We asked a bunch of kids aged between eight and ten to draw their dream cars for us, with no further prompting. Some of them drew fantastic, futuristic designs, with bright colors and weird shapes, but most drew sports cars. The majority of those sports cars were red. And most of them were Porsches (see Figure 4.4). So the dream car was still a dream car to *some* people. People not old enough to be concerned by Porsche-driving junk bond traders, or the movies where the bad guy always seems to be driving a black 911. (Incidentally, we were very struck by the quality of the kids' drawings, with almost loving detail in some of the depictions of the cars. In many ways, this was their best medium of expression. Presumably as we age and become verbally more articulate, those skills desert all but a few.)

Finally, we talked to Porsche drivers and drivers of other luxury and high-end sports cars, and asked them to draw the way they feel about their cars. To our surprise, there was a very marked contrast between the two. Many of the drivers of other manufacturers' cars (BMW, Mercedes, Infiniti, Lexus, and the like) drew the cars as they would see them standing on their driveways. All had the perspective of being on the outside looking in, and many had highlighted features like hood ornaments, airbags, luxurious leather seats, and hi-fi systems. The enjoyment in these cars seemed to lie in the owning and in the way they cocooned their drivers and separated them from the surrounding environment as the suspension and seats removed the bumps in the road and the sound system masked exterior noise.

Figure 4.4   Porsche research drawing: "My Dream Car."

Porsche owners in three cities, in a total of six different focus groups, almost all drew pictures that were virtually identical. With only one or two exceptions, they never even showed the car. Instead, the point of view was from the driver's seat, on a winding road in the mountains, trees all around and sun shining. In their cars they were *part of* the environment, and the whole experience depicted was about the love of driving (see Figure 4.5).

These pictures said more to us than any amount of talking ever could. They brought to life not only the unique truth of what it's like to own a Porsche, but also demonstrated very graphically the way in which the Porsche experience differs from that of another luxury car brand. It led us toward advertising that in print aimed to capture the visceral feeling evoked in the Porsche drivers' drawings, both to reaffirm the specialness of Porsche to existing (and maybe wavering) owners, and to introduce a side of the brand to the nonowners (the ones who would otherwise be thinking or shouting "asshole!") to persuade them that there was more to this vehicle than a place on a pedestal and sneering arrogance. The message was that this was a car designed to be driven, and it should be driven by people who love to drive. Is there anything socially unacceptable about loving to drive? The campaign also used light humor to soften the message, which was a surprise to many who had come to regard the brand as too serious and Teutonic for its own good.

The print campaign always featured the car on the road, a road whose vanishing point was always visible. The 911 Turbo ad, instead of talking purely about speed and acceleration, took the same information and turned it on its head: "Kills bugs fast" (see Figure 4.6). The Carrera Four's superlative road holding was not expressed in technical terms, but by using an everyday metaphor: "Like peanut butter to the roof of your mouth" (see Figure 4.7).

"Bringing out the child" in research respondents is one of my favorite ways of helping them to reveal their true feelings about a subject, because at the same time it tends to focus or

Figure 4.5   Porsche research drawing: "Me and My Car."

Figure 4.6   Porsche: "Kills Bugs Fast."

Figure 4.7   Porsche: "Peanut Butter."

simplify responses *and* it is generally fun for the respondents. I know a lot of moderators who believe that if people are laughing in their focus group, then they, as moderators, are not doing a professional job. In my view, that couldn't be further from the truth, as it has always been apparent to me that the better the mood of the respondents, the better the information they reveal.

There are many other ways of simplifying and bringing out the child beyond the ones I have described—for example, producing collages from pictures torn out of magazines and simple word associations are techniques I use a lot. For the more adventurous moderator there is always the possibility of role-playing exercises—but as this is not meant to be a methodological treatise, I will stop at the Porsche examples and hope that the general point is clear.

GO TO THEM—DON'T MAKE THEM COME TO YOU

In Chapter 3, I spoke of the "unnatural habitat" in which far too much research is conducted, and the way that this environment can limit the ability of respondents to act naturally and reveal their true feelings about the issues under discussion. This is not just a function of the use of a research facility, as many other aspects of the research process can also act as barriers. Consequently, a simple change of location seldom, on its own, provides the solution. But it helps.

My aim, wherever time, money, and clients allow, is to create an environment for respondents that replicates as closely as possible the place and mood that they will be in when they have contact with a brand or a piece of advertising, so that the amount of postrationalizing they are tempted to do about their opinions and preferences is kept to a minimum. There are two main ways in which we have been able to achieve this on a number of different clients' businesses. The first is simply to hold the conversation with the respondent or respondents in a location that seems to fit the task at hand. The other, if that is not possible, is to create tasks for the respondents that allow you to get a unique insight into their world, even if you cannot enter it yourself.

Natural Habitat

In pitching Sega's video game business, almost all of GS&P's exploratory and strategic development research took place in kids' bedrooms. (At times this was a perilous experience. One planner was actually bitten by a respondent's six-year-old brother, who in the middle of an interview, burst out of a closet wearing a cape and sank his teeth into the planner's arm. No explanation for this strange behavior was forthcoming.) We asked the kids to invite over the friend or friends with whom they normally played video games, and for most of the time that the planners were in the houses, they merely sat and watched and listened as the kids played. When they interviewed them, it was always in their own bedrooms, or in the living rooms with a larger group. The combination of their own surroundings and their own friends (as opposed to the strangers who are usually required for most focus groups) made them much more relaxed, and for teenage boys, they really had quite a lot to say.

When conducting Isuzu focus groups, we arranged to have a bus standing by to ferry our respondents to a nearby dealership to shop the cars. Of course the salespeople are always on their best behavior (ten prescreened, already-interested, financially qualified buyers on a plate . . . of course they are on their best behavior), but it does allow us to discuss the vehicles and their features with the actual vehicles as reference, and also talk about the dealer environment as it feels there and then, not as people remember or think they remember it.

We have gone out for the evening with families to Pizza Hut, and with others stayed home and ordered the pizza in. One of my planners, working on a new business assignment for a brand of gin, held a dinner party at a hip martini bar for her respondents, and another held a series of focus groups on board a Norwegian Cruise Line ship, to elicit people's feelings about cruising while they were actually afloat and before their tans had faded.

The Norwegian Cruise Line example is interesting for two reasons: First, the way that respondents talked about their cruise experiences was completely different from the responses we had seen in groups on dry land. People in the onboard groups talked about many of the same things but with much greater intensity, and were much less likely to talk about the rational, tangible aspects of the ship. Second, the planner on this cruise, Mary Stervinou, was accompanied by creative directors Steve Luker and Steve Simpson, none of whom had cruised before and none of whom had expected to particularly enjoy the experience. The three of them snorkeled together, dined together, and no doubt attracted a lot of gossip. Steve Simpson describes the experience as by far the most significant in the development of the campaign. He remembers something "mesmerizing about being at sea," and a physical sensation of "feeling lighter." All experienced the same feeling of freedom that their fellow passengers described, a feeling that was to be a critical building block of the "It's Different Out Here" campaign (which is described further in Chapter 6).

It's an important lesson: In addition to seeking out the people in the general population who use the products we advertise, planners and creatives alike should experience the products for themselves. I suppose that is easy to say and easy to do when the product is a cruise line, but less glamorous products also have to be experienced, if they are to be truly understood.

Homework

If it is not possible to conduct any of the research in people's natural habitat, it is still possible to get a glimpse of the way they live by arranging for them to carry out certain tasks in their own time before coming to a more traditional research session.

I don't talk about too many examples here, as I can't give everything away, but I do mention two particular instances where such a homework assignment reaped great rewards. One of these is some research we did for the California Fluid Milk Processors Advisory Board, where we asked focus group respondents to go without milk for a week before attending the research, to see what effect it would have on their lives to be without milk for a few days. The experiment revealed some tremendous insights into the role that milk played in their lives that I am convinced would have been very difficult, not to say impossible, to extract from the focus groups alone. The full story of that campaign is the subject of Chapter 7, "Serendipity."

The other example, which I describe here in more detail, was a simple pregroup exercise that we asked respondents to complete before attending some Polaroid research.

We knew from Polaroid's own research that their cameras and film had come under heavy assault from 35-mm disposable cameras, one-hour processing, and camcorders that allowed almost instant playback of *moving* images. We wanted to know how people actually used Polaroid cameras. What kind of pictures did they take? Was there a type of picture that Polaroid could *own*, where the aforementioned competitors could not match them?

Focus groups of owners and nonowners were recruited, and each participant was sent a package about a week before the group. To the owners of Polaroid cameras, we sent two films, and to the nonowners we sent a camera and two films. We asked them to take pictures (of anything they liked) and bring them with them to the groups.

The resulting pictures were very interesting. Maybe 90 percent of them were pictures that could have been taken with any camera: dogs, cats, friends, people at parties, people in the park, all album shots that could arguably have been taken more cheaply and at a higher level of quality with a 35-mm camera. The other 10 percent, though, were the type of pictures that only an instant camera could take. One woman had taken several pictures of herself wearing different pairs of eyeglasses, because her husband couldn't come to the optometrist with her and she wanted him to help her choose the right pair. A man had a picture of his dinged car. He explained that he only needed one picture to send to his insurance agent, and for that the Polaroid camera was perfect. Another woman had taken a picture of a pregnant female coworker holding her dress up around her neck to show her how pregnant she appeared to others. And to cap it all, a young man brought along 20 naked photographs of his girlfriend. "I wouldn't want to go and get them developed, would I?" He was so discreet that he brought them and showed them to a focus group of complete strangers.

What all of these pictures had in common was that they were performing tasks for which Polaroid was the unique solution: one picture, instant evidence, no need to be seen by others at the developing lab. All were real-world examples that, incidentally, all the other respondents found most interesting, and they were in turn a catalyst for the "See What Develops" campaign, the story of which is continued in Chapter 5. Once again, I doubt that the same kind of insights could have been collected from traditional focus groups alone, and it would certainly have been harder to sell the idea of the "Architect" commercial (see Figure 5.7) without the assistance of our respondent's envelope of "artistic" shots of his girlfriend.

WATCH THE GAME AWAY FROM THE BALL

A true aficionado of almost any sport that involves teams of players and a ball will tell you that the game that is played away from the ball is at least as interesting, if not more so, than one that is being played with the ball. A soccer player makes a run into space, a tight end makes a key block to open a hole for a teammate to run through, a basketball player sets a pick, the infield moves to double-play positions—all will be missed by a camera that is studiously following the ball, yet all may prove to be pivotal moments in the game.

Roger Rosenblatt wrote that "the journalism I most admire of my colleagues is that which deliberately does not turn its head toward the noise of a moment but instead focuses on a steady condition or continuing process. If one wants to learn about America's poor, one ought not to look at some spectacular event like a city street riot or a march on Washington. The poor are poor all the time." That is the reason that so much of the "pop" research I referred to in Chapter 3 is so often wide of the mark. In its efforts to keep up with the latest trends (competition is now so fierce that these trends have come to be identified before they have even become trends), it deals in such minutiae that it identifies every single tree yet fails to notice the forest.

In similar vein, Bill Bernbach was scornful of the way that many communicators, in their struggle to find a point of difference from a competitor (*any* difference, just find a USP), will move further and further away from the truth of a category's reason for being or the basic instincts that cause a person to want a product from that category in the first place.

"It took millions of years for man's instincts to develop," he said. "It will take millions more for them to even vary. A communicator must be concerned with unchanging man, with his obsessive drive to survive, to be admired, to succeed, to love, to take care of his own."

The campaign for Norwegian Cruise Line is a good example of that philosophy in action. While the cruise industry all chased after the same ball of new ships, onboard entertainment, and deals, NCL took a step back, looked away from the ball, and said, "Why do people want to take a cruise rather than another kind of vacation? What does a cruise have that other vacations don't?"

Critics of this kind of question (and the type of campaign that resulted from it) argue that it leads to a celebration of the *generic*. "Anyone could say that," they scoff, to which I answer, yes they could. If they had gotten their heads out of their asses long enough to spot both the truth and the opportunity. There's a high ground positioning ready for the taking in almost every category. If a company can say it first, or even say the same thing better than someone else is already saying it, their position will be very difficult to assail.

Looking away from the ball, in addition to being a valuable technique at the macrolevel, can be very useful at the microlevel of an individual research project. There are two main ways that I counsel other planners to use it.

Listen Carefully to What the Research Is Not Saying

In a project for KPMG Peat Marwick's Information, Communication, and Entertainment practice in 1995, I came across rather an overt example of this. I was interviewing chief executives and chief financial officers of a number of their higher-profile clients, hearing their perspectives on working with KPMG and hoping to find valuable insights from KPMG that had helped enhance their businesses in some way. Everyone was very happy to talk to me; everyone gave me a lot of general feedback on the relationship; but just as universally, they were unwilling to discuss specifics. The few who would talk at all about the interesting stuff made me turn off my tape recorder and swear that the conversation would go no further than their rooms, which wasn't a great deal of help in my quest to uncover stories to use in advertising.

Then one day one of the clients joked, as he was telling me the same bad news as all the others before him, that he *could* tell me, "but then I'd have to kill you." I realized that I had been watching the ball—my ball—too closely. I had been frustrated because they had not given me an answer to the question I had asked and missed the fact that their reticence to talk was in itself a very powerful and interesting answer. KPMG would love to run advertising detailing its close involvement with certain high-profile clients, but its involvement is, in fact, so high level that confidentiality prevents it from saying anything.

An advertising campaign was developed based on the idea that the message of the advertising was a secret that could not be shared in this public forum. Under headlines like "This message will self-destruct in thirty seconds. Please read quickly," and "You didn't see this. You didn't read this. Do we understand each other?" KPMG executives were photographed, spy-style, running away from the camera or shielding their faces to remain anonymous. Readers were asked to call National Managing Partner Roger Siboni, who would, of course, "officially deny all knowledge of the call." The ads ended with the line, "Good advice whispered here."

Listen with Your Eyes

In Chapter 3 I discussed the problem of people not always saying what they really mean. This is a very difficult problem to identify and overcome. But if as an interviewer you focus solely on what people are saying, then it becomes almost impossible.

I'm sure that any detective would agree with that. Suspects' words of denial may be very convincing on paper, but in person, the slightest physical movement, or the posture of their bodies, or the look in their eyes, might be signs to a professional interrogator that they have something to hide.

In focus groups, I have seen people watching a video of a commercial, leaning forward toward the television screen, eyes alight, laughing at the humor—until the moderator asks them what they think. The smiles vanish from their faces and they say stuff like, "I think some people may be offended by that." Their own body language clearly stated that *they* were not offended by it. They were involved, they got it, and they liked it, yet their comments immediately afterward would suggest the opposite.

When people are truly engaged by a conversation or an idea, they don't easily hide their feelings. The same goes for others who do not understand or do not like what they are seeing or hearing. Folded arms, furrowed brows, and uncomfortable doodling on notepads are all danger signs and should not be ignored, even if those same frowning people say that they thought an idea was good. If my life depended on picking which is more likely to be true, (1) what people say with their eyes, posture, and attention, or (2) what they say with their words, I would choose (1) every time.

DON'T WORRY IF YOU CAN'T FIND THE ANSWER

The worst experiences I have ever had as a planner have occurred when I have gone out on a research project bristling with hypotheses and armed with techniques that will uncover the elusive consumer truth I seek, only to return completely empty handed.

That may be because I haven't done my job properly, in which case I should go out and try again, but there is, of course, the possibility that there is no answer. Nothing can be said about this product that other competing products are not saying already, and there is no real point of difference. In which case, rather than attempt to invent a difference where one doesn't really exist, or take an irrelevant feature and try to blow it up and make it important, it may be better to look to the advertising execution as a potential point of difference.

In which case the brief to the creative team, which will be the subject of the next chapter, will be very brief indeed.

"Can we have a great ad, please?"

5

The Fisherman's Guide
The Importance of Creative Briefing

He said, "They are feeding on drowned yellow stone flies."
I asked him, "How did you think that out?"
He thought back on what had happened like a reporter.
He started to answer, shook his head when he found
he was wrong, and then started out again. "All there is
to thinking," he said, "is seeing something noticeable
which makes you see something you weren't noticing
which makes you see something that isn't even visible."
I said to my brother, "Give me a cigarette and say
what you mean."

Norman Maclean, *A River Runs Through It*

WHAT IS A CREATIVE BRIEF?

CREATIVE

(krea tiv), *adj.* 1. having the quality or power of creating. 2. resulting from originality of thought; imaginative.

BRIEF

(bref), *adj.* 1. lasting or taking a short time. 2. using few words; concise: a brief report.

3. abrupt; curt. 4. scanty: a brief bathing suit.
~ *n*. 5. a short and concise statement or written item . . .

(source: *Webster's*)

The propaganda of many agencies suggests that in the process of developing advertising, there is a pivotal moment where the rational left side of the agency's collective brain completes its work of data collection, analysis, and synthesis, and hands that information, relay baton–style, to the right side, where it can be molded by the forces of intuition and imagination into interesting and unexpected new forms. The delivery of a written creative brief, usually in conjunction with a verbal briefing, is a sign that the intellectual foreplay is over.

Let the creative juices flow.

In its simplest terms, *creative briefing* is the bridge between smart strategic thinking and great advertising (advertising that involves consumers on both a rational and emotional level, and which is capable of affecting a change in both their thoughts and behavior) and is the key tool with which planners and their account management partners can unlock the talents and imagination of their agency's creative people.

Different creative people will argue about the relative importance of this briefing process, although most will tend to agree that if a brief is informative, well argued, and insightful, then their chances of creating better advertising are increased and the process of doing so is made considerably easier. Unfortunately, they are also likely to point out that such insightful briefs are relatively few and far between. Often, they say, briefs are of little help and occasionally even seem to act as a *barrier* to great advertising.

The main task of a creative briefing is not to say "okay, it's finally time for you creative folks to start work," but to *inform* the creative team, and most important, to *inspire* them. To reduce all the information that has been gathered from the client, from consumer research, and perhaps many other sources besides, funnel it down to a single, potent idea, and from that idea to create a sense of possibilities, of great advertising just waiting to happen. So it is at the same time an exercise in synthesis and expansiveness. An interesting, and at times awkward, juxtaposition.

Jeff Goodby, speaking at a conference of account planners in New York in 1995, described creative briefing using a fishing analogy. The brief, he said, is the equivalent of a fisherman's guide—a person who takes you to the best place on unfamiliar water, shows you where to fish, and has some ideas about the best flies to use. The guide doesn't do any fishing but makes sure that the fisherman (the agency creative) has a more enjoyable and successful time than he or she would have had on their own.

In simple, factual terms, a good brief should accomplish three main objectives. First, it should give the creative team a realistic view of what their advertising needs to, and is likely to, achieve. Second, it should provide a clear understanding of the people that their advertising must address, and finally, it needs to give clear direction on the message to which the target audience seems most likely to be susceptible.

You will probably have already noticed that I use the terms *creative brief* and *creative briefing* almost interchangeably, although strictly speaking, the two mean different things. The creative briefing, in many agencies, is a meeting where a planner and/or account person will outline the nature of an advertising problem for a creative team, and start to suggest ways of solving it. The creative brief is a document that summarizes the content of that meeting. But as I have never worked in an agency where a brief is delivered in a single meeting, or for that matter slipped surreptitiously and anonymously under the creatives' door, I prefer to think of both the brief and the brief*ing* as equally appropriate names for a longer, less formal process of communication, whereby planners, account people, and creatives work together to mold the direction that the advertising will take. The boundaries between what is written and what is spoken, in brief or brief-*ing*, themselves blur as ideas constantly evolve and expand.

The longer and less formal this process becomes, the less likely it is that there will be a single, neat transition from logical analysis to lateral interpretation and creation. And to me, that's probably just as well. Where the planning and creative briefing processes work best, creative thinking and interpretation commonly precede the official creative briefing stage, and information gathering never really ceases, as one stage of campaign development merges imperceptibly into the next.

One last general point. Many agencies believe that briefing is the sole province of planners, and that others should not participate in the process, except as recipients of the planners' wisdom. I disagree. Creative people should be involved not as passive recipients, but as active participants, as their thinking at an early stage will improve the quality of the brief *and* act as a catalyst for the process of creative development itself. Throughout the chapter you will also notice that I seldom mention the planner alone when I refer to the process of creating and implementing the brief. I regard creative briefing as a responsibility that is shared by planners and their account management partners. To exclude account management from that process, as many agencies do, is not only elitist nonsense, but counterproductive to the development of great advertising.

THE BRIEF IS A MEANS TO AN END

There is only one reason for anyone to write a brief or engage in briefing a creative team, and that is to help make their advertising better (and easier to create) than it would be if they were left to their own devices. As such, it is a means to an end: the creation of a distinctive and relevant advertising campaign.

There are, however, many common misperceptions (abuses might be a more accurate term) of creative briefing that tend to position the brief more as an end unto itself and thereby prevent it from achieving its full potential.

In the first chapter of this book, I made the point that the best advertising represents a partnership between clients, agency creatives, and consumers. All three parties need to be involved throughout, and advertising strategy should incorporate all of their perspectives. That point is fundamental to the main message of this book, and what I am about to say should not be interpreted as a contradiction of that point of view.

The balance between those different perspectives will necessarily vary at different stages of the process. For example, in setting business objectives for the advertising, clients have the central role; in exploratory research, the focus may be on consumers; and when ads are being developed, the agency creatives take the front seat. That's an oversimplification, but at some point, clients, creatives, and consumers (and their planning representatives) will, albeit temporarily, take a seat on the bench and watch someone else do the work. Creative briefing, I believe, is one of those moments.

1. *Clients should not participate in creative briefing.* A brief is a piece of communication between, usually, a planner and account person on one hand, and a creative team of art director and copywriter on the other. For this to work most effectively, it is important that clients take a back seat.

I realize that many people, clients especially, may raise their eyebrows at this idea. Exclude clients from the creative briefing? Surely that's heresy?

First, let me clarify exactly what I mean by suggesting that clients do not play a direct role in the briefing process, because it is not really as subversive as it may sound. I think that they should always contribute to the thinking that provides the brief's foundation, in the ways described in earlier chapters, and should also be in full agreement with the load-bearing pillars of campaign objectives, proposed target, and the broad idea that the creative team will be asked to communicate. Beyond that, however, they do not need to participate in the verbal briefing of the creative team and should not need to see a written brief at all. As long as they have agreed to the general direction, then the detail should not concern them.

2. *If it's not relevant to the consumer, it's not relevant to the brief.* Throughout the strategic development process, the agency's (and arguably the planner's) most important task is to filter information received from both clients and consumers, and boil it down to the few most useful nuggets. Clients may have a vast amount of information to impart relative to their products, their design, manufacturing process, competitive context, previous communication, and so on, but as important as it is for the agency to be exposed to this information, it is equally important that not all of this information finds its way into the creative briefing. For a start, not all of it will be relevant to the people who are the target of the advertising; and if it's not relevant to them, it should not be included in the brief. But apart from that, too much information can be as damaging to a team as not enough; it creates confusion. Even though it may contain elements that may potentially be very useful to the team, those elements will not be useful if they are hidden under a pile of interesting irrelevancies.

In Chapter 3, I described some of the problems that arise when clients spend more hours each day with their products than with their spouses. They become very attached to them (their products, that is), assume that everyone else feels the same way, and will not hear a bad word uttered about them. In many ways, this is a good thing. It is, after all, very important for most clients on a day-to-day basis. How can they possibly exhort others to sell, buy, and consume their products if they themselves do not appear to love them like their firstborn? Conversely, how could someone get up and feel good about going to work in the morning if he or she thought that their product sucked? But as essential as this affection and belief is to clients' abilities to motivate and to their own personal sanity, it is a serious liability when it comes to guiding advertising communication.

3. *The purpose of the brief is not to praise the product.* If left unchecked, the natural client desire for others to share their belief in their product would manifest itself in a creative brief that reads like a speech at a sales convention. All chest thumping and unrealistic expectations of the way that product x will kick the sorry ass of product y.

There is no place for rhetoric in a creative brief, which has to be truthful to both the capabilities of the product and the expectations of the consumer. This, in turn, means that in the process of briefing, one of the key tasks of the planner and other team members is to begin to translate client language for the benefit of those who are writing the ads and those who will ultimately be addressed by them. And nowhere is this more evident or important than in the area of complex technology, where there is often a yawning chasm of technological sophistication between those who sell, and those who buy, the products.

I once had to brief a creative team at BMP for a campaign for a new Sony camcorder. Prior to doing so, I was taken through a three- or four-hour technical briefing at Sony's office on the new features that the advertising needed to highlight. Two of these features in particular seemed to differentiate the camera from its competitors. It had a very powerful zoom lens and also a new CCD imager with many thousands more pixels than any other nonprofessional camcorder on the market. The pixel discussion alone took more than two hours. For those of you who are wondering, a pixel is a dot of light or color that makes up a video image on television or in print. Pixels are like the dots that make up pictures in newspapers; the greater the number of dots in a given space, the sharper the picture.

I had to find a consumer-friendly way of describing or showing how that worked. In an attempt to make both the zoom lens and pixels merge into one overall benefit, I said:

> The powerful zoom lens allows you to spot
> a bee's balls from ten paces. And the x-

> thousand-pixel CCD imager gives you a pic-
> ture so sharp that you can't just see his balls,
> you can count the number of hairs on them.

Okay, so it was a little irreverent, but my client, who always insisted on signing off on the brief before I spoke to the team, was horrified that I could be so frivolous with this sophisticated, innovative piece of technology that was the cornerstone of Sony's video strategy. The bee's balls had to go.

Now I don't even know if bees have testicles, but that's hardly the point. I was using them as a metaphor, which the creative team, incidentally, felt explained what the camera did very simply and graphically (yes, I had broken the rules by already discussing it with them). I had also pointed out that Sony's advertising required a certain tone and intelligence that would, of course, have been inconsistent with such testicular references in the advertising itself, although I knew from previous conversations that the team understood that without my having to tell them. The sole purpose for the analogy was to explain the technology *to them* in as interesting (and entertaining) a way as possible. They knew that it was up to them to find another example more suitable for mass-market consumption.

4. *Creatives write from a brief, not to it.* The client, however, believed that nothing should appear in the brief that would not ultimately find its way into the advertising, and this flies in the face of the way that many creative people actually use briefs. John Webster once told me that if I were to spend 2 hours briefing him, he would bet that at least 1 hour and 59 minutes of that time would not be directly useful to him in writing an ad. (In fact, I believe that *irrelevant* and *useless* were the words he actually used.) In the remaining one minute, though (which could appear at any point within the two hours), I might be lucky enough to utter a single word or sentence that gave him an idea. That, he said, would be a great briefing.

Many clients are made extremely nervous by the apparently random nature of what Webster describes. They don't like surprises, and if the inspiration could come from *any-where* in the brief, that adds an element of unpredictability that to many is simply unacceptable. In a perfect world, many clients would prefer a creative brief to be a list of instructions to the agency, or a checklist against which to grade the advertising. Whom to talk to, what to say, how to say it, how many times to say it, how much time to devote to the product shot, and even which spokesperson to use. Nothing left to chance. And, as a consequence, little, if any, room for creativity.

A few years ago, I presented a creative brief to a company chairman and founder, who listened stone-faced throughout. When I had finished, he told me that what I had presented was all very fine, but he had a "better idea." That better idea, he went on to elaborate, was to use the popular football coach and commentator, John Madden, as his company's spokesman. "That's the brief," he said. "Use Madden." Please forgive me for not revealing the client's identity, but rest assured that John Madden was about as relevant to this particular product as Michelle Pfeifer would be to a campaign for tractor parts.

Fortunately, the arrival of a new, enlightened company president averted that particular crisis (the ensuing Madden-free campaign helped grow the company's business, won gold awards at all the major creative shows, *and* a gold Effie™ for effectiveness, and ultimately attracted a rich buyer for the company that allowed the founder to retire), but not all agencies (or friends of John Madden) are so lucky.

A planner at GS&P, Andrew Teagle, once commented that he had often heard clients say that creatives write ads "*to* a brief." Wasn't that the wrong way to look at it, he asked? Surely a more accurate description was that creatives write ads *from* a brief? In other words, the clients' phrase described a process where the brief was designed to *limit* the creatives, whereas our own process was designed to *liberate* them. It's not that we set out to give the creatives absolute freedom—far from it, if we are true to our aim of making advertising relevant to its target—but if their advertising is to be distinctive enough to stand out and be noticed, it is vital that they are at least able to explore the possibilities without having their hands tied behind their backs.

5. *The brief is not an opportunity to show off how hard you've been working.* If you are a planner or account person in an agency, it is easy to develop an inferiority complex relative to copywriters and art directors, because they are the only ones who actually have something *tangible* to show for their efforts, in the form of a piece of advertising. However hard or effectively a planner or account person may have worked, they do not have their name *on an ad,* and because both jobs require a great deal of informal maneuvering, it is a very worrying situation when the annual performance review comes around. "Tell me what you did in the development of the campaign for _____," your boss might say, and of course it is often very hard to define exactly what you *did* do.

There is a solution to this problem, which is for planners and account people to be judged on the quality of the advertising, and assume that the end justifies the means. Many agency managers unfortunately don't see it that way, and planners and account people are left to find other ways to justify their existence. Assuming that the advertising itself is off-limits because someone else actually wrote or designed it, they will focus instead on the next best tangible thing that they *can* own, and that is the creative brief.

The creative brief, at least in its written form, may thus become a kind of diary of the planner's or account person's activities over the weeks or months leading up to the creatives first putting pencils to paper. I know how tempting this is, because I have been in situations myself where I have done so much work that a half-hour-long discussion and three pages of letter-sized paper hardly seem to do it justice.

When I knew so much about a product that I could write a dissertation on the subject, I sometimes succumbed to the temptation. I presented an in-depth analysis of a region's economy and history, or explained manufacturing processes in mind-numbing detail, all because I had worked my ass off to unearth this information, and Goddammit, I was determined that it would not go unnoticed.

As I said at the top of this section, "There is only one reason for anyone to write a brief or engage in briefing a creative team, and that is to help make their advertising better," not to prove a point to yourself or to others. Because attempting to do so will invariably make the creatives' jobs even harder.

The Brief Is an Ad to Influence the Creative Team

I once heard a planner ask John Hegarty, the creative director of the top London agency Bartle Bogle Hegarty, what he looked for in a creative brief. He replied that he looked for a very simple, single-minded idea, which is usually expressed in the part of the brief that many agencies term the *proposition*. (I prefer a different descriptor, which I will explain later.) Hegarty said that it was his habit to take that one sentence and write it on a large piece of paper, above or below a picture of the product, almost as if the line from the brief were a headline. Then he would pin it up above his desk and ask himself first whether the juxtaposition of that line and that product made some rational sense, and second, whether it also started to suggest something interesting on an emotional level. If so, then he would think, "There's the first ad in the campaign. It's my job to create something better."

I don't know whether Hegarty really goes through the process of writing out the line, pasting on or drawing a picture of the product, and physically pinning it up as a standard that he needs to surpass, but it really doesn't matter.

What is important is that he sees the brief as a piece of advertising, albeit crude, and tries to react to its main idea as if he were seeing it on a billboard.

In an article in *Campaign* magazine in September 1996, Andrew Cracknell, the chairman and executive creative director of Ammirati Puris Lintas in London, agreed that the brief needs to represent the first creative thinking. "Planners," he said, "take the first leap in imagination." While I disagree with Cracknell's view that planners alone should be responsible for briefing, and for that matter for any leaps in imagination, I believe very strongly that whoever is doing the briefing *should* have the first creative ideas.

For anyone preparing a brief, writing your own ad is a very useful exercise. As Hegarty said, it doesn't have to be a great ad, or even a good ad, but it does have to be interesting on both a rational and emotional level. If the writer of the brief finds it impossible to manifest his or her own thinking in an advertising idea, then it will likely be an uphill struggle for the team assigned to create the actual campaign.

A brief tends to succeed in direct proportion to the level of *creativity* present in both its ideas and presentation. If the creative brief is not itself creative, if it does not suggest solutions to problems, present information in an expansive and interesting way, and interpret that information with imagination and flair, then its authors and presenters have no right to expect anything different from their creative team. Superficial information will spawn superficial advertising, and a dull, unenthusiastic presentation of the possibilities will become a self-fulfilling prophesy in the final work. A creative team has to believe that a great campaign is *possible* before they can begin to create it. Perhaps the most important task of the brief, arguably more influential than the strategic and creative direction itself, is the creation of the *belief* in the team that they will be able to do their very best work on this one assignment.

GREAT BRIEFS: TRIUMPHS OF SIMPLICITY OVER COMPLEXITY

While the physical presentation of the brief obviously plays a key role in raising the expectations and confidence of the creative team, it should not be regarded as some kind of pep rally. Many of the best briefs I have ever seen (as defined by the thinking and presentation of the brief itself, and by the quality of the resulting advertising) avoided the temptation to *sell* an idea altogether, persuading instead through the use of honesty and simplicity of thought and expression. Such simplicity may seem innocent, or even naive, but it is devastatingly effective, not only in communicating the basic truths that are the foundation of so much effective advertising, but also in disarming its audience and preparing them to accept ideas that they might otherwise resist.

The ascendancy of simplicity over complexity is evident in almost every field of human endeavor, although strangely people's perceptions are almost exactly the opposite. They expect that the best solutions must come from the most sophisticated and difficult analysis, and it is rare for anyone who actually achieves these breakthroughs to attempt to dissuade them from this point of view. After all, what great achiever wants to have people think that what they do is *easy?*

One of the pleasures of living in San Francisco in the 1980s and early 1990s was the opportunity to see Joe Montana play for the San Francisco 49ers. One of the greatest quarterbacks of all time, Montana won four Superbowls and was legendary for his ability to bring his team back from deficits late in the fourth quarter of the game. Tom Junod, writing in *GQ* magazine in September 1994, said of Montana, "For a long time, I thought of Joe Montana as a 'thinking man's quarterback,' a 'cerebral athlete' whose game — a greedy, hungry, gobbling thing, based on patience, restraint, even passivity — was an expression of some kind of Zen mastery." His impression, shared by many, I am sure, was that Montana must have a mind like a chess master, capable of computing all possibilities, calculating move, countermove, and counter-countermove, all in a fraction of a second.

The *GQ* journalist asked Montana if at those moments of crisis, with only seconds left on the clock and his team trailing, "he tries especially hard to complete his first pass, because then he knows that the defense starts thinking, Oh no, here comes Joe. . . . And Joe answered that no, he tries to complete his first pass because it's always better to complete a pass than *not* to complete a pass. He feels the same way about the second pass, and the third."

"His simplicity," says 49ers president, Carmen Policy, of Montana, "is his genius. . . . He is able to operate on a simplistic level and come to decisions that others would think of as very complex."

"The Joe Montana of brief-writers." Now that's something to aspire to.

THE BRIEFING ITSELF

Many agencies use a format for creative briefing to ensure that the essential information is included. This format may even extend to a specially designed form, with sections to be filled in by the person preparing the briefing. I personally detest filling in forms of any sort and for that reason have never introduced one in my own agency, but I do suggest a number of questions that I think every brief should attempt to answer.

This is important for two main reasons. First, the very act of posing these questions forces the person preparing the briefing to come up with *answers* to them. It is important that any briefing at least attempts to find solutions, as opposed to simply listing problems that the creative team needs to overcome. Second, a set list of questions does provide focus and discipline, and ensures that the team is given all the basic information they require to do their job.

In the following sections, I go through these questions one at a time, giving examples of the kind of response that is expected and how this information has in turn found its way into advertising campaigns. You will notice one thing about these questions (which I have adapted only slightly from a set first developed by my former colleague, Ewen Cameron, at BMP), and that is that they are all written in plain English. No "marketing-speak" to be seen in any one of them. That is significant because if, as previously suggested, a brief is really an ad to influence a creative team, then it needs to use their language (within certain limits of decency, of course), and not that of marketing executives and management consultants.

Words and phrases like *strategy, positioning,* and *proposition,* that commonly pepper creative briefs, are defined and understood in different ways by different people. Too often, time that should be devoted to solving an advertising problem is wasted in needless semantic arguments about the difference between a strategy and a proposition. The process is hard enough without creating unnecessary problems, and by removing jargon, the path of creativity can be greatly eased. Furthermore, if a question is asked in plain, everyday English, it is more likely to be answered in the same kind of language. In the spirit of engaging and involving consumers, that can only be a good thing.

WHY ARE WE ADVERTISING AT ALL?

Surprising as it may seem, this is often a very difficult question to answer. "Because we always have," "because our competitors do," "because we have a budget and we need to spend it before September," and "for a tax write-off" may all have some truth in them, but are unlikely to inspire a creative team, because they treat advertising as a simple object or commodity. "We have an empty page in a magazine, please fill it," is not likely to excite anyone, and is even less likely to lead to an interesting advertising campaign.

Instead, the question begs a succinct description of the client's current business situation, and the problems that advertising needs to overcome, along with a clear sense that advertising *can* help.

When American Isuzu Motors hired our agency in 1991, our first advertising task was to launch a new version of the Trooper (which had been completely redesigned, taking the price from $13,000 to over $25,000, and taking Isuzu into previously uncharted waters), and to relaunch the Isuzu Rodeo, which had entered the market in the previous year, but with limited success. Increased sales of the Rodeo were critical to Isuzu's business, and very aggressive objectives had been set for 1992.

To develop a campaign for Rodeo, two important questions needed to be answered. First, why had Rodeo not performed particularly well in terms of sales in its first year? And second, why did the people who *had purchased* a Rodeo choose the vehicle in preference to others?

The way most car purchases work is that at some point, an individual decides that they need a new vehicle. Perhaps their old car broke down one time too many, maybe they were in a crash, or maybe they're just bored and want a change. Whatever the reason, they decide to go check out some dealerships. Their choice of which dealerships to visit tends to be defined by the brands and vehicles they know, and most of us carry around such an informal list in our minds, based on vehicles we have seen on the road, things that friends and colleagues have told us, and, I hate to admit it, advertising that we have seen. Generally speaking, people narrow this list down to three or four vehicles, visit the relevant dealerships, and after considering what the car has to offer, how it feels on a test drive, how helpful/sincere/ unpleasant a particular dealer may be, and of course, how the "deals" compare, a purchase will be made.

The important thing to realize about the role of advertising in all of this is that, while it may ultimately reinforce someone's decision to buy, its primary purpose is to draw people to the dealership. After they get to the dealership, a whole lot of other factors come into play, which advertising cannot directly influence.

Industry data on the number of dealerships visited by purchasers of import sport utility vehicles (SUVs) revealed a very interesting fact, which was that the people who had bought either the Nissan Pathfinder or the Toyota 4Runner, the two leaders in the category, had almost all shopped *both* vehicles in the course of making their decision, yet very few had also shopped the Rodeo. Rodeo buyers, on the other hand, had shopped both Pathfinder and 4Runner, and some other vehicles besides; only after that had they shopped Rodeo. In fact, Rodeo buyers tended to visit more dealerships than any other sport utility buyer.

Focus groups elaborated on this issue. Owners of competing SUVs told us that they had simply not heard of Rodeo, which of course would explain why they didn't visit the Isuzu dealership. Some also admitted that they didn't regard the Isuzu brand very highly—Isuzu's own research confirmed this, with 42 percent of intending SUV buyers indicating that they would be "less likely" to purchase a vehicle if it was made by Isuzu. "Poor guy. Maybe next time he can afford a Pathfinder," wrote a respondent when asked in one of our focus groups to imagine the thoughts of a driver stopped next to a Rodeo at the lights. The Rodeo driver's imagined thoughts were defensive. "Well . . . well at least I have four wheel drive. . . ."

But when we showed these people the vehicle, which we had taken to every focus group location, they were very surprised. Its appearance, they said, was very similar to their 4Runner or Pathfinder, and it had almost all of the same features, at a slightly lower price. If they had known that when they were shopping for a car, would they have shopped the Rodeo? Most answered yes.

Meanwhile, Rodeo owners described a purchase process that went something like this. "I really wanted a sport utility vehicle. I was particularly attracted to the Pathfinder and the Toyota—the 4Runner—because they were sleeker, more sporty looking. But when I went to see them, they were too expensive, and I checked out some of the domestics, but either they were too expensive or I didn't like the look, and then I wandered into the Isuzu dealership and found the Rodeo. It had the same look as the 4Runner and Pathfinder, and all the same features. And it was a great deal."

These owner focus groups had begun almost like therapy sessions, with Rodeo owners quiet and even a little embarrassed, when I asked them to tell the group what vehicle they owned. "I, er, have . . ." mumbled the first respondent, eyes lowered, "an Isuzu Rodeo." Others raised their own eyes. Did they hear him right? The second respondent looked at the first and said, almost puzzled, "I have a Rodeo, too." And around the table it went, like the scene at the end of *Spartacus* where everyone claims they are Spartacus. "I have a Rodeo!" "*I* have a Rodeo!" Laughter filled the room (I'm not exaggerating) and conversation, energy level, and body language were all transformed as the respondents realized they were not the only ones. They were delighted to share their sense of discovery, and their intelligence and discernment in having made a smart choice.

The reason we needed to advertise Rodeo was clear—to let people know that the vehicle *existed*. But advertising also had to begin the task of rebuilding Isuzu's reputation. And it dawned on us that while most advertising sets out to say that a product or company is *different* from its competitors, this advertising should start, as strange as it might seem, by trying to convince people that the Rodeo was *the same*. The same as 4Runner. The same as Pathfinder. Because we were confident that if we could get Rodeo onto the lists of people shopping 4Runner and Pathfinder, the combination of Rodeo's comparable features and lower price would win customers.

So at the same time, this description was both an outline of the problems and a glimpse of light at the end of the tunnel. If advertising could successfully position Rodeo in the right competitive context, then Isuzu would have a very good chance of achieving its objectives.

WHAT IS THE ADVERTISING TRYING TO ACHIEVE?

In other words, the objectives. And here it is important to be realistic, because advertising cannot achieve everything. It can't sell a product that's not there (actually, advertising can rarely *sell* anything at all—with the exception of direct response advertising, as just noted in the Isuzu Rodeo example, the most it can do is interest someone enough to go visit a store), and it cannot make up for inherent product deficiencies.

It is vital to be clear about the desired effect, and if it is *effects*, plural, that are being sought, it is important to prioritize. Advertising that seeks, say, to increase frequency of usage of a particular product is different from advertising that is trying to generate trial of the same product. The first objective involves talking to existing users and persuading them to use the product more often, which means changing habits. The second requires addressing nonusers and persuading them to use it for the first time; and that means not only establishing *new* habits, but maybe even overcoming prejudice and misperception.

For the Isuzu Rodeo, the objective was very clear and single-minded:

> The advertising needs to persuade shoppers
> of competing sport utility vehicles to include
> Rodeo on their shopping lists.

In other words, to persuade potential buyers to visit the Isuzu dealership. After that, it was up to the dealer to close the sale.

The only desired effects that should be listed in this part of the brief are the ones that advertising itself can directly affect. For example, it might have seemed like a reasonable objective to say of Rodeo, "We want the Isuzu Rodeo to be the nation's biggest-selling import sport utility vehicle," which, if Isuzu achieved its rather ambitious sales volume, it had every chance of becoming. But that is a business objective, and the briefing needs to recognize that advertising is only a means to that end. To become number one (which Rodeo did within only a few months of the campaign's launch) required a coordinated offensive at every point of the purchase process, so that if advertising succeeded in attracting people to the dealership, the dealers were also equipped to sell the car against the key competitors we had identified. They would need cars on the floor, the right promotional events, and the right lease programs and financing options to close the sale. In other words, it would in theory have been possible for the advertising to succeed in meeting its objectives while Isuzu failed in meeting its overall business objective. Fortunately for us and for them, that did not happen.

While the Rodeo brief had just one major objective, many others may contain more than one. For instance, in developing a new campaign for Polaroid, the objectives were twofold:

1. To get people who already own a Polaroid camera to use it more often
2. To inspire nonowners to consider buying a Polaroid camera

Here, a clear order of priority was being set. Our primary aim was to stimulate increased usage among current owners, but, if our message was compelling enough, it could also interest people outside Polaroid's current customer base. If that happened, it would be an unexpected bonus, and we would be happy. We simply wouldn't *try* to make it happen.

A final example comes from the "got milk?" campaign for the California Milk Processors, where the order of priority that was established, for three separate objectives, was not one of importance, but of *sequence*. Without achieving the first, we reasoned, the second would be unreachable. So, too, the second and third were mutually dependent, although in that case the order could conceivably have been reversed:

1. To persuade Californians to *think* about milk
2. To persuade them to *use* more milk, by creating additional milk occasions
3. To link usage patterns to purchase patterns so that they will *buy* more milk (because if you don't buy more, you can't consume more)

WHO ARE WE TALKING TO?

This question is designed to provide focus; it will rarely, if at all, provide any inspiration. Generally, the answer is a simple demographic description, and while its primary role is to define as precisely as possible the group that needs to be addressed by the advertising, it is equally important for the discipline of deciding whom to *exclude*.

There is an obvious temptation with any advertising campaign to want it to address as many people as possible, and there are some products, like milk, that are so ubiquitous that a target of "everyone" does not seem unreasonable. Even there, though, it should be possible to narrow it down.

Even though milk is present in almost every home, we decided to aim our message only at those people and households that use milk on a regular basis. This decision was driven by the need to obtain immediate results, and the assumption that it would be easier to persuade people who were already happily and regularly consuming milk to consume *more*, than it would be to persuade nonusers or very light users to effectively start from scratch. Such nonusers and light users were thus excluded from consideration. The "regular user" audience was then subdivided further into those who *consume* the lion's share of milk in the home and those who *buy* it (clearly, they are not always the same person). These two subsets were subsequently targeted by different media, in different places, with slightly different messages. The full story of this campaign can be found in Chapter 7.

In its final execution, of course, the advertising may well have an impact beyond the precise target stated in the brief, but I believe that to be much more likely to happen if the brief is tightly focused than if it sets out from the start to appeal to everyone. While a milk campaign designed to address users and nonusers alike may have seemed on paper to be broader and more expansive, the need to find a message relevant to both groups may well have resulted in something that is *acceptable* to both, but motivating to neither. The old "milk is good for you" messages worked that way — everyone knew it (because everyone's mother had told them ad nauseam), very few people disagreed with it, but no one was in the slightest bit *excited* by it.

Even though the answer to the question "Who are we talking to?" may be expressed in very simple terms (for example, for Sega video games, "boys aged 12 to 17," or for Porsche cars, "mostly men, aged 35 plus, with a household income of over $100,000 a year"), finding this answer requires a great deal of thought and may still only represent a part of the true solution. For example, at the risk of stating the obvious, there is a great difference between a 12-year-old and a 17-year-old boy. For that matter the transition from junior high to high school means that there is a very large difference between 13- and 14-year-olds. And "men aged 35 and over with large household incomes" includes Bill Clinton, Billy Graham, Michael Jackson, Michael Jordan, all of the partners at GS&P, Donald Trump, Bob Dole, the San Francisco police chief, and a large number of successful drug dealers. While all these people might have the financial wherewithal to purchase a Porsche, they probably don't share a common interest in, or desire for, a Porsche. Consequently, the description needs to be qualified by the kind of psychographic and behavioral description covered in the next section.

Sometimes an advertising campaign may need to address two quite different groups simultaneously, because resources do not allow for a separate campaign to each. In this case, the solution is not as simple as deciding which group represents the higher priority, because both may be equally important. Instead, it is necessary to find a common denominator that either explicitly unites the two audiences under one thought, or is at least *capable of interpretation* by each group, in its own way, that leaves each feeling it has got what it is looking for.

A case in point is a campaign GS&P created for Bell Helmets, which simultaneously needed to address the children who in many states today are legally required to wear bicycle helmets, and the adults who buy the helmets for those children. On the surface, the differences between those two groups might seem to represent too wide a gap for advertising to bridge. But in answering the next question, a careful analysis of their motivations, and some clever lateral thinking on the part of the planner and creative team, did reveal an opportunity for a single message.

What Do We Know about Them?

The answer to this question stems from a real understanding of the target's lives and minds, and should provide the creative team with an intimate understanding of what makes these people tick. If the demographic description in the previous section is the skeleton of the brief, then this part represents the body and soul. It should take the description down from the relatively abstract definition of a *group* of people to the tangible level of an individual, with whom the writer and art director will be asked to relate as they create their advertising.

The portrait of these people (no longer a number or an average) will be qualitative, descriptive, emotional, and creative. As it is revealed, the team should come to understand how they relate to the particular category or product in question, whether they care about it, how it fits into other parts of their lives, whether it's a product that they use where other people can see them, how they *feel* about it, whether it is easy or difficult for them to talk about it, and what language they use when they do. Personal experiences and anecdotes described in research can be enormously useful in this part of the briefing, because not only can they often make complex issues easily understandable to the creative team, but they may, if played back in the advertising itself, make the same point quite powerfully to the end consumer.

Such personal experiences and anecdotes proved particularly useful in developing a new advertising campaign for Bell Helmets. Advertising for bike helmets is a complicated business, because a very large proportion of helmets purchased are not worn by the people who pay for them; they are purchased by parents to be worn by their children, and a message that resonates with one of these groups will not necessarily resonate with the other. The situation is further complicated by legislation: A number of states have passed helmet laws that require children under a certain age to wear helmets at all times while riding, and this has led to an increasing commoditization of helmets for children. Increasingly, they are sold by mass-retailers, at very low prices, the aim being to enable parents to meet the letter of the law at the lowest price. For Bell, whose distribution had never extended outside specialty bike stores, and whose helmets retailed at much higher prices, this meant talking to an audience who were largely unfamiliar with the company and its credentials, and persuading them that it was worth paying the extra money for a Bell helmet.

Planner Mary Stervinou set up exploratory focus groups so that on the same day she could talk to groups of children who ride bikes and own helmets, and also to groups of their parents. The aim was to explore how attitudes toward bike helmets differed, if at all, between the groups, and if so, what that implied for the purchase process and role for advertising.

In one group, a mother talked about her nine-year-old boy and her obsession with his safety. She told how she bought him a helmet long before any legislation required him to wear one, and that she always insisted that he wear it before leaving the house on his bike. When making her decision about what helmet to buy, safety had been her number one concern, and for a safer helmet she had been willing to pay more money.

In another group, that woman's nine-year-old son told us his side of the story. He described how, as he left the house to go ride his bike, his mother would always check to see that he was wearing his helmet. No helmet, no riding. That was the rule, just as his mother had told us previously. But then the stories diverged dramatically. The boy told us how much he hated the helmet. It looked dorky, and his friends made fun of him when he wore it. So, he would wear it out of the house, down the driveway, and around the corner where, out of his mother's sight, he would hide it under a hedge. Then he would ride, unprotected but looking cool, and finally retrieve it to ride back up the driveway at the end of the day.

This contradiction, between, on the one hand, parents obsessed with their children's safety and, on the other, kids who were more interested in not looking dorky than being safe, was replayed time and time again in the groups. So advertising clearly had two roles to play. First, it had to convince parents that a Bell helmet was worth the price premium, which our discussions suggested could be accomplished by stressing the company's strenuous research and record of protecting the heads of Indy car and Formula One drivers, motorbike racers, and other such high-speed people. As one parent put it, "I guess if they can figure out how to protect someone who drives into a wall at 200 mph, they can figure out how to protect my ten-year-old at 5 mph."

Once the parents were persuaded, though, the advertising also had to work on the kids, to predispose them toward a Bell helmet as opposed to competitors' helmets, *and most important of all, to persuade them to wear it.*

"Think of it this way," said Mary. "The mother can buy the safest helmet in the world for her kid, but if he won't wear it, then it's not very safe, is it?" So, she reasoned, while Bell's reputation for safety would be a powerful message for moms, on its own it would not be enough.

Strangely, the company's heritage in auto racing that had been persuasive to adults in demonstrating Bell's commitment to, and record for, safety, also had an impact on the children, albeit for different reasons. For children, a conversation about helmets in the context of the Indy 500, or motorbike racing, or the Extreme Games, seemed to have a much greater impact than a conversation about helmets in the everyday context of bike riding. And they found it infinitely more interesting than a discussion of research into helmet safety. The reason was that the people who wore Bell helmets in these faster, riskier pursuits were seen as cool. They were not wearing helmets because their moms made them. And the fact that they were wearing Bell helmets seemed to make Bell's *bike helmets* seem cooler.

Different strategies were adopted in different media as a result of these discoveries. Print was used to directly target adults with an explicit safety message in an environment where children would be unlikely to see it. Here, Bell played on its heritage of protecting the heads of race car drivers, et al., and in one execution showed "The 40-year history of Bell helmets, in 2.3 seconds." Beneath the headline were three pictures of various stages of a racing car crash. The first shows a race car hitting a wall and bursting into flames. "00.1, Guy hits wall." The second shows the car exploding into several pieces. "01.2, Car explodes." Finally, the wreckage comes to rest. "02.3. Guy O.K." Interwoven in the telling of the story of Mark Dismore's survival in this apparently horrific crash is information about research and testing, and the news that of the top 33 Indy car drivers, "22 . . . request and wear Bell helmets."

Two other print executions shown here (Figures 5.1 and 5.2) are very simple human stories that require little explanation. In one, a man lies in traction with every part of his body in a cast except for his head. The headline: "Another satisfied customer." In the other, a young girl is pictured wearing an expensive new pair of sneakers, beside a headline that says: "Does your kid have hundred dollar feet and a ten dollar head?" As with the "40 Year History" execution, both of these focus on the research and testing that led to the choice of Bell helmets by more race car drivers and pro cyclists than any other company's helmets. "Because nobody makes a better helmet than us."

A slightly different message appeared on television, where kids were more likely to see the advertising. Here, the idea was to use racers of cars, motor bikes, and bikes alike as role models for the wearing of helmets, and the mes-

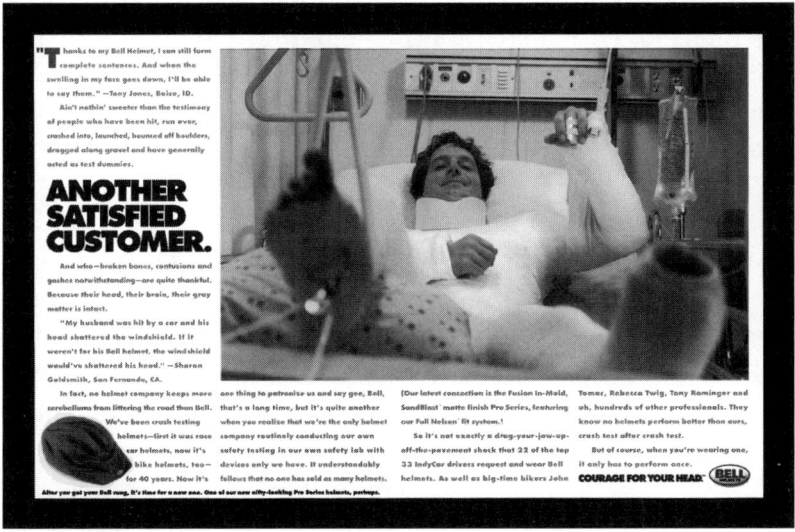

Figure 5.1 Bell Helmets: *"Another Satisfied Customer."*

Figure 5.2   Bell Helmets: *"Ten Dollar Head."*

sage was deliberately kept very simple. The first commercial shows a series of appalling race car crashes, crashing motorcycles, and falling bike riders, all silent, except for the haunting sound of a person whistling. All the unfortunate victims of the crashes are wearing helmets. These scenes are intercut with text pointing out that "humans are the only species with the ability to reason. And sometimes," it concludes, "they actually use it." A human brain is shown, and a Bell helmet attaches itself to the brain with a squelching noise that any child would enjoy. "Bell Helmets," a voiceover says. "Courage for your head." In another, we see footage of a kayaker capsizing in raging white water, with, once again, only whistling for sound. "Here are the possibilities," a card reads. "1. You could hit your head on a rock." The kayaker is underwater. "2. You could drown." Still underwater. "Or . . . 3. You could hit your head on a rock, then drown." Bell Helmets.

The message? Smart people, who could not by any stretch of the imagination be regarded as nerdy, wear Bell helmets.

Another example of a multiple-audience approach is found in the campaign for Isuzu where, as already noted, separate campaigns had to promote the new, upscale Trooper and the more mass-market Rodeo. Aside from the obvious differences in necessary financial resources between potential buyers of the two vehicles, qualitative research revealed two quite different types of personality and motivation among sport utility vehicle owners and intenders. One seemed to lean quite heavily toward the type of vehicle represented by the Trooper, while the other tended to gravitate in the direction of Rodeo and its key import competitors, the 4Runner and Pathfinder. These descriptions of the "Trooper person" and "Rodeo person" appeared in the creative brief:

TROOPER

The Trooper buyer is somewhat wiser than other buyers. But wiser isn't necessarily the result of age; it is more the result of an inquisitive attitude. Trooper buyers are the kind of people who like to discover things for themselves. They are process-oriented, meaning they are just as interested in the process of *how* a decision is made as they are in the actual decision itself. They like knowing all the details before they buy; they don't just *buy*. They don't buy things for what they say, but instead for what they do. They want to know the features and functions. One of the dealers said, "These are the kind of people who when asked why they bought a Trooper could list about a thousand reasons, where other buyers would be hard pressed to list more than a few."

These people are outdoorsy. And while they don't take the "guided tour," they're not trail-blazers either. They've just seen more and like to be prepared in any eventuality. They are looking for an SUV that can handle anything that might be thrown at them.

RODEO

> Rodeo buyers see themselves as different. They are cooler, more adventurous, fun, and "in the know" than most buyers. While they certainly aren't as studied as Trooper buyers, they know their stuff . . . and know what they want. They want their vehicle to be a sort of a tool, to help act out and express their active lifestyle. . . . These people are doers, so their vehicle has to work. It has to be able to be pushed, and they will push it to the limits. These are the kind of people who will want to get their vehicle covered in mud on the first day they own it.

In summary, we said, Rodeo was the vehicle for people who wanted to find adventure. Trooper was for those who wanted to be prepared whenever adventure came looking for them.

WHAT'S THE MAIN IDEA WE NEED TO COMMUNICATE?

This is the part of the brief that many agencies call the "proposition," and an important point needs to be made about the precise phrasing of this question. The emphasis should be firmly on the message that should be communicated to people, rather than on what the advertising should directly *say*. In other words, the focus should be on what people *take away* from the advertising, as opposed to what the advertiser puts in.

Of all the questions in the brief, this is the most important, because its answer should encapsulate everything else that appears *and* represent the first creative leap that John Hegarty and Andrew Cracknell spoke of earlier. Ideally, it should be a single idea that is expressed in a single sentence. If it is any more complicated or lengthy than that, the chances are that it will lead to advertising that is equally ponderous.

What is this one idea? The one thing that is most likely to make people reconsider their views on an existing product or form new opinions about a new product, and take some action as a result. It can be based on the product, on an observation about the consumer, or even an attribute of the category (although in this last case, unless the execution of the idea is exceptional, the idea is in danger of being generic).

The Cuervo example I cited in Chapter 3, "Good drinks, fun times, real people," attempts to capture product, consumer, and category attributes simultaneously. It is not *a* main idea, but *three* main ideas. By comparison, "A party waiting to happen," which was the main idea in our preferred brief, is single-minded, and arguably much more true to both the product and its core users.

The main idea of the Isuzu Rodeo brief previously discussed comprised more of a lifestyle benefit that puts the vehicle firmly into the sporty context of Pathfinder and 4Runner, while playing off the audience's clear desire for adventure:

> The normal restrictions don't apply with an
> Isuzu Rodeo.

The resulting advertising interpreted that idea in a way that presented the Rodeo as a kind of escape vehicle for people who still held on to the spirit of their youth. In one TV commercial, a seventies mom is hanging out the laundry in a suburban back yard and harnesses her small boy to the clothes line by a long cord. As she turns to hang the clothes, he takes off, popping pegs off the line as he runs. She is oblivious as he dives head-first into a large mud puddle and begins to throw mud all around. "They say our personality traits are formed at an early age," a voice-over says, as the boy covers both himself and the camera in mud. The music then cuts to a pounding rock track, and the picture to a Rodeo tooling through the mud on a mountain trail. We realize that it's the boy, now grown up, but still enjoying getting dirty. The voice-over says, "Introducing the 3.1 litre V6 Isuzu Rodeo. So growing up does have its rewards . . ." as the Rodeo disappears down the trail.

In another spot (see Figure 5.3), a man is wheeling his young son around a toy store in a cart. "Okay," he says as he selects a potty, "we're out of here." Easier said than done, as the boy is oohing and aahing and making grabs for toys that take his fancy as they pass within his range. "No, please keep your hands in the cart. . . . We'll come back for that later. . . . That one needs batteries. . . . No, you're gonna get daddy in trouble. . . . 'Scuse me. . . . No, that one definitely has too many parts. . . . We gotta go. . . ." He's almost home free, but as he rounds the corner and enters the last aisle, we see the kid point at something new and let out an appreciative "ooooh. . . ."

Dad is frozen in his tracks. His eyes widen, and his jaw drops.

We see a full-size Isuzu Rodeo, packaged like a toy car. It looks huge, and Dad has clearly fallen in love.

"Ooooohh . . ." he murmurs.

As he continues to ogle, a line appears on screen that says, "Isuzu Rodeo. Grow up, not old."

Trooper, not surprisingly, went in another direction. Knowing that potential buyers would be interested in a vehicle like Trooper for more *defensive* reasons (that is, if they had a problem while driving, Trooper could deal with it), we decided to focus on the features of the vehicle that gave it its practicality and ability to deal with those problems. The

THE RODEO.
GROW UP. NOT OLD.

Figure 5.3 Isuzu Rodeo: *"Toy Store."*

Trooper had been designed with the specific needs of SUV drivers in mind, and in the original design brief, written by a Japanese engineer, we found an analogy that we were more than happy to appropriate. He described his vision for Trooper as a "Swiss Army Knife of SUVs," and our brief focused on that very thought:

> Trooper is exactly the right equipment for
> life's great expedition . . . it's the Swiss Army
> Knife of SUVs.

A campaign was developed based on what we called "the unwritten laws of driving," automobile equivalents of Murphy's law that were universal observations on the problems of driving, parking, and indeed any part of life that related to the use of a vehicle. And for each of these unwritten laws, Trooper had a feature as the antidote to the problem.

The 5th unwritten law of driving was "if there's a hole in the road, you will hit it." With that in mind, Isuzu had developed a double wishbone suspension system for Trooper that would absorb the impact of potholes in the mountains, or in this case, on decaying city streets.

"The attraction of shopping carts to automobiles is one of the strongest forces in the Universe," stated the 9th unwritten law, before presenting a unique, nine-coat paint treatment that among other things was "grocery cart-proof" (see Figure 5.4). And law number eight, over a picture of a baby with all the paraphernalia that accompanies a child on even the shortest journey, raised the eternal truth that "the smaller the person the more space they will occupy." The solution was, of course, a "cavernous" 90 cubic feet of cargo space.

The main ideas of the briefs for both Rodeo and Trooper remained at the hearts of their respective campaigns for a number of years. Even as new models have appeared, the market and consumer have changed, and the campaigns for both vehicles have evolved accordingly, the aforementioned ideas have stayed central to the way we have all thought

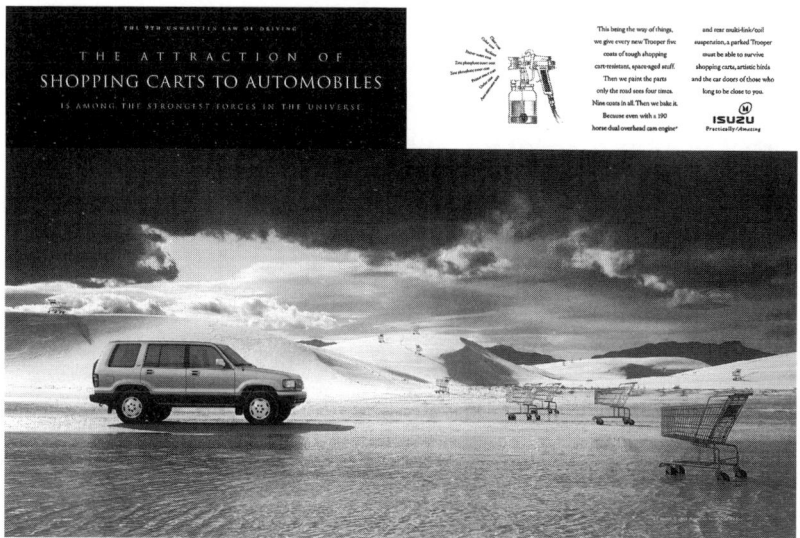

Figure 5.4   Isuzu Trooper: *"Grocery Carts."*

about the two models. Even if advertising has had slightly different tasks to accomplish, it has remained consistent with those first ideas.

WHAT IS THE BEST WAY OF PLANTING THAT IDEA?

Some call this the *strategy,* or the *how* part of the message, as opposed to the *what* of the main idea. Even when a main idea has been honed in the way demonstrated in the preceding section, there are many possibilities for different ways to execute it. Four different teams, given the exact same brief and main idea, will invariably interpret it in different ways, and four quite different campaigns may result, all anchored on the same basic idea, but coming at it from different angles. When I write a brief, this is always the part where I am most likely to experiment and include a lot of ideas that I know may be immediately rejected, in the hope of one sticking and providing some inspiration.

Here I will give just one example, and again it represents the continuation of a story whose earlier parts have been told in other places in the book. This is Polaroid, whose brief, based in large part on the unique ability of an owner to take one picture at a time and use it for immediate effect, had as its main idea:

> With Polaroid, the picture is only the beginning.

What's the best way of planting that idea? Planner Kelly Evans-Pfeifer had several thoughts, only some of which are shown here:

> Maybe highlight innovative or unusual ways that people are using Polaroid—at home and at work.

> Show Polaroid as a participant . . . a means, not an end.

> Perhaps focus on the effects of a Polaroid picture . . . the chain of events that it sets in motion.

> I took the picture *so* something would happen, *for* a certain reason, *to* achieve a particular objective.

> Think about how Polaroid is a tool for communication, how the pictures can be a language in and of themselves.

Note the use of language like, "maybe," "perhaps," and "think about." These are suggestions, not instructions.

The resulting "See What Develops" campaign built on many of those ideas. "See What Develops" itself is a line that is simply a much more interesting (and, given the way a Polaroid picture does appear before your eyes, relevant) version of "the picture is only the beginning." It's one of those moments that defines who in the agency is creative and who is not, because it says what we (the noncreative ones) really wanted to say in half the words and with far more style.

In print (see Figure 5.5), the victim of a neighbor's dog's indiscriminate toilet habits is able to catch the dog in the act with a Polaroid picture and prove to her neighbor that his dog isn't as well trained and behaved as he thought. And the unfortunate head of a company called "Wow" productions (Figure 5.6) is able to send a picture to a company to show them that they screwed up when hanging his building sign. The sign, upside down, reads, "Mom." His letter is succinct. "Dear Hung-Rite Sign Company. You Morons."

On television, one spot (Figure 5.7) opens in the middle of a tense meeting in an architect's office.

"That's right, that's exactly right," says one of the group, placing his pencil on the plans to emphasize his words.

Figure 5.5 Polaroid: *"Dog."*

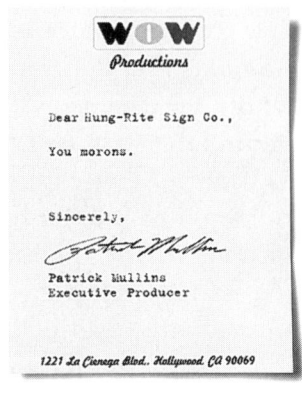

Dear Hung-Rite Sign Co.,

You morons.

Sincerely,

Patrick Mullins
Executive Producer

1221 La Cienega Blvd., Hollywood, CA 90069

Polaroid *See what develops.*

Figure 5.6   Polaroid: *"Mom/Wow."*

His partner isn't satisfied. "How am I supposed to explain that to the client?"

The phone buzzes, and the first guy picks it up, as the fourth member of the group, a woman, protests, "We have no time!"

"This is Jeff," he says, tersely.

"Hi, it's me," a woman's voice purrs.

"Hi. Er, what's up?"

"How's work?"

His colleagues roll their eyes, gesture at their watches, and exchange frustrated glances.

He moves as far away in the small office as his phone wire will allow, and in a low voice answers, "It's busy, very busy. What's up?"

"Well, do you want to meet me at home for lunch?"

More impatient glances from his colleagues.

"No . . . no . . . I . . . I . . . I can't do that right now. I'm in the middle of something and I can't get away. It's a big meeting. Big meeting." He gestures to his colleagues to indicate that he'll be right there.

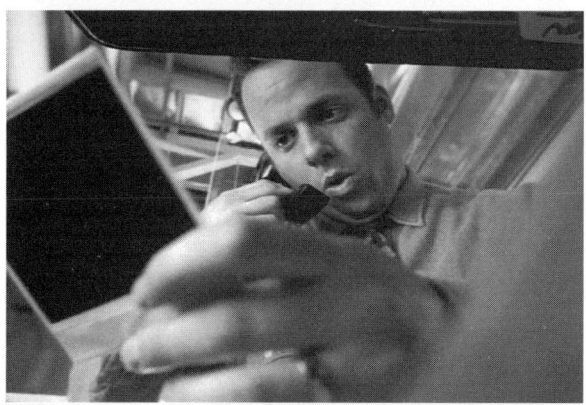

Figure 5.7   Polaroid: *"Architect."*

"Have you looked in your briefcase yet?" the voice on the phone asks.

"You're killing me," he mutters, as he reaches for his briefcase, phone tucked under his chin. Our point of view is from inside the briefcase, as he rummages impatiently. "Come on, come on. . . ."

"I left you something this morning," she continues, as he pulls out a Polaroid picture. We only see the back of it, but his eyes widen, and he lets out a gasp. As the Polaroid logo and "See What Develops" comes up on screen, we hear him mumble, "I'll be . . . I'll be home in ten minutes."

Only a Polaroid can do that.

And in a second spot (Figure 5.8), a dog is being scolded by his owner for upsetting the trash. "Very bad dog," she admonishes, wagging her finger, and the doleful dog, powerless to defend himself, takes his punishment quietly. "Bad, bad dog." Meanwhile, an evil looking cat sneers from the other side of the kitchen.

The owner goes out, and the dog goes to sleep, but he is awakened by the sound of the cat advancing across the counter toward the trash. The dog, knowing he'll be blamed again, has a flashback. He imagines the finger wagging in his face and hears the angry words, "Very bad dog," as the cat starts to root for food. He's desperate and looks around in panic for ways to stop the cat. A rolling pin is tempting, but out of reach. So too a meat cleaver. Then his eyes alight on a Polaroid camera, and "ping!" he has an idea. "See What Develops" appears on screen, and we return to the dog, sitting in the hallway as the door opens and his owner returns. In his mouth is a Polaroid picture of the cat, astride the trash with a chicken bone in its mouth. "Oh dear," we hear her say, as the picture fades.

How Do We Know We're Right?

Where's the evidence? Is there any support for the points of view that have just been expressed? If there is, then be sure

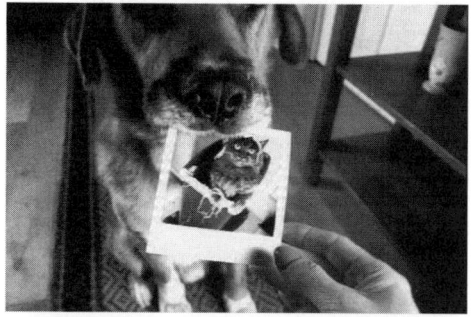

Figure 5.8   Polaroid: *"Dog and Cat."*

to at least refer to it (actually, that may be covered in earlier parts of the discussion, if you like to name your sources as you go), but if not, and if the brief reflects only guesswork, then be sure to admit it. If you're wrong, the creative team won't thank you if they've already spent two weeks working on your spurious hunch on the assumption that your direction was really based on solid fact.

A Good Brief Cannot Be Prepared in a Vacuum

I can say with complete confidence that the best briefs I have ever written have really been written by my creative colleagues.

Whenever possible, I like to discuss any half-baked ideas I may have with the team, or at least one of the team, who will ultimately have to write ads from my brief. There are several reasons why I like to do this, foremost of which is that they are invariably much better than I at finding the right words to express the all-important main idea. While planners may say, "The picture is only the beginning," creatives might say "See What Develops." Our words sit on the page, logical but passive, while theirs invariably crack like a whip and command attention.

It is also important to gauge whether the direction that I am leaning toward makes sense to the team. It's all very fine for me to come up with impressive abstract ideas, but if they turn round and say, "We can't write an ad to that," then I have wasted both my time and theirs. They have to be intrigued by the direction, and an immediate and most reliable test of its potential is whether they are able to add ideas of their own.

When GS&P pitched the Sega business in 1992, the research among gamers described in Chapter 4 had revealed an interesting insight into the relative appeal of the Sega 16-bit system and its better-established rival from Nintendo.

While the majority of kids owned and played only Nintendo, a few had played with both systems. And those who had played both felt that in many respects, Sega's was the superior system. The differences were subtle, but if they had to choose which had the best graphics, they would say Sega. The fastest gameplay . . . Sega. The best colors . . . Sega. And many described how once they had tried the Sega system, there was "no going back." Somehow, Nintendo seemed to pale by comparison. I told this to creative director Dave O'Hare and added that my first, half-assed idea for a brief was that moving from a Nintendo system to Sega was like "getting called up to the majors." Sega was "The Show" to which all gamers could aspire.

O'Hare was quiet for a moment, then said, "If you were to put that in gamers' language, it wouldn't be 'The Show,' would it? It would be the zone. The next level. How about 'Welcome to the next level?' " Dave really knew how to piss me off. I had been trying to figure that out for, oh, about two weeks, and he nailed it within 30 seconds. "Welcome to the Next Level" became the core idea of our brief. The advertising wasn't about getting there, but *being there,* being at the next level of games, of graphics, of colors, of speed, and of attitude. It was not just a "Congratulations, you've arrived," kind of phrase, but a challenge. A challenge to the advertising to find and retain a new level within each execution, and between each execution and its predecessor. Not only did it become the main idea of our brief, but it also became the tagline for the campaign itself. Generally, I am very nervous when a line from a brief finds its way directly into the advertising, but on this occasion, given that it was a writer and not I who had come up with it, I didn't feel so bad.

I don't know why so many planners and account people toil over briefs alone when it would make their task so much easier (and the end thinking probably much better) if they were to solicit the ideas of others at an early stage. Don't get me wrong—I'm not suggesting that they should let the creatives do their work for them; rather, that once they have a solution in sight, they should expose it to the creative team both to assess its potential and to see if the initial thinking can be expanded and enhanced. If it does make sense, and if they *can* enhance it, it gives them a powerful stake in the strategy and the brief. They are less likely to feel backed into a corner by it, and it also gives them a considerable head start in terms of thinking time.

On the other hand, I have seen both planners and account people deliver previously undiscussed briefs to creatives as if they are carved in tablets of stone, and the results are often not pretty.

"We have spent weeks figuring this out, and the logic is irrefutable," I once heard a planner say in frustration to a team who were questioning his lengthy creative "brief"—the result of his 40 days and 40 nights in the wilderness, conducting and analyzing research, and creating what he thought was a watertight intellectual argument.

"The logic might be irrefutable," the art director replied, irritably, "but I'm sorry to say that this particular piece of irrefutable logic isn't going to help me write a fucking ad."

In a situation like that, the only option may be to start over, and in that case it won't just be the creative team who are upset. The client's deadline may also be in jeopardy, and missing an airdate is never high on a client's list of favorite things. But talk to a team early on, and such an appalling situation is much less likely to happen.

"Can We Have a Good Ad, Please?"

As noted above, planners and their account management partners need to begin these discussions with creatives with at least some ideas of their own, to set the ball rolling. But I have to admit that there have been occasions where despite access to all the data I required, the opportunity to craft my own research, and the time and money to ask all of the questions I wanted to ask, I have still found myself standing pathetically in front of a creative team, admitting that I don't have a clue what the answer is.

On some of these occasions, I had only myself to blame. The answer was there, but I was simply looking in the wrong place, or just wasn't thinking properly. There were other times when I don't think I could have found a great insight if I had looked for ten years, because in the end, the only thing that could have truly differentiated the product was a great creative execution.

In doing our homework for a campaign for Foster Farms chicken in California, we looked at Foster Farms' product—California-grown fresh chicken—from every conceivable angle. We talked to the people who buy it, the people who eat it, the people who decide which brands to stock in stores, the people who deliver it, and even the people who breed, feed, and process the chickens. And here's what we found out: People who buy fresh chicken think that the most important attribute of that fresh chicken is . . . (wait for it) its freshness; phrases like "corn-fed" and "natural" connote freshness; and fresh chicken is better than frozen chicken.

Foster Farms fresh chicken has two chief competitors—another California-grown brand called Zacky Farms, and out-of-state birds that are usually sold under stores' own brand labels. As most stores stock only one California-grown brand, Foster Farms and Zacky Farms rarely compete directly in any one store: Their battle is at the distribution level. In the stores where it has the distribution, Foster Farms tends to compete in the display case with the store's own brand.

Advertising thus had two tasks, the first of which was to help Foster Farms in its battle for distribution with Zacky Farms. Foster Farms and Zacky Farms were similar in many respects—both were California brands, both had similar feeding regimes for their chickens, which both delivered to stores within 24 hours, and both had described themselves as "fresh and natural" in previous advertising. Key grocery chain buyers could perceive no significant point of difference between the two, and we have yet to meet a consumer whose store preference was outweighed by his or her preference for a brand of fresh chicken. Advertising needed to give Foster Farms an edge over its rival to get it into the store.

Once there, the second task for advertising was to persuade shoppers to purchase the usually more expensive Foster Farms chicken over the own-brand/out-of-state alternative. Even this was difficult, because people generally do not think that there might be any differences between the two. Fresh chicken is fresh chicken is fresh chicken.

In the absence of a clear, tangible tie-breaker, we realized we had to create a *perceptual* advantage.

We had to suggest, to paraphrase George Orwell, that all chickens are created fresh, but some fresh chickens are fresher than others. And the only way we could do that was to ask for our advertising to talk about freshness in a more interesting, distinctive, and compelling way than our competitors. As I said, "Can we have a good ad, please?"

Writer Bob Kerstetter and art director Tom Routson came up with the idea that instead of talking directly about what Foster Farms' chickens *were*, they would show what they were *not*. They were not frozen. They had not taken advantage of some legal loophole that allowed them to describe themselves as fresh even though they had been kept, let's say, "very cold" on a long journey from Arkansas to California. Bob and Tom imagined Foster Farms as a kind of elite among chickens, in the same way as the Marines in the military: "The Few, the Proud, the Foster Farms chickens. . . ."

Creative director Jeff Goodby and the creative team invented two chicken characters named, for some reason, Bob and Tom, who had traveled from out of state with the express intent of becoming Foster Farms chickens. Like their namesakes, these chickens were not exactly well-groomed, and their diet certainly left a lot to be desired, but they lacked nothing in enthusiasm. They would do anything to become the best of the best — Foster Farms chickens.

The first TV spot (see Figure 5.9) began with a car passing a sign saying, "Welcome to California." Inside the car, an old clunker, are the ragtag chickens, who cheer, "Foster Farms, here we come!" The words are scarcely out of their beaks when a siren sounds, and they see a cop's flashing light in their rear-view mirror. "Stay cool," advises Tom, the driver.

The cop's flashlight illuminates their Arkansas plates, and he walks slowly to peer into the car's interior (I suppose you could call it the cockpit). "Hi officer," says chicken Tom.

"Identification, please," says the officer.

"We're just heading home, back to Foster Farms," says Tom, as the cop and his flashlight examine the debris on the dash: half-eaten pizza, doughnuts, empty soda cans, burger wrappers, and the like. Bob, shaking behind his bag of potato chips, adds, "We're not from out of state or anything!"

Always natural. Always fresh.

Figure 5.9   Foster Farms: *"Cop."*

The cop's flashlight catches Tom's wing.

"Foster Farms chickens are never frozen," he says, sternly. "This looks like freezer burn to me."

"No, no . . ." Tom starts to protest, and again Bob interrupts: "It was a curling iron accident!"

"Would you mind stepping out of the car, please?" asks the officer, at which point we see Tom's foot hit the gas. As the wheels begin to spin and dust kicks up, we see a beautiful plate of chicken, and a voice-over says, "Foster Farms. Always natural, always fresh."

Then we cut back to the impostor chickens, who are in full flight, with the cop car in pursuit. "AAARGH!" screams Tom as the picture fades, "WE'RE FUGITIVES! AAAARGH!"

In other executions, the "Foster Impostors" try to hijack a Foster Farms truck, attempting to trick the driver into stopping with the offer of free doughnuts, and to convince an old lady in the parking lot of a grocery store that they are Foster Farms chickens. Both the truck driver and old lady are too smart for them, and their quest to become members of poultry's chosen few continues. And just in case you were wondering, the campaign was extremely successful, both in gaining retail distribution for Foster Farms and in building sales.

Did the planners and account people shirk their responsibilities? I don't think so. Planners and account people are only human and cannot possibly come up with the right answer every time (is there a creative team that has never failed to come up with an idea? Never failed to come up with a *good* idea? If they exist, I would love them to come and work at our agency). But aside from that, the parity between so many products in so many different categories makes it inevitable that the advertising becomes the point of difference, and that difference is as likely to be executional as strategic. Which in turn perhaps means that a solution is *more likely* to come from a creative person than from a planner or account person.

I agree that in an ideal world it would be terrific for every brief to provide a clear and compelling creative direction. Last time I looked, though, it was not an ideal world. If after all the analysis, interpretation, and interdisciplinary discussion is done an answer still does not suggest itself, isn't it better to be honest about the fact that you don't have a clue, than try to fashion an irrelevant point of difference out of nothing?

No Brief at All

One of my partners at GS&P, Harold Sogard, recently asked me for copies of the original briefs that were written for eight successful agency campaigns, most of which appear at some point in the pages of this book. The campaigns covered a period of several years and a wide variety of types of clients.

I was only able to find four of those briefs. There was a simple reason I could not find the others—there was no such thing as the "original" brief. They had never been written.

Looking back, the four "missing" briefs were all for campaigns that had been presented as part of GS&P's new business pitch to the client. Briefings *had* taken place in the frenetic atmosphere of the previous days and weeks, but all as informal conversations. No one had written anything down. At some point, all the different agency departments had coalesced around a simple idea—like Sega representing "The Next Level" of video games, or people only thinking milk was important when they didn't have any—and executed that idea without pausing to worry over the nuances of words in the description of the target audience. Having agreed on the broad direction and idea, all their energies, quite rightly in my opinion, went into creating advertising.

Subsequently, the clients also bought into that general direction and idea and ran the advertising. They also never asked to see the creative brief. And the results of all four campaigns have been outstanding.

The briefs that I *did* find had all resulted from a lengthier process, where both inside the agency and between agency and client, almost every sentence of every section of those briefs had been the subject of lengthy discussion. Single words were haggled over and revision after revision negotiated, presented, and represented, until they were honed to perfection. Sometimes, however, this process of finessing had taken so long that by the time the brief was finally approved, the creative team had already written the campaign. They had been party to the key thoughts contained within it, but while the semantic discussions raged, they went off and turned those thoughts into advertising. And that advertising, consistent with the ultimate direction and idea of the brief, was both creatively distinctive and commercially successful.

The reason I prefer the former over the latter process is that it more closely reflects my belief that the brief is a means to an end, while in the more formal, discussing-the-brief-to-death approach, the brief really seems to take on a life of its own. Until the day comes when we put creative briefs in consumer magazines or run them on the Superbowl, I think that the time spent noodling over detail in a brief is wasted time. Well, perhaps not entirely wasted, but it could at least be better spent.

The bottom line is, you don't have a good brief until you have a good ad.

6

Ten Housewives in Des Moines
The Perils of Researching
Rough Creative Ideas

We don't ask consumers what they want. They don't know. Instead we apply our brain power to what they need, and will want, and make sure we're there, ready.

Akio Morita, Sony Corporation

"TEST IT"

The planner has completed the exploratory research. The creative team and account director have taken the factory tour. An account executive has spent a week on the road with a salesperson. Industry analysts have been consulted. Numerous meetings have been held with the client's marketing group. The target audience has been identified, advertising objectives agreed on, and a strategy defined. The brief has been carefully crafted. The creative team has come up with a campaign, which seems to be "on strategy," and which everyone on both the client and agency teams likes. The rough scripts have been sent to the first-choice director, who says that the campaign is the most exciting new material he has seen all year. Everything's looking good.

"It's very good," the client says. "Let's test it."

"Absolutely," says another. "Let's run it up the flagpole and see who salutes it."

The creative team's faces drop. They think that they have already "run it up the flagpole." They ran it up in front of their creative director, who, for the first time in recent memory, saluted their work. They ran it up again in front of the account team, and they, too, raised their fingers to their foreheads. And here they are once more, running it up in front of a roomful of clients, and the room is standing firmly to attention. It's been saluted by their boss, their peers, and the people holding the purse strings, so what is the point of going through yet another stage?

The usual answer to this question is both predictable and logical. "Well, we all love the idea, but what *we* think isn't really important. The only opinion that really counts is that of the *consumer.*"

To this, the creatives may rightly point out that consumer opinions *have already* been heavily solicited. The strategy was based on consumer input, the creative brief was inspired by consumer input, and the resulting advertising seems, at least to everyone gathered in the marketing conference room, to reflect that consumer input. So, they conclude, what is there to be gained by talking to them again? Having learned everything there is to be learned about consumers in this category, isn't it time for *us* to make some decisions? Aren't we experienced and highly paid marketing and advertising executives? Surely, based on everything we know, we can judge for ourselves whether it will resonate with consumers?

"Why the hell," a creative once asked me, "should I be told how to write or produce a TV commercial by ten housewives in Des Moines? They don't know what they want . . . they have no idea from a script or a storyboard what I really mean . . . they can't see what I see . . . there's an art to this thing that they just won't get until they see the finished spot." He laughed derisively. "And probably not even after the spot is finished."

While not all art directors and copywriters feel that way, I do understand why some do. After all, there's a gestation period for many advertising campaigns that is at least as long as the period between the conception and birth of a human baby. The process is sometimes just as painful. And after going through all that, who wants to take their new baby to a focus group of nonparents and listen to them saying that it's ugly, it makes too much noise, and it smells bad?

On only one or two occasions have I encountered clients who actively avoid asking consumers what they think of newborn advertising ideas. One such client is Scott Bedbury, who in a previous life directed Nike's worldwide advertising, and who is now senior vice president of marketing at Starbucks Coffee Company. He regards "traditional research" as the first enemy of creativity (I agree). While he accepts that research can play a useful role at the front end of the process, in strategic development, he considers the exposure or testing of embryonic creative ideas to be tantamount to a criminal act. In an article about Starbucks in the *Los Angeles Times Magazine,* in September 1996, he talked about the way that he had used (or, more precisely, *not* used) research to evaluate creative ideas in his days at Nike. "We never pretested anything we did at Nike, none of the ads. Wieden (Dan Wieden, founder of Wieden & Kennedy) and I had an agreement that as long as our hearts beat, we would never pretest a word of copy. It makes you dull. It makes you predictable. It makes you safe."

Nike's advertising over the years has been anything but dull, predictable and safe. It has constantly been among the best, if not *the* best in the world. Even so, there are very few other clients who would buy the argument that conducting research on rough creative ideas is a bad thing. Most of them do not *deliberately* set out to be "dull" (even if their words and the appearance of their advertising suggests otherwise), but they tend to regard "safe" as *good.* Even "predictable" has a positive ring to it. A television advertising campaign can cost millions of dollars to produce, and running it may cost tens of millions more. Clients want to be able to predict how consumers will react to it. So, in their minds, a few thousand dollars spent on a series of focus groups, or even a hundred thousand dollars spent on an extensive quantitative copy test, is a small price to pay, even if the research results turn out to be hunky-dory and simply confirm everything they already thought. On the other hand, if the research surprises them and exposes some problems, then it may be the best few thousand dollars they ever spent.

The desire to test rough creative ideas in part reflects the natural desire on the client's part not to make a mistake. I am sure that if *I* were responsible for signing a multimillion-dollar production estimate, or committing to a media budget greater than the annual expenditure of 50 percent of the world's governments, I too would want to have at least *some* evidence that I was doing the right thing.

But it also reflects the sad fact that many clients do not fully trust their agencies. Some fear that the agency desire to be creative and win awards far outweighs the desire to do the right thing for the clients' business. As previously noted, creativity does have a vital role to play in "doing the right thing," but the more distinctive and original the advertising idea, the more nervous many clients become, not only of its potential for failure, but also of the agency's underlying motivations. Research conducted on rough creative ideas thus becomes as much of a test of the agency as of the campaign. Is the agency recommending the right thing? Is it trying to go further than necessary in the search of a more creative approach? Is it more interested in awards than in meeting the client's business objectives? Testing advertising ideas, with consumers enlisted as allies, may provide the client with the means to curb creative excess and keep the agency in check.

ROUGH CREATIVE IDEAS?

Before I explore some possible ways of resolving the conflicting views and expectations of clients and creative people relating to research conducted on rough creative ideas, let me pause to provide some clarification on what exactly I mean by "research conducted on rough creative ideas."

Rough is the key word. And by rough, I largely mean advertising in any one of a number of forms that is not *produced*. In other words, big money will not have been spent to film a commercial, photograph a print ad or billboard, or record a radio commercial. This is important because it means that the advertising could be *affected* in some way by the research. (Affected in a way that is less dramatic and painful than throwing away a commercial that costs a million dollars to make.) If the research can have no possible effect because all the money has been spent, time has run out, and it is too late to change anything, then there is no possible reason for doing it.

The rough forms of advertising of which I speak cover a very wide spectrum of cost, complexity, and degree of finish, from ideas scribbled on the back of napkins to videos that look to the untrained eye much like finished commercials. Apart from some general points about the degree of finish that is desirable for eliciting the best consumer response, however, I do not spend much time debating the relative merits of presenting ideas in the form of scripts, narrative tapes (with or without key frames), animatics, photomatics, or videomatics. I have used all of them on many different occasions and have had success with every one. The choice of stimulus material should be based on the nature of the idea being exposed, the instincts of the creative team for which method will best communicate their idea, the precise nature of the research methodology, the preference and skills of the person conducting the research, and, of course, time and cost considerations.

Given all those variables, it is hard to make any general rules. The only thing that is important is that whatever form the stimulus material takes, it should be capable of communicating the idea. Sometimes that means, in addition to exposing the idea itself, that it is necessary to show addi-

193

tional stimulus material, like photographs, or clips from movies, or even other advertising, to establish a mood, or a particular visual style, or to flesh out characters.

When multiple ideas are exposed, there is often considerable pressure from clients to "compare apples to apples," and ensure that each individual idea is exposed in exactly the same form. Thus, it is argued, all will have the exact same chance of success or failure, and none will enjoy an unfair advantage over another. I see the point, but I do not agree with it, because the same form of stimulus material will often give an unfair advantage to some ideas and unfairly disadvantage others. To create a truly level playing field, it is necessary to find the form of stimulus material that gives each individual idea its best chance of being understood. If that means different material for different executions, so be it. Any advertising idea that does not have the benefit of beautiful film, actors' performances, professional editing, and sound design has a tough road to travel, and it should be given all the help it needs to communicate. The shortcomings of the stimulus material should not be allowed to act as yet another barrier.

"Someone to Say No to Me"

My main interest in writing this chapter is not to discuss the minutiae of what is exposed and to whom, but to explore the larger issue of why and how research on rough creative ideas should be conducted in the first place.

First and most important, I do not believe that rough advertising ideas should be "tested," or put through research whose sole aim is to give them a thumbs-up or thumbs-down rating. In fact, I never refer to this kind of research as testing at all. I prefer to call it *creative development research,* where the aim is not to attach an absolute value to a piece of advertising (or, more accurately, to a rough representation of a piece of advertising), but to elicit a response to it, understand why people are responding in that way, and explore possible ways of improving it.

It is in this area of understanding people's relationships to an advertising idea and exploring that idea's potential for improvement that the real power of creative development research lies.

When Stanley Pollitt wrote of the beginnings of planning in his *Campaign* article in 1979, he stated as fundamental a "commitment and a belief that you can only make thoroughly professional judgments about advertising content with some early indication of consumer response." It is fundamental not only to the planning philosophy that he inspired, but to the structure and process of any agency that is serious about advertising effectiveness. And it is fundamental to the central theme of this book, that if consumers are involved *throughout* the process of developing advertising, then better advertising will result.

Consumers cannot be involved only up to the point where a brief is delivered to the creative team, because however solid the strategy, however smart and inspiring the brief, and however closely the planner is involved as the creative team gives birth to advertising ideas, mistakes can still be made. And they are often made not because the agency is deliberately setting out to be naughty, but because people in agencies are in most cases different from the people who represent the target for a particular advertising campaign. They know and understand different things; they laugh at different things; and in the course of developing an advertising idea, they may slowly and inexorably drift off course. It may only be a degree or two, but just think about the difference that a one-degree mistake in navigation would make for a plane crossing the Atlantic. Passengers who had bought tickets from London to New York would not be happy disembarking in Canada.

A 30-second TV commercial may represent the distillation of several weeks or months of thought, and occasionally some wrong choices can be made about what information to include or leave out. Thinking that was fundamental to the creation of the idea itself may come to be taken for granted and excluded, but without it, members of the viewing public may find the idea hard to understand. Conversely, the best-intentioned attempts to explain an idea may result in information overload and, once again, consumer detachment from the advertising.

In Chapter 4, I spoke of the need for open minds in the process of designing and conducting research. Nowhere is this more important than in creative development research, because it is here that clients, creatives, planners, and account people are most likely to encounter points of view that conflict with their own. A campaign that seemed so right in an office in the creative department, or in a client conference room, may after only one night of consumer research seem so wrong, and the reasons for its failings so obvious. An idea that had seemed so simple to its creators may be mired in confusion. The ironic humor that everyone enjoyed so much in the first client presentation may go completely over the heads of the target audience. The execution that the client thought captured the essence of their brand so perfectly may be rejected as irrelevant or boring. And on the other hand, an idea that the client thought too creative, too complex, or too peripheral to the product, may be enthusiastically endorsed by real people, for whom the desired message is communicated in a very involving way. Sometimes, creative development research reveals that *everyone,* agency included, was being too conservative, and that consumers can be pushed a whole lot further than even the creatives thought possible.

The "on the other hand" scenarios just described provide, for me, the most powerful argument with which to persuade creative people that such research can *help make their work better.* If the advertising gets produced, then it's presumably better than if it doesn't.

The Foster Farms campaign described in the last chapter was first presented to the client in GS&P's new business pitch. The day after the meeting, Bob Fox, Foster Farms' president, came by for a second visit. He had enjoyed the meeting, he said, and felt that both the chemistry and our understanding of his key business issues were powerful reasons to hire us. The one thing that gave him pause for thought, though, was the campaign that we had presented. He felt that it was not appropriate for the company and said that he would not feel comfortable even presenting the Foster family with a campaign featuring delinquent "puppet chickens" whose sins included smoking and drinking alcohol. If he hired us, he asked, would we be prepared to develop other campaign ideas?

His comments were fair. Looking back, the chicken characters in their original incarnation were not unlike the character Nicholas Cage later played in *Leaving Las Vegas*.

We developed three new campaign ideas, all of which Bob Fox considered more appropriate. But at the same time we revisited the "puppet chicken" campaign and tried to make the characters less down-and-out. Instead of alcohol and nicotine abuse, their weakness would be junk food. It would be their poor diet that prevented them from ever being Foster Farms chickens. Bob was still not convinced, but indicated that he was happy for us to at least expose the revised campaign alongside the new ideas.

In the research, all three of the new campaigns were well-received, but all on more of a rational than an emotional level. People understood what they were saying, felt that the message was right for Foster Farms, but never got excited by them. Meanwhile, every group went nuts over "those damn puppet chickens." Having seen the same response in several different groups without any prompting from the agency, Bob Fox said that he thought he had been wrong. He now saw the power of that campaign and had decided that he should run it. It would have been much easier to stick to his guns and say, "Listen, I told you not to show that campaign, and I'm not changing my mind . . .," but he chose not to.

Ultimately, I believe that it is the ability to face up to one's mistakes that separates the best agencies and clients from the rest. Agencies and clients who have more of a stake in finding the right solution than in *being* right themselves are much more likely to produce more effective advertising campaigns.

My partner, Colin Probert, often annoys me by suggesting to prospective clients that the most important role played by the planners at the agency is to take out all creative work in embryonic form, gather consumer opinion, and make recommendations based on that feedback. It annoys me, not because I disagree with the level of importance he attaches to creative development research, but because it implies that planners don't do anything else that is important. I believe that it is at the front end of the process, through exploratory research, strategic development, and creative briefing, that a planner can routinely exercise the greatest influence over the outcome of a campaign. But in the final analysis, he's absolutely right, in that all of that front-end work is worthless if the creative team then go off on their own and execute an idea in a way that does not, for whatever reason, connect to target consumers.

When I met Jeff Goodby for the first time in the summer of 1989, we talked a lot about the effect that the introduction of planning would have on an agency like Goodby, Berlin & Silverstein. As far as I could see, there wasn't exactly anything that needed *fixing*. I thought that the agency's advertising was both distinctive and smart; it was winning new business; and, although I didn't know it at the time, *Advertising Age* was to name GBS "Agency of the Year" for its 1989 performance. But Goodby thought that planning could help him and Silverstein and their creative department do better work. How? By giving them more information and insights than they could come up with on their own. And most important of all, he said, by letting them know when they had crossed the line and produced advertising that was not communicating what it set out to, that did not make sense, or that was more appealing to us on the inside than to real people on the outside.

"I want someone to say no to me," he said, and went on to explain that it was important for any agency that was serious about effectiveness to have a built-in control mechanism in its own philosophy and working method. And this mechanism, he believed, would be more effective if it was led by us than if it was imposed from the outside, because we could develop our own system, not only for doing the research, but for implementing its findings and adapting our work accordingly.

"Planners," he has said since on many occasions, "have a black ball in the process, a right of veto," so that if they discover an idea is not working, they can stop it in its tracks. As a creative director, he says, he may not always be *happy* about that, but as an agency principal he knows that it is in the agency's long-term interests for advertising to work. It's really quite simple—if a campaign works, an agency can enjoy a long and fruitful relationship with a client. If it doesn't, the agency will get fired. Therefore, any opportunity to hone the advertising and increase its chances of effectiveness should be embraced.

In July 1992, an *Adweek* feature about account planning, embarrassingly entitled "The Knights of New Business," told the story of our agency's pitch for Sega video games earlier that year. The opening paragraph read as follows:

> Less than two weeks before Goodby, Berlin & Silverstein was due to make its presentation to Sega of America, Jon Steel, the agency's director of account planning, called the principals into a meeting and said flatly, 'We can't show this work.' For weeks, GB&S planners had visited and practically lived with close to 100 kids to understand their passion for video games. Armed with those insights, Goodby roughed out some commercials for Sega . . . but the kids GB&S had studied so assiduously found the ads a total bore. Only after quickly recasting the

campaign did Goodby win the $65-million account.

It was a dramatic start to the story. The planner's right of veto being exercised in a showdown with the agency principals, right in the heat of a new business pitch (which, coming as it did on the heels of Andy Berlin's departure from the agency, represented even more pressure than usual). It was gripping stuff, but it was not exactly what had happened.

It was true that planners had spent weeks living the lives of teenage gamers. In the course of those interviews a clear picture had emerged of the video game as a world that was the exclusive preserve of kids and teens. Inside the game was a place where they could escape from the pressures and influence of adults and for once be in control of their own destinies. Kids had their own language, their own codes, and their own hierarchies, and adults tended to understand none of it. While a kid could spend hours going through the different levels of a game, an adult would be greeted by the GAME OVER message within minutes. The game was the only place where the *kid* was the master.

We thought that was interesting and developed a television advertising campaign based on the idea. In one commercial, fast cars race across the screen, and a dry voice says, "They can drive cars." (Odd words appear in the corner of the screen: "Speed . . . babes . . . can . . . bite . . .") The voice speaks again. "They decide how much ice cream goes on their cake. They decide when they go to bed . . ." (More words: "can . . . midnight . . . dawn . . . can . . . sex . . .") The scantily clad body of a woman gyrates in silhouette behind a leveler blind, and the voice says, "They can go to R-rated movies. . . ." Loud music cuts in, and we see game footage from Sonic the Hedgehog. ". . . But it will be a chilly day in hell," the voice continues, "before an adult gets this far on Sonic 2. Sega. Welcome to the Next Level."

In another, a young boy called Mitch is playing Sonic 2 and has just realized his ambition of reaching level seven.

His dad, a nerdy-looking guy, tells him that if he doesn't shape up and do some work instead of playing video games, then Mitch will not grow up to be like his dad. As a result of this advice, we are told, Mitch's new ambition is to reach level eight. Sega. Welcome to the Next Level.

We shot both of these spots on video and were very pleased with the results. The clients from Sega who saw them thought they were "right on," and we went optimistically into consumer research.

Focus groups with teenage gamers were organized. On the first night, while another planner, Irina Hierakuji, moderated, I sat in the viewing room with Jeff Goodby, Rich Silverstein, and a bunch of agency creatives who had worked on the campaign. The first words out of the mouth of one of the respondents on seeing the video were not encouraging:

"That sucks." (Isn't it great how kids will always tell you exactly what they think?)

An avalanche of criticism followed, which was almost exactly replicated in subsequent groups. The advertising, they thought, was slow, boring, lacked enough game footage to give a full impression of the game, and contained no new news.

"We know our parents don't know how to play the games. Tell us something new."

"Sega shouldn't be insulting our parents."

"That footage you showed wasn't from Sonic 2—it was from the original Sonic, and it was from level two, which isn't hard at all . . ."

And then the lowest blow of all:

"Those commercials look like they were written by adults."

"The guys who made it weren't good enough to get to the difficult parts!"

At some point, behind the mirror in the viewing room, Goodby and Silverstein concluded that they had better start over.

Other creatives nodded their assent.

Only then did they ask for my opinion. I said I thought they had already decided what was right, without me.

That's what happened. No fist pounding. No veto. The planners had simply created an environment where the creatives could see and hear for themselves how their campaign was being received. And when they realized that they had missed the mark, they made up their own minds that they had to do something different.

So they did start over and came up with a campaign that I will not even attempt to show in storyboard form or describe, because they decided that if kids thought their original ideas were too slow, they would speed them up. A lot. If there wasn't enough information or game footage, they would cram in more. Sixty seconds' worth into fifteen seconds in some cases. Which meant that in some commercials there were more than 70 different cuts. The ads would make no mention of the "kids' world" idea, but their frenetic pace, volume, and language was designed to exclude adults in the same way as the games themselves. Each ad would represent the next level of speed, noise, and in many instances, bad taste. And in subsequent research, while both we and the Sega clients, as adults, hated it and found it offensive, the kids loved it.

We were hired, and within months Sega, on the back of their anarchic new advertising and hot new Sonic title, had overhauled arch-rival Nintendo and taken the number one spot in the expanding video game market.

To Group, or Not to Group?

If creative-development research can be defined in the way I outlined at the start of the previous section—namely, as a means of eliciting consumer response to advertising ideas, *understanding* that response, and seeking ways to *improve* the response of future viewers or readers—then I believe that only research that is qualitative in nature and almost always in the form of focus groups is suitable for the task.

I know that many in the industry have different preferences. Focus groups, they assert, are "too unreliable." Respondents are too easily led by others for a group's individual and collective opinions to mean anything. If one person loves it, they'll all love it (and vice versa), is the general criticism. Such criticisms are, of course, quite justified if the focus group in question is being moderated by an idiot. My preference is based on the assumption that the moderator will be of a higher caliber. (I talk more about exactly *who* should moderate later in this chapter.)

Even among those who agree that qualitative methodologies are better (than quantitative methodologies) for creative development research, a significant difference of opinion exists on the relative merits of focus groups and one-on-one depth interviews.

Why Focus Groups and Not One-on-Ones?

A depth interview, I have heard many people argue, is likely to yield a much more "pure" response than a focus group, because the respondent is not influenced in his or her reactions by the opinions of others. It is just the moderator and the one respondent, alone in a room. Alone, except for the 23 observers who are hanging on their every word from behind the viewing mirror.

If I were conducting a research project that sought to find out about people's sexual habits, illicit drug use, or criminal activities, I would probably use one-on-one interviews, figuring that some degree of privacy (video cameras, tape recorders, and observers notwithstanding) was going to be an important prerequisite for extracting the information I needed. If I needed to interview a bunch of heavy-hitting chief executives, I would most likely do so one at a time, to avoid the inevitable clash of egos in a group setting and to overcome the probably insurmountable logistic difficulties of getting ten CEOs in the same room at the same time. And if all I wanted to do in creative development research was to gather opinions on what people think of an advertising idea, then one-on-one interviews might again seem like a good idea.

But to understand those opinions and figure out ways to shift them by manipulating the advertising, I prefer to have more than one person's opinion to play with at any one time. I am not suggesting that neither heightened understanding nor improvements to ideas are attainable using one-on-one interviews, but that both can be taken to a *higher level*, much more rapidly, in focus groups, by using the very group dynamic that many researchers fear.

One of the mistakes that many people make when thinking about creative development research, especially if they adhere to the previously described theory of "research-as-test" is to think that objectivity is the only legitimate method of inquiry and analysis. While objectivity, in whatever impure form it really exists, may play a role in assessing how closely an advertising campaign meets its objectives and identifies problem areas, it is very unlikely that it alone will uncover a deeper truth or begin to suggest solutions. The same points that I have made about objectivity throughout this book become most acute in the area of creative development research, where the planner or other person conducting the research has to be at once a logical, analytical researcher, and a lateral, intuitive, creative thinker. This requires a significant amount of subjectivity and flexibility on the part of the moderator, and a research environment that is conducive to creative thinking and expression.

Almost all the best ideas that I have extracted from focus groups have come from people who would not have made the profound comments they did, if they had not been stimulated by the comments of others. If a conversation in a focus group is allowed to run free with a minimum of moderator interference, then respondents will build on each other's comments and, if the moderator is lucky, become ever more inventive as they go. The "Fresh TV" campaign for Chevys Mexican Restaurants, included later in this chapter, and the "got milk?" campaign featured in Chapter 7, both benefited from this type of free-ranging, self-stimulating conversation in creative development research. While it is not impossible that the same answers and ideas could have come out of one-on-one research, I consider it very unlikely.

One of the main advantages of focus group research, in the hands of a skilled moderator, is that high energy levels are much easier to create and sustain than in one-on-one interviews, and higher energy levels are necessary if respondents are to feel comfortable in expressing their opinions. They are especially important if respondents are going to be creative, whether by accident or design. I have conducted many depth interviews, and observed many more, and on the whole the experience has been about as interesting as watching paint dry. That is less true of interviews that are conducted in the respondent's natural habitat. But in my experience, while most clients are happy to embrace such anthropological research at the strategic stage, their desire to keep an eye on the agency at the creative development stage almost always means that they want to be able to observe, and that means going to a facility.

The last point that I'll make about one-on-one interviews is that they are a logistic nightmare. Whereas 60 different respondents can be spoken to in six focus groups over two or three days, it will take weeks to meet that many if they are brought in one at a time. The sheer quality and quantity of information that can be extracted from focus groups makes them more *productive* than one-on-ones in an absolute sense. And when cost and time considerations are added in, they are also more *efficient* in a relative sense.

Why Not Quantitative?
Many of my readers may take issue with my earlier point that only qualitative research is useful in eliciting and understanding the response of consumers to rough creative ideas,

and in finding ways to improve the response of future readers or viewers. I have already touched on my reasons for preferring focus groups as a medium for creative development research, namely, the flexibility, energy, and opportunity for creativity that they offer. I would, however, be negligent if I did not say a few words on the subject of the quantitative research that may be done at this stage, generally known as *copy-testing*. As with several other areas that I cover in this book, copy-testing is a huge subject, and a great number of books and papers have already been devoted to it by authors much better qualified than myself (references to some of these are included in my bibliography). I do, however, want to make a few brief but important points.

The use of quantitative copy-testing is the source of much controversy and friction between clients and agencies. While many clients insist on copy-testing their advertising for reasons of risk-management and efficiency, seeking to remove the possibility of human error from their decision making, their agencies often regard such tests as counterproductive to the aim of producing distinctive advertising.

It may appear from my earlier statement that my opinion lies on the copy-testing-is-counterproductive side of that argument, but that is not so. Qualitative and quantitative research at the creative development stage are useful for different reasons and at different times, and I believe that treating them as alternatives is not particularly constructive. It is necessary to distinguish between true *creative development research*, where the aim of understanding and improving response is best met by qualitative research, and *creative evaluation*, where the desire for hard facts and numbers to give confidence to decision makers is probably best provided by some form of copy-test.

Copy-tests tend to fall into one of two types, although some techniques are all encompassing. The first measures the ability of an advertising execution or campaign to shift attitudes or "persuade," and it is based on the assumption that any change in attitudes or claimed propensity to buy a product around the time that a respondent is exposed to the advertising is predictive of later behavior in the marketplace. In the most common tests, respondents are asked, under some pretext, to make a choice between a number of products, one of which is the test product. Then they view a TV program (which they have been led to believe is the sole reason for their being in the research), in the course of which they see a commercial break that includes the test commercial. After the show, they repeat the product-choice exercise, and the difference between their pre-advertising and post-advertising choices represents the advertising's ability to persuade.

I have worked with a number of clients who live and die by these persuasion scores, and it is easy to see why they are regarded as such a critical measure. Unfortunately, there is a growing body of opinion, led by Gordon Brown of Millward Brown, that such measures are not really predictive of anything, as changes in attitudes toward brands occur over a much longer time period than these tests typically measure, and are influenced by a number of indirect factors, not least of which is real-world contact with the product itself. If Brown and others are correct (which I, for one, believe them to be), then the founding principles of these persuasion tests are fatally flawed, and so too the results that emerge.

The second type of copy-test is multidimensional. It is less concerned with persuasion, focusing instead on the ability of a commercial to break through clutter, to be remembered (and linked to the brand), to communicate a message to its target, and to be understood, liked or disliked by respondents. Typically, it will also include a battery of diagnostic questions that explore detailed attitudes to the message and executional style of the advertising. This type of copy-test, by the nature of the questions it poses, is clearly more open to interpretation than the pass/fail persuasion test. But once again there is considerable disagreement over the absolute and relative importance of its various measures. Some companies and authors place great importance on recall measures. Others champion brand linkage. Many recent studies have concluded that the degree to which viewers *like* the advertising eclipses all other measures in terms of its ability to predict success in the marketplace. There's certainly no easy answer, although common sense suggests that the more people notice and remember the advertising, link the message to a specific brand, and like what they see and hear, the better the ad will perform. The question that I have yet to see satisfactorily answered is whether the environment and methodology of the tests themselves provide a truly accurate representation of the way people really feel about the advertising ideas. If finding the truth depends, as I have suggested, on establishing an intimate relationship with consumers, then most copy-testing methodologies are the exact opposite of what should be done.

Paul Feldwick, the Executive Planning Director of BMP DDB in London, in an excellent, concise paper for the United Kingdom's Account Planning Group (*A Brief Guided Tour Through the Copy-Testing Jungle*), writes:

> This type of research, if done well by an
> experienced and sensitive advertising
> researcher, can be enormously rich and help-
> ful. But it can also turn into a depressing and
> frustrating experience for the advertising
> agency as sloppy questions, poor coding, and
> nonsequiturs of interpretation based on
> invalid models of advertising, misrepresent
> the reality of consumer reaction.

Almost all of GS&P's large clients copy-test their advertising prior to it going on air, some of them having a particular bias toward persuasion testing, while others favor the more multidimensional, diagnostic approach. I have often asked myself whether, if it were my money, I would spend it on these copy-tests; and I have always concluded that I would not, because I have yet to learn anything from a copy-test that I could not divine for myself (directionally at least) using qualitative methodologies. Of course, it is not my money, and never will be, and while I do not enthusiastically recommend copy-tests, I certainly do not fear them or feel that they get in the way of good advertising. In the tests that I have experienced, exceptional advertising ideas have always scored well on most of the key measures, and I thus regard copy-tests as a kind of benign force that neither helps nor unduly hinders the process.

The reason I tend to feel better about copy-tests than most of my industry peers is that all of my clients who copy-test do so in addition to earlier qualitative strategic and creative development work, and the material they put into the quantitative test is generally a pretty advanced rough-cut or finished commercial. So the earlier research has informed and shaped the advertising, which greatly reduces the possibility of problems of comprehension, relevance, and appeal, and the test material has the added benefit of production values. If everyone has done their jobs properly earlier on, it is rare indeed for the copy-test alarm bells to sound.

WHO SHOULD CONDUCT CREATIVE DEVELOPMENT RESEARCH?

The subject of who should actually conduct creative development research is the source of considerable debate between agencies and clients, and once again, the argument hinges on the issue of objectivity. Many clients, looking at the research as a simple pass or fail exercise, may wish to have it conducted by an objective, independent researcher. That person, they say, will be detached from any emotional issues surrounding the campaign's development, and as an independent, his or her opinions will have more influence on senior management than those of an agency planner.

I have heard these arguments from many clients who are more than happy to let an agency planner conduct exploratory research but who say that "this type of research is different." I disagree. The same barriers that stand in the way of consumers revealing their true feelings, as described in Chapter 3, can be as problematic in creative development research as they are in strategic research. The same methods of opening minds and generating ideas, described in Chapter 4, may be applied with equal success, whether the aim of the research is to test a strategic hypothesis or to gather reactions to a creative idea.

If creative development research is different at all, it is so only in requiring, more than any other type of advertising research, a moderator who is not only well versed in the realities of the client's business, but who also has an understanding of, and sensitivity to, the creative process. This is the principal reason that agency planners should conduct all creative development research.

Most planners have developed their research skills in the environment of an advertising agency. This means that besides their abilities as researchers, they ideally have highly developed creative skills. It is their job to learn creative ways of thinking, creative ways of interpreting, and creative ways of applying the results of their work to the process of developing advertising ideas. Most people who work as independent researchers, on the other hand, developed *their* research skills in research companies. While technically they may be superior researchers to their planning counterparts, many do not have the creative training to fully understand the intricacies of many advertising ideas, and most important of all, do not themselves have the creative skills to begin to suggest interesting solutions to problems.

In an excellent chapter on creative development research in the United Kingdom's Account Planning Group's book, *How to Plan Advertising*, Leslie Butterfield makes the point that the planner's job is to be the representative of the consumer within the agency.

> As such, the most vital part of their job is the
> understanding of the consumer. The best

> way to understand consumers is to talk to them — and the best way to talk to them is first hand. If a planner is not good at talking to consumers first hand, he probably is not a very good planner. Therefore, a good planner ought to be a good qualitative research moderator. The planner is the person closest to the brand and its advertising on a continuous basis; he understands the context within which the advertising has to work better than anyone else. Thus, by definition, no outsider will ever be as well briefed to tackle creative development research, since no briefing can substitute for the accumulated knowledge of the brand that resides in the planner.

I think that Leslie's logic is flawless, and I couldn't agree more with what he says.

On the subject of *objectivity* and detachment, this may be useful, as previously noted, in the area of creative *evaluation*, but not in creative development research. Again, Butterfield notes that "qualitative research is about participation and ideas, not distance and observation." My own experience has shown that an inverse relationship often exists between the degree of detachment exhibited by the moderator, and the usefulness of the research. A planner doing his or her job properly has lived at the heart of the creative development process and understands as well as the creative team themselves its core ideas, executional nuances, and desired response. They are therefore better placed than anyone to identify weaknesses and to suggest changes and improvements.

This brings us to the area of implementing the research findings, both within and outside the agency. Influence does not come automatically with independence; it is more often wielded by those with the most knowledge and the communication skills to make that knowledge seem important. That, too, is the job of agency planners: to have all the information at their fingertips that key decision-makers need to make their decisions, and to communicate a powerful point of view that leads them in the right direction (note: I said the right direction, not the agency's direction). Planners are much more likely than outsiders to be able to work with a creative team to implement findings from creative development research, because they work together, they know each other, and they see each other every day. A successful debrief on this type of research does not take place in one meeting and a document, but in a series of (usually informal) conversations that are obviously not possible if the moderator and creatives work for different companies.

Some agencies and clients will argue that if the planner is *present* at the research, then it doesn't matter who is moderating. I reject that notion, for the same aforementioned reason that Leslie Butterfield described and for the reasons outlined in Chapter 3 when I spoke about the O.J. Simpson trial. If you are not in the room, talking to consumers yourself, you will never be able to truly understand them.

Keeping a Great Idea Alive

The campaign that GS&P produced for Chevys Mexican Restaurants in the early 1990s is an excellent example of the advantages of intimacy with the development of a campaign idea when conducting creative development research. Albeit on a regional scale, the Chevys campaign was one of the most effective campaigns the agency ever produced, driving a dramatic increase in sales, attracting outside investment to finance the chain's expansion, and garnering numerous awards for both creativity (gold lions at Cannes and gold pencils at the One Show) and effectiveness (gold Effie™). Yet the campaign almost died in the first stage of creative development research. And I remain convinced that it *would* have died in the hands of a researcher who was not familiar with the genesis of the campaign, and who was not empowered to take liberties with the creative ideas in attempting to understand people's negative reactions.

Chevys was, at the time we were hired, a chain of around 30 restaurants in Northern California. A colorful, lively place with singing servers and free sombreros for guests celebrating birthdays, walls fashioned from Corona cases, and floor-to-ceiling Cuervo posters, it promised the freshest food of any Mexican restaurant. On its menu it featured a "Fresh Mex Pledge," a list of ten guarantees to its diners.

There will be no cans in our kitchen.
Chips will be served warm at your table within two
minutes of your sitting down.
Our guacamole is made from fresh avocados. If you
don't believe us, we'll bring you a pit to plant.
And so on.

The creative team had come up with an idea that the advertising itself should reflect the freshness of the food at Chevys. A TV commercial would be shot on video and aired on the same day, after which it would be thrown away and never used again. The next day, another "Fresh TV" commercial would be made. Each commercial would focus on a particular aspect of the fresh food at Chevys. It would also contain some proof that the commercial had actually been made that day—maybe a newspaper headline, perhaps a reference to some breaking news. Whatever it was, it had to be something that could not possibly have been prepared in advance.

Everyone, both at Chevys and the agency, was excited by the idea, particularly because we could imagine that same-day commercials might have enough news value to generate some PR, and hence additional exposure for our very small budget. Both of us, however, wanted to run it by some customers for two reasons. First, we obviously wanted to see whether they were as turned on by the idea as we were. But most important, we also wanted to know whether it could actually be done, because it looked as though it was going to be a logistic nightmare. Part of each spot could be shot beforehand, namely, the food in the restaurant, with tomatoes being sliced for a spot about salsa, tortillas rolling off "El machino," sizzling fajitas being delivered to tables, and people generally having a good time. But the bulk of each commercial, the part that proved the freshness of the commercial itself, would have to be shot starting at around four in the morning. Shooting would wrap by eight, and the spot had to be edited by ten, when the client would arrive at the studio to approve it or request changes. By noon, the finished spot had to be delivered by hand to San Francisco TV stations, and sent by satellite to the stations in Sacramento.

Focus groups were set up for the evening of May 15, 1992, in Sacramento. Steve Simpson, the copywriter, and Tracy Wong, his art director partner, would shoot and edit the commercial as described above, only instead of delivering it to a TV station, they would give it to me, and I would drive to Sacramento and show it to two focus groups.

This pilot commercial is shown in storyboard form in Figure 6.1. It was dated, interestingly enough, by that day's *San Francisco Examiner,* whose headline carried the news of the indictment of some Los Angeles Police Department officers for the videotaped beating of an African-American named Rodney King.

"Friday, May 15, 1991," said an *Examiner* employee, as the newspapers rolled off the presses. A title card announced that "this commercial was made today." A second added, "just like everything at Chevys." As the specials board was shown, a voice-over said, "Lunch at Chevys. The fresh fish today is thresher shark. That's served with a pico de gallo sauce." Quick cuts showed steaming food being brought to tables, waiters weaving their way through the crowded restaurant, and diners enjoying their meals. "Well, since you've already missed lunch," the voice-over continued,

Figure 6.1 Chevys Mexican Restaurant: "Pilot Film."

"maybe you can try it at dinner. If you come early enough." The spot closed with another scene of piles of newspapers rolling along a conveyor belt. "Chevys Fresh Mex. There's hardly anything fresher."

It was finished according to schedule, and I drove safely to Sacramento. Everything was going as planned, until respondents in both groups told me, in no uncertain terms, that it was the worst advertising idea they had ever seen. They hated it.

"It's boring."

"It's insulting."

"Who gives a damn about thresher shark?"

"What did all those newspapers have to do with anything?"

"Have the people who made that ever *been* to Chevys?"

"They said it was made today, but I don't believe them."

"Where did it say that? I didn't see anything about 'made today.' Isn't that impossible?"

"The quality's awful. It's all shaky and blurry. The food looks terrible."

"I hate that guy's voice."

The voice on the tape belonged to Steve Simpson, the copywriter, who I knew was watching from behind the viewing mirror. I imagined him trying to hang himself, using his belt and shoelaces.

Most of the respondents had clearly not gotten the message that the commercial had been made that day. The typed card, reading "This commercial was made today," seemed to have escaped the notice of the majority.

The few who had seen that card did not believe it. Some thought it physically impossible. Others thought it had been faked in some way. (Presumably they thought Chevys had orchestrated the beating incident, released the video to the press, and waited until indictments were issued before releasing their previously prepared advertising. Not even Oliver Stone would buy that one.) While many criticized the rough video style, some cited the typed cards as evidence that the commercial was "too polished" and must have taken longer than a day to make.

If they didn't know, or didn't believe, that the commercial had been made that day, then the only explanation for the rough *video* style was that Chevys simply didn't care about the quality of its commercials. Which was in turn taken to mean that Chevys probably didn't care about the quality of its food. In other words, it seemed to be having quite the opposite effect to that which was desired.

In the second group, reactions were so vehement that after about a half hour, I told the respondents that I had gotten their message loud and clear, removed the tape from the VCR, and dropped it into the wastebasket.

"Let's talk about something else," I said, and gave each of them a copy of the "Fresh Mex Pledge" from the menu, which most of them had surprisingly never seen. (We later realized that the reason they had never seen it was that it was positioned on the back part of the foldout menu, where nobody would ever look, except by accident.) This got a much more positive reaction than the advertising.

"That's cool."

"Why don't they talk about this in the advertising?"

"Yeah. That's what the advertising should have said. This 'fresh' stuff is great."

I asked them whether anyone thought that the advertising that they had just seen might have been *trying* to say that. No. No one had gotten that message.

Was it the thresher shark that was the problem? Wasn't there a point in the pledge list that they had read that mentioned fresh fish specials? The specials were a good thing, they agreed, but thresher shark . . . they weren't sure. I asked how many of them had ever tried thresher shark. None of them had.

The pledge points that they all wanted to talk about were the ones relating to salsa, chips, tortillas, and guacamole: the universal appetizers that many regarded as the real test of the quality of a Mexican restaurant.

"If this stuff about the tomatoes and the warm chips is true, then that's real good," said one respondent. "I can taste it just thinking about it."

"If the advertising people were to do a commercial about salsa, or about chips being delivered warm to your table within two minutes of sitting down," I asked, "would that be more interesting?"

Everyone agreed that it would.

"But I still don't see what it has to do with those newspapers," said a devil's advocate. The others agreed. Pretending to be made that day? What was the point?

My office at the agency was just across a small corridor from Rich Silverstein's, and as our doors virtually opened onto each other, we could always hear every word of the other's telephone conversations. A few days earlier, I had overheard Rich talking to a friend about an idea we had for a new campaign for Chevys. He was clearly very excited, and he told his friend that "for the freshest food, we're going to do the freshest advertising." Now, as respondents began to attack the irrelevancy of the advertising idea again, I realized that Silverstein's description, which was so succinct and interesting, did not currently appear in the advertising. Perhaps that was the missing link.

"I'm not sure about this," I told the group, "but I think what the advertising people *meant* to do with this commercial was show that for the freshest food — the pledges you all said you liked so much — they would create the freshest advertising. So for fresh salsa, they would do a fresh TV commercial."

"Why didn't they say that?" asked a respondent.

"That's much better than what they did."

"They should say that. I like that a lot better."

"So is that why they had the newspapers?"

When I say that planners should spend more time listening, perhaps I really mean that they should spend more time eavesdropping on other people's telephone conversations. *That* would be difficult for an outside researcher.

On May 9, a commercial aired in the Bay Area and Sacramento that opened on Steve and Tracy, armed with a video camera, in hot pursuit of early morning joggers on San Francisco's Marina Green (see Figure 6.2). A lively Mexican mariachi track played throughout. "Scuse me! Scuse me!" shouts Simpson in a vain effort to attract a lady jogger's attention. One male jogger does stop. "Could you tell me today's date?" Simpson asks.

"It's . . . er . . . it's the ninth of . . . er . . . May."

A voice-over speaks as we see the date on the man's watch—"5-9." It is circled as if with a bright, vibrant green marker pen. "We made this commercial a few hours ago. We call this fresh TV." The words FRESH TV appear on the screen in the same shaky, vibrant style. A funky red-and-green border emphasizes the words. Now we see tomatoes and onions being chopped.

"At Chevys," the voice-over continues, "we made our salsa just minutes ago. We call this Fresh Mex." The words FRESH MEX appear on screen.

"Fresh TV," repeats the voice-over, as Steve and Tracy run after yet another jogger. "Fresh Mex. I dunno, so far we're a lot better at the Fresh Mex part than the Fresh TV."

The lady jogger we saw at the start of the spot disappears into the distance. "Don't be frightened," Simpson shouts, as he and Tracy fall behind. "I just wanna ask you a question."

On June 20 (Figure 6.3), another spot opened with the same mariachi music, and Simpson shouting, "free lie detector test, one day only!"

A man, shown being hooked up to a polygraph, is asked by Simpson, "can you tell me today's date?"

"June twentieth," he replies, and a bell rings to show he's passed the test.

"This commercial was made today," says the voice-over.

Now a nun is hooked up to the machine. "June twentieth," she says with a smile, and the bell rings once more.

"We call this Fresh TV," says the voice-over, and the words FRESH TV appear on screen. Now we see guacamole

Figure 6.2 Chevys Mexican Restaurant: "Salsa."

Figure 6.3 Chevys Mexican Restaurant: "Polygraph."

being made from fresh avocados, with juice being squeezed from a lemon. "At Chevys," the voice-over continues, "our guacamole is made fresh every day. We call this Fresh Mex." FRESH MEX shimmers on screen. "At Chevys, we make *every-thing* fresh every day. Hey—would we lie?"

A priest is now connected to the machine and is asked, "Have you ever cheated at golf?"

"Yes, I have," he replies, sheepishly, and the bell rings. The interviewers laugh.

"Do you usually cheat at golf?"

"No. Rarely." His response is greeted by the sharp sound of a buzzer, and a big, red cross on screen highlights his sin.

Creative-Development Research Is a Negotiation

At a convention of packaging designers in 1963, Robert Pliskin observed that "Market research can establish beyond the shadow of a doubt that the egg is a sad and sorry product and that it obviously will not continue to sell. Because after all, eggs won't stand up by themselves, they roll too easily, are too easily broken, require special packaging, look alike, are difficult to open, [and] won't stack on the shelf."

However good a product, it is always possible to find something wrong with it. The Chevys campaign is only one of a number that I could have used to make the point that a bad consumer response in creative development research isn't necessarily the end of the world. It is rare for any advertising campaign, however great, not to attract negative comment. The real skill of the planner is in distinguishing between those negative comments that are relevant and need to be addressed and those that are either irrelevant to the ideas as they currently stand, or that can easily be dealt with in production.

The late Akio Morita, founder and chairman of Sony, writing in *Made in Japan* about the launch of the Walkman, made the argument that a company whose strength lies in innovation does not wait for consumers to tell it what they want. "The public does not know what is possible," he wrote, "but we do." The same argument he makes in the context of technological innovation can also be made about consumer response to creative innovation. Most people have a frame of reference that extends only as far as their existing experience. Their ability to predict how they might feel at some time in the future, about a piece of advertising that they are seeing only in embryonic form, is often severely limited.

In creative development research, advertising ideas are frequently exposed to consumers in a form that bears little resemblance to the way they would look, sound, and feel as finished advertising, and the consumers who are expected to pass opinions on them often have neither the experience nor the imagination to fill in the gaps. Their responses are thus likely to be as incomplete as the creative stimulus material being exposed and must be tempered with creative vision and client confidence if they are to be useful. And like any negotiation, this isn't always easy.

I recently put together a reel of advertising from Goodby, Silverstein & Partners that contained many of the TV commercials featured in the pages of this book: "Aaron Burr" and "Heaven" from the "got milk?" campaign; "Architect" and "Dog and Cat" for Polaroid; "Mud" for the Isuzu Rodeo; "Laws" and "Fantasy" for Norwegian Cruise Line; and many others besides. With the benefit of hindsight, I know that all of those commercials stood out, not just in their respective categories but from the body of advertising in general, and all were extremely effective in building the client's business. Yet all could easily have died in creative development research had consumer comments been listened to literally, creatives not been allowed to express their differing opinions, and the client in each case not had the courage to say, "I hear what they are saying, but I will not change my mind about running this advertising as a result."

In the case of "Aaron Burr" (Figure 7.5), consumers were very hung up on "other people" not knowing who

Aaron Burr and Alexander Hamilton were. We (agency and client) simply decided that it didn't matter. The point was, lack of milk prevented the character from answering the big money question that he'd been waiting for all his life, and the more esoteric the question, the better.

Many of those who saw "Heaven" (Figure 7.13) in rough form were horrified that someone actually got *killed* in the commercial. It's hard (especially when the idea is being presented in script form) for respondents to imagine someone getting run down by a truck and it being *funny,* but all along, Jeff Goodby, who directed the spot, knew that he would shoot that scene in a way that was almost cartoonlike. The client trusted his judgment, and I never heard a single person complain about bad taste on seeing the finished spot.

Isuzu's "Mud" commercial raised all sorts of parental concerns about encouraging kids to be disobedient and suggesting that it was a good thing to dive face first into mud puddles. Polaroid's "Dog and Cat" (Figure 5.8) was criticized by some because "dogs can't take photographs." Really. And the "Architect" spot (Figure 5.7) attracted a lot of early criticism because in its first iteration, we described the actual picture that the architect drew from his briefcase. While the "Mud" and "Dog and Cat" comments were largely ignored, the issue of the picture in "Architect" was taken a little more seriously. The picture being used by the architect's wife or girlfriend to get him home was central to the story, and without it the whole idea would have been dead, but there was a simple solution — to show only the back of the picture and let the architect's face and the viewers' imagination join up the dots. In the end, people tend to imagine something far more raunchy than we could ever have *shown,* but that, we thought, was their problem and not ours. Hey, it could have been a picture of his favorite tuna sandwich. What sort of minds do you people have?

The Norwegian Cruise Line campaign was a negotiation from start to finish. GS&P had worked with NCL's parent company, Kloster, for several years, first on Royal Viking Line and more recently on NCL. But NCL had just appointed a new president, Adam Aron, and as anyone in advertising knows, a new president usually means a change of agency.

On his first visit to the agency, his opening words did not augur well.

"Why the hell do I have an agency in San Francisco when my office is in Miami?"

Before anyone had the opportunity to offer an opinion, he said that he would cut to the chase and say that although he thought the campaign that was currently running was okay, he had a better idea for a new campaign, which he would like us to produce for him. In a previous job at Hyatt hotels, he had been responsible for the "Hyatt Touch" campaign, my own recollections of which revolve mostly around sensual music and naked women having suntan lotion applied to their backs. The idea of the Hyatt campaign, Adam said, was to show the hotels as places of more than business, as places where couples could go, relax, and rekindle relationships. If that had worked at Hyatt, he said, he was certain it would work at a cruise line.

"All people want to do is go on a cruise and have sex," he said to the stunned team from the agency. He wanted a campaign that captured this thought, and imagined the way that Calvin Klein might advertise a cruise ship.

"Could it be about other things, too?" asked Steve Simpson, the creative director. "You know, maybe the sexual thing you are talking about could be wrapped up in a larger idea?"

"Are you the planner?" responded Adam. "You talk like a planner."

Over the next two weeks, Simpson and his partner, Steve Luker, as well as the real planner, Mary Stervinou, took the cruise mentioned in Chapter 4 and found the larger idea that Simpson had postulated at dinner with Adam. Cruising, as they saw it, was in a larger sense about freedom and escape, about having a weight lifted from one's shoulders and feeling lighter, as if the rules of gravity no longer applied. Simpson captured this idea in a line of copy, "the laws of the land do not apply," and a tagline that said, simply, "It's Different Out Here."

A video was produced in an attempt to capture this idea, both to present to Adam and to show to focus groups. The script was very similar to that which eventually appeared on the "Laws" commercial: "There is no law that says you can't make love at 4 in the afternoon on a Tuesday . . . that says you must pack worry along with your baggage . . . that says you must contribute to the GNP every day of your life . . . because the laws of the land do not apply . . . it's different out here." This was spoken over beautiful, sexy black-and-white imagery of relaxed and amorous couples. At one point, we even saw writhing bodies and bouncing bedsprings.

"You've gone too far," said Adam Aron.

"You've gone too far," said the focus groups. In fact, some respondents were absolutely appalled.

But while the bodies and bedsprings were enough to prevent some people seeing anything else in the spots, others were able to see beyond them to the bigger idea that Simpson had been trying to communicate, and they loved what they saw. This campaign polarized people as much as any campaign we have ever exposed. Because it was so different visually ("can't you make the sea blue instead of black and white?"), the characters depicted were not typical of cruisers, and the overt sexuality was off-putting to many. In many ways, I have come to believe that a campaign *needs* to polarize people if it is going to be effective. It has to elicit an emotional response, for good or for bad, if people are going to notice it and think about it. I would much rather, as was the case with NCL, have a couple people in a group *loving* it, a couple more *hating* it, and some in the middle who are uncomfortable because they're not sure which way to jump. At least it's moving them so they know they're going to *have to* jump. That kind of advertising will be much more successful than a campaign that ten respondents mumble is "okay," or "good." It will be acceptable to all, and exciting to no one.

Figure 6.4 Norwegian Cruise Line: "Fantasy" (TV).

Figure 6.5   Norwegian Cruise Line: "There Is a Place."

In the end, the sexuality was pared back so that the feel of the campaign was more *sensual* than sexual, which felt right to all parties concerned, but the beautiful models and black-and-white imagery remained. They, it was felt, along with the wonderful Cowboy Junkies' version of "Blue

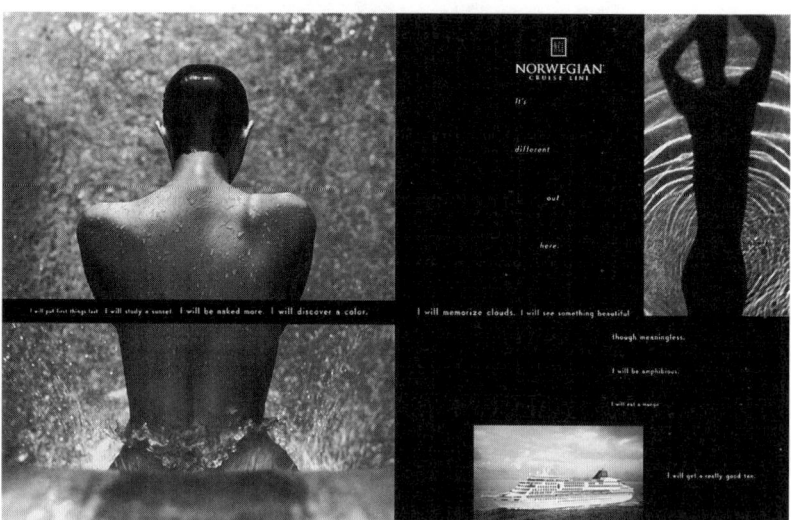

Figure 6.6   Norwegian Cruise Line: "Fantasy."

228

Moon," were vital to the feeling of beauty, nostalgia, and fantasy (see Figures 6.4–6.6). In the end, people could read into it whatever they liked.

A few months later, I took my first cruise, on the Norwegian Cruise Line *Windward* to Alaska. My wife and I emerged from the dining room at about 10 p.m. on the Saturday night and observed two couples, both in their sixties, standing by the elevator. One of the couples was obviously ready to retire for the evening, and the others were trying hard to change their minds, with appeals like "the night is still young . . . let's go gambling" and "what about the midnight buffet?"

The others would have none of it and stepped into the elevator. There was time for one last appeal from their friends outside:

"Come on, it's much too early to go to bed."

Inside the elevator, the 60-year-old woman looked at her elderly husband and then back at her friends. She raised an eyebrow suggestively, and purred, "It's Different Out Here."

The color drained from her husband's face, and the doors closed.

7

Serendipity
"got milk?"

That is the essence of science: Ask an impertinent question, and you are on your way to the pertinent answer.
Jacob Bronowski, *The Ascent of Man,* 1973

INTRODUCTION

So far in this book, I have discussed a number of different advertising campaigns, but always in parts and always to illustrate a certain broader point. Thus a particular campaign may have been used to illustrate a particularly insightful approach to strategic research, or a specific aspect of creative briefing or creative development research, or maybe even all three. But nowhere, so far, have I attempted to tell the whole story of a campaign from start to finish. The simple reason for that is that I didn't want this to be a book of case histories. It would take up far too much space to provide a full story of several campaigns. I also know from both presenting case histories to existing or prospective clients and acting as a judge for effectiveness awards that the more case histories you hear, the less interesting they become. For obvious reasons, there's a fairly standard content and order to these things, with a standard sequence of background information, campaign objectives, strategic insight, creative solution, and results (that hopefully meet or exceed the objectives), and that, after a while, can become very tiresome.

I did, however, want to include just one full story, which will hopefully illustrate a number of the different observations and suggestions that appear in the preceding chapters. I do not belabor any of those points as I go, preferring simply to tell the story as it developed, and allowing you to make the connections for yourselves. That assumes, of course, that you have read some of the previous chapters.

The campaign that I have chosen to feature is "got milk?" for the California Fluid Milk Processors' Advisory Board (CFMPAB). In case you are wondering, I am not presenting it as an example of advertising perfection (I am convinced there is no such thing), but rather as a fortunate alignment of a number of unrelated factors: a client who was prepared to fly in the face of industry experience and wisdom; some hunches that proved to be more right than wrong; research that walked hand-in-hand with hypotheses and proved that neither expense nor sophistication are necessary to make a profound contribution; a powerful creative idea that gained its momentum from the ideas of several different people; and perhaps a healthy dose of good fortune besides. On the subject of good fortune, though, an old sporting adage asserts that "luck is what happens when preparation meets opportunity." So maybe any luck that came our way was not entirely accidental.

CRYING OVER SPILLED MILK

In May 1994, Bruce Horowitz began an article in the *Los Angeles Times* with the statement that "There are just two things in the world more boring than whole milk: low fat and skim. While Pepsi has its own generation, Milk can't muster one palpitation . . . Milk—is even on its best day—a real yawner."

About a year before that article appeared, Goodby, Silverstein & Partners had received a visit from a man named Jeff Manning, the executive director of the newly formed CFMPAB. He was looking for an agency to advertise milk in California. Although he came with a very large budget, some $25 million to spend in the first year alone, many in the agency would have agreed with Horowitz, feeling that whatever he and his board were considering spending, milk was a lost cause, and "there is nothing that advertising can do to help." Many were of the opinion that this was a review in which the agency should not even enter into contention.

There was much evidence to support their case. As recently as 1980, the average Californian (yes, the Californian with one breast and one testicle) was consuming 30 gallons of milk a year. By 1993, that figure had declined to 24.1 gallons, a loss of 20 percent. In most categories, such a decline would be almost catastrophic, but the Californian farmers and dairies had been fortunate enough to be protected by California's steady population growth. In other words, even though individuals were consuming less milk, the absolute number of individuals was climbing fast enough to keep the state's *total* milk consumption constant. By the late 1980s, though, the decline in per capita consumption was steep enough that even population growth could not keep pace, and total milk consumption began to shrink. Two percent one year. Three percent the next. From 1992 to 1993, 3.6 percent less milk was consumed by Californians.

It was this decline that had brought Manning to the agency. An experienced advertising man, he had worked on a number of commodities accounts in previous lives at J. Walter Thompson, McCann Erickson, and Ketchum Advertising, including campaigns for national boards representing eggs, beef, raisins, prunes, bananas, and potatoes. (At Thompson, he also had the distinction of playing first base on a softball team whose third baseman was Jeff Goodby. A losing, error-plagued softball team, I suspect.) This extensive and diverse experience had qualified him uniquely when the CFMPAB had started its search for an executive director.

The board itself had been formed out of dissatisfaction with the results of advertising expenditure from other bodies representing the dairy industry—bodies to whom they were contributing their own money, yet who seemed to be providing very little return. All of the CFMPAB's members owned or ran dairies. They got the raw milk from the farmers, processed it, and then sold it on to retailers. In forming their board, they pledged three cents for every gallon of milk they processed to fund an advertising campaign that they hoped might halt the decline, and they gave themselves two years in which to make a difference. If in that time they had failed to make any impact, they would disband the board and stop wasting their money.

"That makes for a pretty unique situation," observed Jeff Manning on his inaugural visit to the agency. "It means that I'm only interested in one thing, and that's selling milk. Because if we don't sell more milk, the board will disband. If the board disbands, I will no longer have a job. And if I don't have a job, neither do you."

A WIDE-OPEN BRIEF

A long-running Gallup survey has tracked attitudes toward milk and milk purchase and consumption behavior on a national basis and has consistently highlighted three key reasons people are consuming less milk, both in California and the rest of the country. First, many people are concerned about milk's fat content. I have heard many express their fears that milk may be unhealthy; when asked to elaborate, they have pointed out with great conviction that even with semi-skimmed milk, half of what you are drinking is fat. I'm not sure what they think is left in nonfat, or skimmed milk, when all the fat has been removed, but one can only assume that it isn't milk. The second problem is that milk is often regarded as a "kids' drink." Perhaps our mothers spent too much time telling us to drink it because it was good for us, with the unhappy consequence that once we had our driver's license, we figured we didn't have to drink it any more. Industry data shows a very steep decline in consumption as kids move into adolescence, and again as they transition from adolescence to adulthood. Perhaps associated with this is the third problem, which is the feeling that by comparison with other beverage choices, especially sodas like Coke and Pepsi, milk is boring.

In summary, the industry had concluded, milk had an image problem. And to correct that problem, a number of advertising campaigns had been developed over a number of years that attempted to directly refute people's concerns and misconceptions. "Milk is good for you," we were told in a variety of ways, and healthy, good-looking people of all ages with lustrous hair, perfect teeth, and fine muscle definition jogged with milk cartons, danced with them, and sang to them. Milk was healthy, milk was for everyone, and with its lively music tracks and jingles it certainly wasn't boring.

The Gallup survey showed that this advertising had been successful in shifting *attitudes* toward milk. For example, in 1982, 40 percent of Californians had agreed with the statement: "I should drink more milk than I do." By 1992 that number had risen to 52 percent.

"All that shows," said Manning, "is that image means nothing. Because as milk's image has improved, its sales have declined." It was true. A chart on which both key image dimensions and consumption were plotted on the same axis showed a classic scissor shape. As image went up, volume seemed to go down.

> So I'm not interested in image. If all we do is affect image, we will all lose our jobs. We need to affect *behavior.* People have to buy more, and they have to consume more.
>
> That's the objective. And I don't give a damn how we get there. If you think that

persuading people to take baths in milk will
get them to buy more, and you can persuade
me that you're right, I'll go with it. I'm not
going to tell you that you have to do anything like the milk industry has done before.
Because whatever they have done, it hasn't
worked. I don't know, maybe we don't even
have to see milk in the advertising. If you
want to spend all the money promoting
cereal sales in California, getting people to
eat more cereal, maybe that's the answer.
That may sound weird, but what else are
they going to put on their cereal? What I'm
saying is that it's wide open.

There can be no better brief for an advertising agency
than one that says, essentially, start from scratch. Assume
that there are no rules. And if Rich Silverstein is right when
he says that clients get the advertising they deserve, here was
a client who deserved something very good. If he didn't get
it, then we would have no one to blame but ourselves.

FISHING WHERE THE FISH ARE

A study of milk consumption habits commissioned by the
CFMPAB showed that 70 percent of Californians claimed to
use milk "frequently," while 30 percent did not. It also
seemed that the majority of previous milk advertising had
been aimed at the 30 percent who, for whatever reason, were
not using milk at all, or at least using less than they used to.

In any category, persuading people who are *not* doing
something to do it, whether again or for the first time, tends
to be a much harder task than persuading people who are
already doing it to do more of it, or do the same thing more
often. If a company, for whatever reason, wanted people to
run three miles a day, they would undoubtedly have the most

success initially among people who are already running one or two miles a day. For them, the change is merely one of degree, while those who do not run have to learn a whole new pattern of behavior, and anyone who has ever started running for the first time will know how difficult (and painful) that can be.

As we talked about this in the agency, we quickly arrived at the conclusion that if our task was to influence behavior quickly, then trying to amplify existing behavior, by persuading people to use more milk, or use it more often, gave us a much greater chance of success. Those who were not using milk, or using less of it, were often doing so for reasons that were quite deeply ingrained, and it seemed to us that advertising was not likely to make a difference, at least in the short term.

If we were right to talk to the user group, then the immediate question we had to answer was "how do they use milk?" Again, Jeff Manning had an insight that he wanted us to consider.

"A few years ago at Ketchum, I worked with [creative director] Ken Dudwick on a speculative campaign for one of the milk industry organizations, and we had this notion we called '____ and milk.' If you think about it, you hardly ever use milk on its own. The '____' part is brownies, or cereal, coffee. . . . those things taste so good with milk, and you can't imagine eating them without it." At the time, he said, the clients had not been willing to buy into the idea, but he remained convinced that there was something powerful in a food and milk story.

A tracking study designed to investigate this particular hypothesis and conducted by MARC research, revealed that almost 88 percent of milk is consumed in the home, a figure that makes advertising images of people chugging from milk cartons while jogging in the park seem somewhat ridiculous. Marketing people often look at the absence of consumption among a particular group or in a particular location as an "opportunity," but in this case there were very good reasons people didn't take milk with them on their travels. Like the fact that it spills once opened, and if not refrigerated it smells and tastes really bad.

Not only did the research confirm that most milk was consumed in the home, but it also showed that very little milk is consumed in isolation. As Manning had postulated, it is usually a complement to a food item, and as such is rarely the center of attention implied by much previous milk advertising. Cereal, not surprisingly, accounted for the lion's share of occasions where food is consumed with milk (some 45 percent), followed by breakfast pastries, cookies, peanut butter and jelly sandwiches, graham crackers, and brownies.

In focus groups, we asked people to talk about milk in relation to these foods. In some groups we showed respondents a beautiful photograph of a glass of milk and asked them to talk about the first things that popped into their heads. Their resulting imagery was very diverse, and not all of it positive. Many people didn't really know what to think at all, feeling that it was, "Uh, just milk." There really wasn't that much to say. In marked contrast, other groups were shown beautiful shots of chocolate chip cookies and brownies, and the response was almost unanimous. They were attracted by the food and immediately imagined a glass of milk alongside it.

"I'm hungry!"

"That cookie and a glass of milk would be pretty good right now."

Importantly, though, it was clear that people wanted the food first and the milk second. The food was always more interesting and emotive than the milk, but the milk was still an essential accompaniment. In a way, the two were codependent, in that most people could not imagine consuming that particular food *without* milk. But it had to be "____ and milk." "Milk and ____" just wouldn't be the same

Milk, it seemed, could not create its own desire. On the other hand, these appetizing, sometimes naughty companion foods (with the exception of cereal), seemed capable of creating a powerful craving that could only be satisfied with milk as part of the equation. With milk, respondents told us, these foods were perfect. Without milk, they were ruined. And this, we discovered, was the only time that people even seemed to think about milk at all—when they wanted it, and it wasn't there.

A theory began to emerge, stimulated by threads of evidence from research, by the hypotheses that Jeff Manning had brought to the table, and by our own experiences as milk consumers. Perhaps, we thought, the companion food items mentioned above could be used in advertising to stimulate desire for milk. With the exception of cereal, these food items had largely been ignored by years of milk advertising, because the industry—not surprisingly—considered them to be unhealthy. But if they were the sole reason many people consumed milk, we reasoned, why should we shy away from them?

Moreover, when people described situations where they had the food but not the milk, we were intrigued by the level of emotion in their descriptions. It wasn't merely inconvenient; they were angry, upset, frustrated; and it showed not only in their words but in their hand gestures, their posture, their facial expressions, and even in their artwork. We asked them to draw pictures depicting running out of milk, and many showed themselves screaming, tearing their hair out, and trying to hunt down the culprit who had drunk the last of it.

As any one individual described such a scenario, others could clearly relate to it. You spent most of your life not giving milk a moment's thought, then along comes a moment when you really need it, and it's not there. "It's traumatic," one person told us, and their fellow group members pursed their lips and nodded sympathetically. So beyond the simple food association (something that Jeff Manning was later to describe, jokingly, as "milk and food—yum yum—half a good idea"), maybe there was something in these emotional reactions relating to *not having milk* that we could exploit.

To explore the full potential of this area, an experiment was conducted with some standard focus groups. People were recruited for the groups with the offer of the normal 50-dollar respondent incentive, but with an additional 25 dollars if they would agree not to use milk for the week immediately preceding the research. Most agreed with alacrity. "No problem." An easy 25 bucks, they assumed.

One week later, we held focus groups in both Northern and Southern California. The respondents brought with them a diary we had asked them to keep, detailing everything they ate or drank over the previous week, as well as what they were doing, who they were with, and how they were feeling on each such occasion.

"When you offered us the extra 25 dollars," said one middle-aged woman, "I figured it wouldn't be difficult, but I guess I was thinking about glasses of milk. It didn't occur to me that I wouldn't be able to get my latte on the way to work."

"No kidding," added her neighbor. "I forgot about coffee, too. I hate coffee without milk."

Another, a single mother, described a terrible day at work. She had been inundated with problems, her boss had shouted at her, the commute was awful, and to cheer herself up she had bought two decadent chocolate chip cookies on the way home. When she got home, she had to deal with the kids, who were behaving badly, but finally, around nine o'clock, she had got them to bed and settled down in front of the television with her cookies. She needed something to drink with them, and instinctively made for the fridge to pour herself a glass of milk. The carton was in her hand when she remembered the promise she had made, not to consume milk for that week. "It was awful," she remembered. "I didn't know what to do. I thought about drinking some and coming here and lying, but that wouldn't have been right. So then I thought maybe I should come clean, but then perhaps you'd throw me out and I wouldn't get paid. So I put the milk back. And the cookies just weren't the same. Actually it was a bad end to a bad day."

What only half an hour earlier had been a normal research group now came to resemble a support group. Other respondents nodded gravely as the lonely cookie scenario was described, and other, similar experiences began to emerge. All agreed that the last week had greatly heightened their awareness of milk, and that their experience had been like every previous time they had ever run out of milk, only worse because this time it had lasted for seven days. Some indicated that they would be stopping at the store on the way home from the group to make sure that they were stocked up. After all they had been through, they agreed, they didn't want it to happen again for a while.

We wanted Californians to think about milk in a way that they did not normally do, and this experiment had certainly shown that to be a possibility. Somehow, *advertising* had to affect their minds in the same way, but more than affecting their minds, it also had to affect their behavior. From what we had observed in our initial research, where simply talking about food items like brownies and chocolate chip cookies made people want to eat them and wash them down with milk, we thought that it might be possible to create more milk occasions, so that people would *use* more milk. But that on its own would not be enough. Usage patterns had to be linked to purchase patterns, so that people would not only use more, but also *buy* more. Drawing a distinction between the two may seem like splitting hairs, but in fact there is a logical reason for doing so. If people were to use more milk without buying more, they would simply run out faster, and the industry would have gained nothing. Both sides of the equation needed to be affected simultaneously.

CONVERGENCE

The strategy consequently went beyond the combination of food and milk to suggest combining complementary foods and *no milk*. In other words, a deprivation strategy. We wanted to find a way, in advertising, to feature a food with which milk was the perfect complement. Desire would be created for the food, and in turn for milk. The twist was, there would never be any milk, and as a result both the food and the moment would be ruined.

In both creative and media terms, a number of separate ideas began to converge. The first, which somewhat unusually came up in isolation from an overall campaign idea, was a rather unusual tagline. A few weeks before the proposed strategic direction was even agreed with Jeff Manning, the subject of deprivation had come up in a conversation with Jeff Goodby. Some agency team members asked Goodby if he could come up with an interesting phrase that captured this deprivation idea, that they could put on a presentation board for a meeting. He came back with a line that to him "seemed kind of weird"; and by his own admission, he didn't really know what to do with it, but it seemed interesting. If copywriters were to be paid by the word, Jeff wouldn't have gotten rich with this one, because it was only two words:

got milk?

Goodby remembers that when he first showed this phrase to the account team, certain (unnamed) individuals felt that it lacked clarity. Shouldn't it say "have you got enough milk?" Fortunately, he ignored them.

As the evidence began to mount in favor of a deprivation strategy, "got milk?" began to take on a life of its own. Another writer, Scott Burns, had some ideas for television commercials that were like small streams of consciousness, celebrating certain moments when one might need milk, and the foods with which milk was the perfect companion. In every one of these poetic pieces, expectations are raised and then dashed as it is revealed that there is no milk. All finish with the flat question, "got milk?" He hadn't thought much about the visuals, but we agreed we would expose them to people in focus groups anyway. To get around that problem, we simply asked people to shut their eyes, listen as the scripts were read aloud, and use their imaginations. It would be interesting to hear the images that *they* conjured up as a result of our stimulus material.

NIGHT

The earth turns its back on the sun. Sirens sing lullabies, and the heart asks questions of the head that send you tossing and turning for answers. And you wrestle doubt from one room to another until you stand face to face with the refrigerator asking it for something to make morning seem a little closer. Something like a glass of milk which usually does the job, unless you don't have milk in which case, well, you better hope you have friends on the other side of the world you can talk to on the phone.

got milk?

COFFEE

Steamin' joe. Java. A bit of the bean. Coffee is proof of civilization every bit as much as government or professional sports. Charged with caffeine like a race car, or made peaceful as a pup, it's there for you in the morning with the paper, and it tells you that dinner's done—let the conversation begin. And nothing improves coffee like milk. Cuz, without it you're just staring down at hot brown liquid worrying about burning your tongue.

got milk?

BROWNIE

There's not a lot that can go wrong in your life that a brownie can't fix. A bad relationship, the loss of a job, a rainy day or a minor illness are each and all burdens lightened by a chewy brownie fresh from the oven. Store bought or home-made, just the word "brownie" is usually enough to bring a smile to young and old alike. Unless of course you don't have any milk, in which case a brownie is likely to lodge in your throat and send you stumbling around the room wishing you were someone else instead.

got milk?

CEREAL

Hot or cold, day or night, a bowl of cereal is a great way to celebrate having a mouth that connects to your stomach. There must be over a hundred kinds of cereal, each one made out of wheat, corn, sugar, granola, oats . . . just about anything mankind can put in a box and make up a name for. Best of all and not to be forgotten, all you need is a bowl and spoon . . . and that means not much clean up for a whole lot of food fun. And of course you'll be needing milk, or else you're just holding a bunch of dry seeds in a curved dish wondering what stores are open.

got milk?

Reactions to these ideas were fascinating. All seemed very evocative, and most respondents in our groups said that they could relate in some way to each one of the scenarios. Everyone has a sleepless night once in a while, they said, and everyone knows what a brownie tastes like without a glass of milk to wash it down. In the latter example, people told us they could imagine someone staggering around blowing brownie crumbs out of their nose in panic, an amusing prospect indeed. Coffee was somehow a less effective tool, perhaps because many people like to drink it black anyway, and somehow the cereal scenario seemed, well, almost too *rational.* Perhaps it was because cereal, and coffee too, are more matters of habit than the kind of craving or treat represented by a brownie, or the kind of food that satisfies the late night munchies. Unlike the brownie scenario, people couldn't *feel* the deprivation in these other descriptions; and if they couldn't feel it, we concluded, they were unlikely to take any action as a result. It still felt like even in the most powerful brownie scenario, people were in a sense observing someone else's pain. We needed to find a way to draw them into the scenario themselves.

The first clue to an answer came from the agency's media department. This may come as a surprise to people in many agencies where the media department generally plays little part in the creative process — the media and creative departments live on separate floors and do not communicate with one another on either a strategic or creative level. On this occasion, while the agency creatives were firing off their first, exploratory idea salvoes, the media people were trying to figure out ways to talk to people at times, and in places, where they were most likely to be able to take some action as a result of seeing or hearing the advertising.

Given that most milk is consumed in the home, it was not difficult to figure out that for the consumption part, at least, television was the most likely medium through which to talk to people within easy reach of their refrigerator. A media plan was presented to Jeff Manning that consisted of a simple floor plan of a house. A circle was drawn, centered on the refrigerator, to represent a 30-foot diameter. Advertising, we said, had to reach people within 30 feet of the fridge if they were going to be able to take any action as a result. Television ads would run to coincide with particular meal or snack occasions, with executions selected to air at specific times based on a particular food that was featured. For example, if a commercial contained a peanut butter and jelly sandwich, it might appear at morning or afternoon snack time, or late at night, in the hope of setting off a craving; the same with brownies, cupcakes, or chocolate chip cookies. Instead of traditional media dayparts, the "got milk?" media plans continue to define their dayparts as "breakfast," "snack," "dinner," and so on.

The same logic that suggested people were most likely to be persuaded to *consume* milk when they were within easy reach of the refrigerator, also applied to the *purchase* process. If we wanted to set off a craving for a chocolate chip cookie, it made sense to do so in a place where people could conceivably buy one. So why not, the media director suggested, strategically position billboards around grocery stores and near freeway exits, to make people crave our foods and act as a reminder to stop, shop, and avoid the horror of running out?

A very simple creative idea brought this poster idea to life. A beautiful, appetizing, chocolate chip cookie was photographed with a bite taken out, and in the space left by the bite appeared the words, "got milk?" A tray of brownies, fresh from the oven, a succulent peanut butter and jelly sandwich, and a pair of cup cakes all got the same treatment (see Figures 7.1–7.3). These new executions were once again taken out to focus groups, along with some new TV scripts. Among them was a hastily written script from Scott Burns, which more than a few people thought would go nowhere. It was about a strange guy who collects memorabilia relating to Alexander Hamilton and Aaron Burr. His big chance to translate his obsession into riches comes with a big-money question on a radio show, to which he alone knows the answer. Unfortunately, when he receives the call, his mouth is filled with a peanut butter and jelly sandwich, and he has run out of milk. He cannot talk, and as a result, blows the chance to win $50,000.

"People won't know Alexander Hamilton and Aaron Burr," said the naysayers (who will again remain nameless).

"It's too esoteric."

"It's too contrived. I mean, it's a hell of a coincidence that the radio show just happens to call the biggest Aaron Burr freak on the planet. People won't believe it."

Figure 7.1   California Fluid Milk Processors Advisory Board (CFMPAB): "Chocolate Chip Cookie."

They did more than believe it. They loved it. We presented the idea to the groups using just a script (see Figure 7.4), making use of a mouthful of cookie which I, as moderator, was able to spray over the respondents for dramatic effect. Their response, once we had cleaned up, was very encouraging. First, their body language showed that they were completely sucked in by the story. They laughed, and at the moment our hero was desperate to talk but couldn't, you could almost see their mouths filling up too (like when you are really involved in a movie, and someone's underwater and you find you're trying to hold your breath as long as they do).

Figure 7.2   CFMPAB: "PB&J Sandwich."

They related to the feeling of peanut butter in your mouth without milk to wash it down; they related to the feeling of knowing the answer to a prize question on the radio (and not getting the chance to answer it); and they also enjoyed the absurdity of the whole situation. Far from distancing people through its potential logic flaws, as had been feared, it had engaged them on a visceral level. It was a powerful metaphor for the agony and frustration of running out of milk.

What did it say to people?

"Don't let this happen to you," said one man. "Let this be a warning!"

Figure 7.3   CFMPAB: "Cupcakes."

Aaron Burr

Visual: Guy in apartment. Apartment is the hovel of a man totally absorbed with the lives of Alexander hamilton and Aaron Burr. His walls are covered with curios to this effect. Rare books and portraits surround him. His radio is on. He is having a pbj sanwhich.

Radio: And today's question, "who shot Alexander Hamilton?" We'll see if anyone's home.

sfx ringing

Guy (under his breath): Aaron Burr, Aaron Burr.

sfx ringing

Guy: whooooooo! (takes bite of pbj picks up phone)

DJ: Good evening sir, today's 50,000 dollar give away question, who shot Alexander Hamilton...

(choking, whispering, trying to blurt out the answer through the peanut butter lodged in his throat. He runs to fridge, no milk)

DJ: Don't be shy...No need to be nervous here. Who shot...

Super: GOT MILK?

Figure 7.4   CFMPAB: "Aaron Burr" (first draft script).

Others began to talk about experiences in their own lives that felt like the one they had just "seen" through the script rendition. Almost all their descriptions involved frustration, and they were doubly painful because they were avoidable. "All you have to do is stock up, and it won't happen." It seemed like they were getting the intended message.

Some respondents mentioned the way that running out of milk "brings out the worst in you," and makes you do things, or at the very least *think* things, of which you are later ashamed. One man started to tell a story from one day the week before, when, as was his routine, he stumbled downstairs at 7A.M. to have his morning cereal. He got his plate, poured in the cereal, sliced up a banana on top, then went to the fridge to get milk. The carton was empty. A murmur rose up from the other respondents. Heads shook. Eyes rolled. They'd been there too.

"Someone had drunk it and put the damn carton back empty. I was so mad . . ." More sympathetic nods. They all had such a "someone" in their lives, too. The victim had been forced to eat the banana slices, encrusted with dry granola, had thrown the bowl of cereal away, and got to work hungry. It had, he said, ruined his day, because he had started in a bad mood that just never went away.

In a situation like that, offered another group member, "it (feels) so bad that you'd even steal it from your kid." The others laughed. Yes, it was that frustrating that you would go to almost any lengths. You were capable of bad things. "Never mind stealing it from your kid," said another. "I'd steal it from my *cat*." (The creative people watching the group from behind the mirror agreed that this scenario, conjured up by the respondents themselves, was pretty terrific. It was later to form the basis of a very popular TV commercial. See Figure 7.6.)

The groups were next shown the billboard ideas, and their appetites were seriously piqued. Almost universally, they were upset that I had none of the featured foods and glasses of milk available for immediate consumption.

The combination of the television ideas and poster executions seemed to be very powerful. Overall, the message that respondents told us they got from the incipient campaign was that they should check their refrigerators to make sure they didn't run out of milk. If there wasn't enough, they should go buy some. If there was, well, maybe they should have some right now. If I had wanted to cheat and pay respondents to say the right things, I wouldn't have dared to ask them to play back our strategy so closely.

Jeff Goodby put his finger right on the way that the campaign seemed to be working. "The food and milk together is pretty interesting. Then you take the milk away, and it gets even more interesting. But you give someone a *mouthful* of that food and no milk, then you've really got their attention."

A week after the focus groups, we conducted a small follow-up telephone survey among the respondents. We wanted to see what, if anything, they remembered from the discussion, and more important, whether they had done anything differently in relation to milk in the six or seven days that had elapsed since they were exposed to our first advertising ideas. It was the first time I had ever done anything like this, and I was somewhat nervous about establishing a very dangerous precedent. (Clearly, their responses could not be regarded as anything more than anecdotal, or directional, and I was concerned that not everyone would take them that way.) The feedback we got, however, was both surprising and encouraging. First, individual executions that had been presented were recalled with incredible clarity and detail, especially the "Aaron Burr" TV idea, and the outdoor campaign. And second, more than two-thirds of those respondents we were able to contact claimed that their milk-related behavior had deviated from the norm over the past few days.

One woman told us that she had surprised even herself. "Before I came to that research," she said, "I don't think I'd had a glass of milk in, oh, probably 15 years." She did use milk, but only as an ingredient in coffee and on cereal. "But on the way home," she continued, "I stopped at a Seven-Eleven and bought some chocolate chip cookies and a gallon of milk, and I actually drank a glass. And I've had one every night since." Hers was the most extreme conversion, but others noted that they had bought extra milk on normal visits to the store, "just in case," and a number of respondents reported unusual consumption of the featured foods, like brownies, peanut butter and jelly sandwiches, and cookies, as a result of cravings that they attributed directly to our discussion.

Even though we could make no projections based on what we were hearing, one thing was very clear—the idea was having *some* effect, on both consumption and purchase. Jeff Manning and his board were delighted and gave their

251

blessing for the campaign to go to the next stage. For the first year's production and media, it was a 25-million-dollar decision, and they made it based in part on the evidence of the agency's focus groups, but largely, I believe, on gut feelings. As people whose entire professional lives had been spent in the diary industry, but also as family men, the idea simply felt right. Which is even more remarkable considering that the 25 million dollars they were spending was their own money.

The outdoor campaign was produced almost exactly as concepted, the only difference being that the food shots became even more appetizing. It was supplemented by drive-time radio commercials, designed to remind people on their way home from work to stop off and stock up, just in case.

The majority of media dollars, though, went to television, where four commercials launched the campaign. The lead spot was the "Aaron Burr" story (Figure 7.5), rewritten and extended to 60 seconds in length, and with a depth of detail brought by director Michael Bay that made an already strong idea quite remarkable. In another 30-second spot, "Couple," a young man finds his partner in the kitchen late at night. "What's the matter, couldn't you sleep?" he asks. She gives him an icy stare in return. "Did you think I wouldn't find out?" she responds, icily. He knows he's been busted and makes the fatal decision to save himself by coming clean. The problem is, he doesn't know what he's supposed to have done. "Is this about the ring I gave you?" No response. "Listen, cubic zirconia looks just like a real diamond." She stares at her ring and glares at him. "Is this about my time in prison?" Now he's really in trouble. Another moment's silence, then she finally speaks. "You drank the last of the milk." He notices the bowl of dry cereal in front of her and smiles weakly (as if smiling's going to do him any good) as an announcer's voice says, "got milk?"

Another of the opening spots, "Baby and Cat" (Figure 7.6), was a tribute to the experience and wit of our deprived focus groups. A bleary-eyed man arrives at the breakfast table, greeting his baby, who is drinking milk from a bottle.

Figure 7.5 CFMPAB: "Aaron Burr" (TV).

Figure 7.6   CFMPAB: "Baby & Cat."

Figure 7.6   *Continued*

"Hey, boopy!" The family cat, drinking milk from a bowl, watches the guy as he pours out a bowl of cereal. He goes to pour on the milk, but all he gets is a trickle. He's desperate. He eyes his child's bottle, as the music to the gunfight in *The Good, the Bad, and the Ugly* begins. The baby returns his stare. The guy looks at the cat and her bowl of milk. The cat stares back. He has to do something, and his arm stretches out toward the baby's bottle. The baby leans back, protecting his milk, and under his breath mutters, "I don't think so, baldy!" The voice-over asks, "got milk?" and as the visual fades to black, the last sound we hear is the indignant hiss of the cat.

CLOSING THE DEAL

The relationship between milk and its companion foods also gave rise to some ideas outside the realm of mass media that gave the campaign a much greater presence than advertising alone could have achieved, and most important of all, brought the message right into the stores, where advertising usually cannot reach.

The first element was a promotional campaign, which was based entirely on companion food items, the logic being that if people would use more of that food, they would also be sure to use more milk. A number of national advertisers entered into joint promotions with the CFMPAB, including General Mills, Kraft General Foods, Nestle, Nabisco, and Mother's Cookies. Both General Mills and Nabisco cooperated on joint "got milk?" TV advertising with their Trix and Oreo brands (see Figures 7.7 and 7.8). In addition, General Mills allowed a poster to run with "got milk?" in place of its Wheaties logo (Figure 7.9), printed "got milk?" on millions of packs of Wheaties, Cheerios, and Total, and on-pack promotions on a variety of brands allowed customers instant redemption off their milk purchases.

In addition to the promotional efforts, point-of-purchase displays were set up in stores across the state, with "got

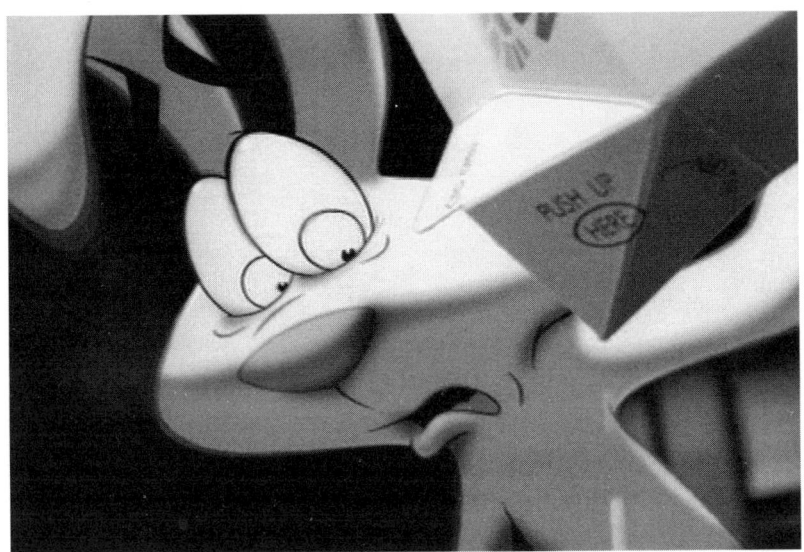

Figure 7.7 CFMPAB: "Trix."

Figure 7.8 CFMPAB: "Oreo Kane."

Figure 7.9   CFMPAB: "Wheaties Box."

milk?" shelf-talkers set up not in the milk aisle but in aisles that sold companion foods such as cookies and cereal (Figure 7.11). Small versions of billboards were placed on grocery carts (Figure 7.10), and in convenience stores "got milk?" ads were even placed on the floor to lead people to the dairy section. If all else failed, "got milk?" checkout dividers (Figure 7.12) were also produced, to provide a final reminder as the groceries made their last journey along the checkout conveyor belt.

Campaign Expansion

The campaign was launched in November 1993, and between then and the time of writing, in June 1997, Californians have been exposed to 23 different "got milk?" poster executions, 25 TV commercials, and 25 radio commercials.

Figure 7.10   CFMPAB: "got milk?" (grocery cart advertising).

Figure 7.11   CFMPAB: "got milk?" (shelf-talker).

Figure 7.12   CFMPAB: "got milk?" (checkout divider).

Milk deprivation has been used as a means of breaking a hardened criminal in an *NYPD Blue*–style interrogation and has caused a priest to forget who he is for a moment and beat up a faulty vending machine. In my personal favorite from the campaign, "Heaven" (Figure 7.13), milk was used as a device to torture an evil yuppie.

The spot opens on the aforementioned yuppie, talking into a cellular phone as he swaggers down the street. "Tom, can I make a suggestion?" he says, then shouts "YOU'RE FIRED" and barges onto a crossing, pushing past an old lady who falls down. He ignores her and doesn't see the huge truck bearing down on him. When he sees it, it's too late. The horn sounds, and the spot fades to black.

A white dove flutters, and a beautiful woman murmurs, "Welcome . . . to Eternity." Gentle music starts as the yuppie takes in his new surroundings, and the woman shuts a door. He is in a large, white, sunlit room. There are beautiful white flowers, a white goldfish swims in a bowl, and on a table is a large plate of enormous chocolate chip cookies. He takes a bite, takes one more look around, and laughs in delight. "Heaven!" he crows, heading for the refrigerator.

He opens the huge door, and inside there are hundreds of cartons of milk. "YES!" he exults, and punches the air. Funny . . . the first one is empty. And the second. And the third. His puzzlement turns to concern, then confusion, then panic as he pulls empty carton after empty carton from the shelves. "Wait a minute," he gasps, on his hands and knees in front of the fridge, "where am I?" His answer is supplied by the words, "got milk?" which just happen to be in flames.

Hungry and thirsty children and kittens have glared from billboards, daring passing motorists and pedestrians to stop and buy milk or risk the wrath of their own families, and radio commercials have evoked the horror of a "town without milk," ending their description of the inhabitants' misery with a gentle statement that "of course you've got milk in your fridge . . . don't you?"

Figure 7.13   CFMPAB: "Heaven."

The California Fluid Milk Processor Advisory Board

got milk?

Figure 7.13 *Continued*

GOT RESULTS?

This story began with the opening paragraph of an article written by Bruce Horowitz in the *Los Angeles Times* in May 1994, just six months after Californians had seen "got milk?" for the first time. Much to his and everyone else's surprise, he wrote, that "yawner," milk, was the subject of an advertising campaign that in a very short period of time, had "developed a near-cult following." The campaign had already passed the long-running "Does a Body Good" milk advertising in terms of awareness, and both qualitative and quantitative research revealed that "got milk?" was a favorite of *all* advertising campaigns among Californians. People even admitted that they were *affected* by it: Cravings were triggered for the featured foods, and trips to the store were triggered out of fear of running out.

This was very encouraging, but generations of milk researchers had probably been encouraged by the "I-should-drink-more-milk-than-I-do" numbers, too. And as Jeff Manning was always quick to point out, people liking the campaign and saying nice things wasn't going to keep him (or the agency) employed beyond the initial two-year commitment.

Fortunately for the CFMPAB, Manning, and ourselves, the anecdotal evidence we were hearing in our initial research was not just talk.

First, the number of Californian households claiming to use milk on a regular basis appeared to have increased. Nielsen's Household Panel showed an increase in milk's penetration from 70 percent of households in 1993 to 74 percent in 1995. This news came as a bit of a surprise, as it had really not been our intention to gain additional households; but if it meant additional volume, we would accept it without argument.

Our primary aim had been to persuade people who already consumed milk regularly to consume more, and prior to the campaign launch, we had commissioned a tracking study through MARC Research to monitor our target's milk usage. Between October 1994, before the advertising broke, and the end of 1995, the average number of occasions on which people claimed to use milk had risen from 3.9 times in the past 24 hours, to 4.3 times. Nielsen's Household Panel also showed increases in milk consumption over the previous year in all but the first two months of the campaign. Where California had previously trailed the rest of the United States in per capita and household milk consumption, it quickly overhauled the other states and has since extended its lead. As consumption in the rest of the United States continued to decline, it provided further confirmation that something different was going on in California.

In terms of milk *volume*, the intention of the CFMPAB from the start had been to stem the decline in their sales, which in 1993 were down 3.6 percent over the previous year. It soon appeared, though, that the campaign had helped to do more than stem the decline, as milk sales in California began to rise. In 1994, the first year of "got milk?", California Department of Food and Agriculture figures show that milk sales *increased* by 0.7 percent over the previous year — an increase of 5.2 million gallons, with a retail value of $13 million. This was the first increase in milk sales recorded anywhere in the United States in the last decade (or, for what it's worth, anywhere in the world). Sales in 1995 were down by a percentage point, in 1996 were up slightly over 1995, and in 1997, the campaign's fourth year, they appeared to yet again be on the rise. *Note:* The California Department of Food and Agriculture has revised its figures after identification of some errors in data collection, which means that some of these numbers may differ slightly from those previously released.

On the surface, those numbers may not appear very impressive, but if the previous steady decline is considered, the 1994 numbers alone represent a *swing* of 4.3 percent, or

33 million gallons, or $83 million. The California Milk Processors estimate that if the decline had remained unchecked (they compare their actual performance to a "nose dive" scenario, whereby they assume a continued 3 percent annual decline), they could have lost a total of 170 million gallons of volume between 1993 and 1998. I personally regard that scenario as too extreme, but it is quite possible that about 10 percent of their volume, or 75 million gallons, has been protected over the life of the campaign.

In the summer of 1995, the DMI (the body representing all dairy producers, or farmers, in the United States) decided, on the basis of the success of "got milk?" in California, to adopt the campaign to run nationally, with an $80-million annual media spend. They pay the CFMPAB a royalty to run their campaign, and the CFMPAB ploughs the money back into media. The DMI, incidentally, has subjected the campaign to extensive quantitative copy testing, which in almost all respects confirmed the findings of our own, less scientific (and much cheaper) qualitative research. They concluded that "got milk?" was "memorable and entertaining," "most likely to generate awareness and interest in milk," clearly communicated "need or strong desire for milk," and generated "increased expectations of drinking milk in the next week." The campaign consistently and greatly outscored control samples and historical milk databases on many key measures. Thank God for that.

In the first year that "got milk?" was broadcast nationally, milk volume increased by a similar amount to that seen in the campaign's first year in California.

"Got milk?" remains among the most popular advertising in the United States, with *USA Today's* Adtrack study ranking it as the second most popular campaign in America in March 1996. For the methodological reasons outlined in Chapter 3, I don't regard that as great cause for celebration, but as my dad likes to say, it's better than a poke in the eye with a sharp stick. And I suppose that while a sample representative of the population at large may be misleading for Isuzu or Porsche, it can't be that far wrong for a product as ubiquitous as milk.

One of the surest signs of a campaign's success in the real world is the degree to which it is able to enter popular culture, and "got milk?" has appeared unsolicited in cartoons and on popular television shows, like *Cybill*, *Mad About You*, *The Cosby Show*, and *The Tonight Show with Jay Leno*. On an episode of *Roseanne*, Roseanne poured an entire gallon of milk over her sister's head, then asked her if she'd "got milk?" In San Francisco, we've seen "got porn?" on signs on the outside of sex clubs, graffiti on the side of a bus where the not-too-substantial breasts of a well-known "waif" model had been covered with the words, "got milk?", and (my personal favorite) one of our copywriters recently spotted a billboard at a county fair, featuring a large picture of a goat and the line, "goat milk?"

The campaign has also been very successful from a merchandising point of view. My children wear "got milk?" baby clothes and drink from "got milk?" bottles. Adults too can wear the logo on their T-shirts and drink coffee from "got milk?" mugs. Sometimes I wonder whether it's gone too far (apparently, special shirts for nursing mothers were regarded as too much), but I must admit when I see the stuff in stores or on people I still get a little kick out of it.

One day, about three years into the campaign, Jeff Manning got a telephone call from someone at Mattel. He later admitted that he thought they must have dialed him by mistake, but it turned out they really did want to talk to him. Would he be interested, they asked, in allowing Mattel to produce a "got milk?" Barbie™ doll? Manning said that it took him all of about two seconds to make up his mind (of course, he said yes).

So, advertising really does work in some mysterious ways.

People often ask me what lessons can be learned from the campaign's success, and in many cases, what they really mean is, how can they do "got milk?" for *their* client? The answer is, they probably can't, any more than we could do "got milk?" for any other of our clients (or would even have done it for the California Milk Processors at a different point in time). A deprivation strategy such as that which provided the foundation for "got milk?" only works when not having the product creates a crisis, and for most products it would simply not be true. I suppose it could be said that running out of toilet paper at certain moments represents a crisis of massive proportions, but a deprivation strategy would not necessarily help any individual *brand* of toilet paper. An advertising idea, however powerful, cannot simply be painted over other categories, products, or consumers. It has to start from the inside and work out.

If there are any general lessons to be learned from "got milk?" they have more to do with the *approach* to the campaign than with the nature of the solution itself. I hope that the preceding description provides good illustrations of some of the more general points I have made throughout this book: that the best ideas result from the combination of many different points of view; that industry wisdom is sometimes not so wise; that research should not start with a blank sheet of paper but with hypotheses; that research needs to be as creative and expansive as the process of developing advertising ideas if it is to succeed in uncovering the truths of consumers' relationships with any product or category; and that the success of a research project is not directly proportional to its level of sophistication and expense.

The best research and strategic thinking in the world is absolutely worthless without a creative execution of similar stature. Indeed, the power of the strategic thinking of "got milk?" and many of the other campaigns mentioned in this book was not apparent until someone (not the planner, I must stress again) came up with a great creative execution. As my old boss in London used to say, "you don't have a strategy until you have an ad." Only a memorable advertising execution can prove that an abstract, intellectual strategic idea is capable of tangible, emotional execution and response.

Finally, the beauty of "got milk?" lies in its simplicity, and the simple, obvious solution is nothing to be ashamed of. As Albert Szent-Gyorgyi, the Nobel laureate biochemist, once put it, "Discovery consists of looking at the same thing as everyone else and thinking something different." And that is the essence of planning.

Acknowledgments

I would like to thank a number of people for their direct contributions to this book.

I wrote it for one reason, which was simply because Andrew Jaffe, the Executive Editor of *Adweek* magazine, and Ruth Mills, of John Wiley & Sons, asked me to. I would like to thank both of them for extending the offer and sincerely hope that they will not regret it. In particular, I would like to thank Ruth for her support, guidance, and feedback at every stage of the book's development. Thanks also to Linda Witzling and Monika Jain of John Wiley & Sons and Christine Ducker and Christine Furry of North Market Street Graphics.

My friend, Adrian Morgan, designed the jacket. Actually, he designed a lot of jackets, redesigned them, and started over once I changed the book's title. Thank you, Adrian, and please forgive me.

In addition to making my life easier and keeping me sane over the past four years, my assistant, Lynn Rubenzer, has provided invaluable logistic and creative support for this book. Without her help, I would have quite simply failed to complete it. Bess Cocke, the incomparable Ron Urbach, Ruchele Eisenman, and especially Michelle Lamphere provided the legal advice and attention to detail in the complex area of permission to reproduce advertising images that hopefully will protect me from litigation. Thanks also to Greg Martinez, Max Fallon, Suzie Watson, Suzee Barrabee, Michael Stock, Beau Bouverat, and Stacy Higgins, who produced the visual materials; to Scott Burns for his recollections and original scripts from the "got milk?" campaign; to Maria Thomas and Rachel Elgin, who helped track down some of my stranger and more elusive facts and figures; and to Bruce Gifford, for his endless supply of weird stories. Thanks also to Lionel Carreon and, again, Stacy Higgins for their help in compiling the credits.

Several other of my friends helped out in various capacities: Roger Williams provided encouragement and a much-needed explanation of the finer detail of publishing contracts; Mark Barden, Tim Hollins, and Jerome Conlon were willing to discuss new scientific theory and recommended much interesting reading material on the subject; and Kevin Dundas read my manuscript as I wrote it, suggested changes, and was prepared to read it again once I had made them. Without his feedback and enthusiasm for the project, I probably would not have finished.

I would also like to thank Jeff Goodby and Sue Smith of GS&P; Mary Carole Bahr, a student from the Ad Center at Virginia Commonwealth University; Professor Kathy O'Donnel from San Francisco State University; and Sheira Furse of Hewlett-Packard, for their helpful comments on what at the time I naively thought was my finished manuscript.

For giving their permission for me to include their advertising in the book, and for their support along the way, I would like to thank the following people: Stephen Palmer and Niall Murdoch of the British *Guardian* newspaper; Sean Clarkin of the Partnership for a Drug-Free America; Carol Eleazer and Diane Cantello of UNUM Corporation; Joel Ewanick of Porsche Cars of North America; Mary George of Bell Helmets; Dick Gillmore of American Isuzu Motors; Ken Mills and Julie Petrini of Polaroid; John Bartelme and Bob Fox of Foster Farms; Bruce MacDiarmid and Tina Salem of Chevys Fresh Mex; Jean Patterson of KPMG Peat Marwick; Signe Bjorndal of Norwegian Cruise Line; Jeff Manning of the California Milk Processors Advisory Board;

and Rhonda Ihrke and Pam Becker of General Mills. Too numerous to mention here are all the photographers, agents, actors, and models who gave me permission to use their work and likenesses, and who are all identified in the credits on page 288. Thank you all.

That is already a very long list of people, but I ask for your indulgence to allow me to step back from the book for a moment.

My only ambition, until I graduated college, was to spend the rest of my days teaching geography and coaching cricket in some rural English school. The fact that I'm now working in advertising never ceases to surprise me, never mind writing a book on the subject, so whether they meant to or not, I am very grateful to the following people who created the series of accidents that led to the book.

Without Toby Nash and Ivan Pollard, it would never have occurred to me to even apply for a job in an advertising agency. I *think* I should thank them for that. There are many other things I could say about them, but I'll save that for another book.

I would also like to thank the guy who turned down the trainee job at BMP in London in 1984, to become a stockbroker. I was fourth on BMP's list of three, so without him I would probably still be selling dog food from the trunk of my car. Whoever and wherever you are, I hope you survived the stock market crash in 1987.

At BMP I was fortunate to work with some truly remarkable people. Nick Hough opened the door to the agency's Courage business and a host of opportunities. Peter Field, Andrew Ockwell, and James Best trained me; and when Peter left to join another agency, it was James and Andrew who suggested that I might like to step into Peter's vacant planning job. That is how I inadvertently became a planner. David Cowan agreed to let me transfer into his department, despite the fact that I had a degree in geography, and Ross Barr, Chris Cowpe, and Paul Feldwick tolerated my continued presence there in later years. I would like to thank them all for the opportunities that they presented to me. To Chris Cowpe and Chris Powell I owe a special debt of thanks. They had the confidence to let me make a new business presentation after only two years in the agency, and after I had screwed that up, they let me make another. I know I wouldn't have let me do it. Thanks also to Tom Rodwell for the cricketing adventures and the realization that it was only advertising, and should never be taken too seriously. In that regard, this list would certainly be incomplete if it did not include Bill Lea and Derek Morris.

Many of the aforementioned were also instrumental in my move to the United States, to affiliate agency Goodby, Berlin & Silverstein. For that I must also thank Andy Berlin, who had the idea in the first place; Peter Jones, who helped arrange an intercompany transfer; and let's not forget my trusty immigration attorney, Richard Pettler, thanks to whom I have so far avoided deportation.

Jeff Goodby, Rich Silverstein, and Colin Probert hired me, and they and the other GS&P partners, Harold Sogard, Steve Simpson, and Robert Riccardi, continue to inspire and challenge me. Their collective philosophy is unique in our industry for its devotion to excellence, combined with true respect and affection for the people around them. Sure, people are hired at GS&P for the quality of their work and for their intellect, but also for who they are as people, and whether a six hour flight with them from San Francisco to New York would be an interesting and enjoyable experience. I know it is an environment that has encouraged me to do my best work, and for that I thank them and everyone else at GS&P with whom I have worked.

Hundreds of people have passed through the door of GS&P since I joined the agency in 1989, and all have changed the place in their own ways. I would like to mention four people in particular who really helped to establish planning: the creative teams of Steve Simpson and Tracy Wong; and David Page and Dave O'Hare, who, with their work for Chevys, the Northern California Honda Dealers, and Isuzu, proved to both the agency and the outside world that planning, when used correctly, could inspire, guide, and even save great creative ideas. Finally, at GS&P, I must give thanks to the planners themselves: Carole Rankin, Dan Baxter, Mary Stervinou, Irina Heirakuji, Jeffre Jackson, Kieran Darby, Linda Casey, Jo-Anne Fernando, Cathy Clift, Emily Reid, John Thorpe, Debbie Mobley, Laura Forman, Andrew Teagle, Kelly Evans-Pfeifer, Sue Smith, Barbara Borst, Diana Kapp, Josh Mandel, Pam Scott, Kari Marubbio, Rosemary Hallgarten, Maria Thomas, Rachel Elgin, and Margot Bogue.

Almost done. Stepping even further back from the book and work, I would like to thank three teachers who encouraged my interests in reading, writing, and acting, all of which seem to be useful in the advertising business. I was lucky to be taught English at the same time by two remarkable men: John Charlesworth, who set the highest standards imaginable and who, as he reads this, is probably shaking his head and wondering what happened to all the grammar I was taught, while making corrections with his trusty pencil; and Robin Gracey, who lent me *The Electric Kool-Aid Acid Test* and cast me in the lead role in my first big stage production. Robin, you were an inspiration.

The third of these teachers was my own father, David, who was the principal of my elementary school and taught me personally from the ages of 8 to 11. It was great, except that it was a small, rural school of only four teachers, another of whom was my mother, Bridgett. My mother was an exceptional teacher, but the presence of her and my father in the same building meant that whenever another kid got into trouble, I would be dragged out into the schoolyard and beaten up (by the kid, not my parents). But that taught me to fight dirty, and that, too, is useful in advertising.

My parents taught me the value of hard work, humility, and respect for others, as well as imbuing in me a spirit of independence. For all the opportunities you gave me, thank you both very much.

Finally (yes, finally), the most important thanks of all—to my wife and best friend, Lynda, who has moved 5,000 miles from her family, and endured the traveling, late nights, and bad moods that accompany a job like mine without complaint. Well, not exactly without complaint, but close enough for me to be a very lucky man. She supported my taking the time to write this book, even though we have, as of September 1997, a two-year-old son, Cameron, and a six-month-old daughter, Hannah (call myself a planner?), and there have been times when I would probably have been much better employed changing diapers and tidying the kitchen than typing. Thanks too to Cameron and Hannah for their ability to sleep at night. Without that, none of this would have been possible.

If the above list seems excessive, don't hold it against me. There are far too few opportunities in this life to say "thank you" to the people who have really made a difference, and I am delighted to be able to do so now.

Jon Steel
September 1997

Bibliography

The following is a selection of books and articles that have informed and inspired certain parts of this book. You will notice that very few of them are specific to account planning and research. I consider this a good thing.

Alexander, Christopher, et al. *A Pattern Language: Towns; Buildings; Construction.* New York: Oxford University Press, 1977.

Bendinger, Bruce, ed. *The Book of Gossage.* Chicago: The Copy Workshop, 1995.

————, ed. *The Copy Workshop Workbook.* Chicago: The Copy Workshop, 1993.

Bernbach, William. "Facts Are Not Enough." *Paper from the 1980 AAAA Annual Meeting.* New York: American Association of Advertising Agencies, 1980.

Bronowski, Jacob. *The Ascent of Man.* Boston: Little, Brown & Company, 1973.

Brown, Gordon, et al. *How Advertising Affects the Sales of Packaged Goods Brands.* Leamington Spa: Millward Brown, 1991.

Butterfield, Leslie, ed. *Excellence in Advertising: The IPA Guide to Best Practice.* Oxford: Butterworth-Heinemann, 1997.

Caples, John. *Tested Advertising Methods: How to Profit by Removing Guesswork.* New York: Harper & Brothers Publishers, 1947.

Capra, Fritjof. *The Tao of Physics.* Boston: Shambhala, 1991.

Capra, Fritjof. *The Turning Point: Science, Society and the Rising Culture.* New York: Bantam Books, 1983.

Channon, Charles. "The Difference Between Effectiveness and Efficiency." Speech delivered at the ADMAP/ *Campaign* seminar. London: March 1990.

Collins, James C., and Jerry I. Porras. "Building Your Company's Vision." *Harvard Business Review* 74, no. 5 (September–October 1996): 65–77.

Cowley, Don, ed. *How to Plan Advertising.* London: Cassell Educational Ltd./Account Planning Group, 1987.

———, ed. *Understanding Brands: By Ten People Who Do.* London: Kogan Page Ltd., 1991.

Delaney, Tim. "Planning: Are We in Need of a Reformation?" Speech delivered at the UK Account Planning Group, July 1988.

Feldwick, Paul. *A Brief Guided Tour through the Copy Testing Jungle.* London: The Account Planning Group, n.d.

Fortini-Campbell, Lisa. *Hitting the Sweet Spot.* Chicago: The Copy Workshop, 1992.

Gladwell, Malcolm. "The Tipping Point." *The New Yorker* (June 3, 1996): 32–38.

Hedges, Alan. *Testing to Destruction: A Critical Examination of the Uses of Research in Advertising.* London: Institute of Practitioners in Advertising, 1974.

Hopkins, Claude. *Scientific Advertising.* New York: Lord & Thomas, 1923 (Crown, 1966).

Jaworski, Joseph. *Synchronicity: The Inner Path of Leadership.* San Francisco: Berrett-Koehler Publishers, Inc., 1996.

Jungk, Robert. *Brighter Than a Thousand Suns: A Personal History of the Atomic Scientists.* New York: Harcourt, Brace & World, Inc., 1958.

Lodish, L. "The How Advertising Works Project." *Proceedings of ARF Key Issues Workshop on Marketplace Advertising Research.* New York: November 1991.

Machiavelli, Niccoló. *The Prince: And Other Political Writings.* London: Everyman/J. M. Dent, 1995.

Maclean, Norman. *A River Runs Through It.* Chicago: The University Of Chicago Press, 1976.

March, Robert H. *Physics for Poets.* New York: McGraw-Hill, 1996.

Morita, Akio. *Made in Japan.* London: William Collins Sons & Company Ltd., 1987.

Ogilvy, David. *Ogilvy on Advertising.* New York: Random House, 1983.

———. *Confessions of an Advertising Man.* New York: Atheneum, 1963.

Ohmae, Kenichi. *The Mind of the Strategist: The Art of Japanese Business.* New York: McGraw-Hill, 1982.

Peters, Tom. *Thriving on Chaos: Handbook for a Management Revolution.* New York: Harper Perennial, 1991.

Pollitt, Stanley. "How I Started Account Planning in Agencies." *Campaign,* (April 20, 1979): 30.

Popcorn, Faith. *The Popcorn Report.* New York: Doubleday, 1991.

Reeves, Rosser. *Reality in Advertising.* New York: Alfred A. Knopf, 1961.

Rosenblatt, Roger. *The Man in the Water: Essays and Stories.* New York: Random House, 1993.

Strean, Herbert, ed. *The Use of Humor in Psychotherapy.* Northvale, NJ: Jason Aronson, 1994.

Toobin, Jeffrey. "The Marcia Clark Verdict." *The New Yorker* (September 9, 1996): 58–71.

Watson, James D. *The Double Helix.* New York: Mentor, 1968.

Wheatley, Margaret. *Leadership and the New Science: Learning about Organizations from an Orderly Universe.* San Francisco: Berrett-Koehler Publishers, Inc., 1992.

Wing, R. L. *The Art of Strategy: A New Translation of Sun Tzu's Classic The Art of War.* New York: Dolphin/Doubleday, 1988.

Wright, Frank Lloyd. *An Autobiography.* New York: Horizon Press, 1977.

Index

Index

Credits

I would like to thank the following people whose expertise and talent made possible the advertising featured in this book, and whose support and permission enabled me to reproduce it.

Fig. 1.1   Title: "Points of View"
           Client: *The Guardian*
                    Marketing Director: John Gordon
           Agency: Boase Massimi Pollitt
                    Account Mgt: Peter Herd
                    Account Planner: Adam Lury
                    Copywriter: Frank Budgen, John Webster
                    Art Director: John Webster

Fig. 2.1   Title: "Long Way Home"
           Client: The Partnership for a Drug-Free America
                    Vice President: Amy Maximov
           Agency: Goodby, Silverstein & Partners
                    Creative Directors: Jeff Goodby, Rich Silverstein
                    Copywriter: Jeremy Postaer
                    Art Director: Jeremy Postaer
                    TV Producer: Cindy Fluitt
           Director: Jeff Goodby
           Talent: Robert Johnson (Kid)

Fig. 4.1   Title: "Bear & Salmon"
           Client: UNUM Corporation
                    VP, Corp. Adver.: Carol Eleazer
                    Dir., Corp. Adver.: Charles Hurdman
           Agency: Goodby, Silverstein & Partners
                    Creative Directors: Jeff Goodby, Rich Silverstein
                    Copywriter: Harry Cocciolo
                    Art Director: Jeremy Postaer
                    Account Mgt: Tom Hollerbach
                    Account Planner: Irina Heirakuji
                    Print Production: Suzee Barabee

Photographer: Galen Rowell/Mountain Light
Represented by Gary Crabbe (510) 601-9000

Fig. 4.2   Title: "Father & Child"
        Client: UNUM Corporation
                 VP, Corp. Adver.: Carol Eleazer
                 Dir., Corp. Adver.: Charles Hurdman
        Agency: Goodby, Silverstein & Partners
                 Creative Directors: Jeff Goodby, Rich Silverstein
                 Copywriter: Dave O'Hare
                 Art Director: Mike Fazende, Bob Pullum
                 Account Mgt: Tom Hollerbach
                 Account Planner: Irina Heirakuji
                 Print Production: Suzee Barabee
        Photographer: Michele Clement/San Francisco
                 Represented by Norman Maslov (415) 641-4376

Fig. 4.6   Title: "Kills Bugs Fast"
        Client: Porsche Cars North America
                 President/CEO: Frederich Schwab
                 VP, Vehicle Sales & Mktg.: Rich Ford
                 GM, Marketing: Joel Ewanick
        Agency: Goodby, Silverstein & Partners
                 Creative Directors: Jeff Goodby, Rich Silverstein
                 Copywriter: Bo Coyner
                 Art Director: Rich Silverstein, Todd Grant
                 Account Mgt: Julie Chandik
                 Account Planner: Irina Heirakuji
                 Print Producer: Max Fallon
        Photographer: Clint Clemens
                 Represented by Jae Choi (212) 206-0737

Fig. 5.1   Title: "Another Satisfied Customer"
        Client: Bell Sports, Inc.
                 President/COO: Mary George
                 VP, Helmet Mktg.: Graham Webb
        Agency: Goodby, Silverstein & Partners
                 Creative Directors: Jeff Goodby, Rich Silverstein
                 Copywriter: Paul Venables
                 Art Director: Jeremy Postaer
                 Account Mgt.: Brian Hurley
                 Account Planner: Mary Stervinou
                 Print Production: Max Fallon
        Photographer: Heimo/San Francisco (415) 621-8260
        Talent: Tom Crumb/Boom Models & Talent

Fig. 5.2   Title: "Ten Dollar Head"
        Client: Bell Sports, Inc.
                 President/COO: Mary George
                 VP, Helmet Mktg.: Graham Webb
        Agency: Goodby, Silverstein & Partners
                 Creative Directors: Jeff Goodby, Rich Silverstein

Credits

Copywriter: Paul Venables
Art Director: Jeremy Postaer
Account Mgt: Brian Hurley
Account Planner: Mary Stervinou
Print Production: Max Fallon
Photographer: Heimo/San Francisco (415) 621-8260
Talent: Caitlin Barrett/Gossett Entertainment Management

Fig. 5.3 Title: "Toy Store"
Client: American Isuzu Motors, Inc.
Dir. of Marketing: Dick Gillmore
Natn'l Adver. Mgr.: Chris Perry
Agency: Goodby, Silverstein & Partners
Creative Directors: Jeff Goodby, Rich Silverstein
Copywriter: Chuck McBride
Art Director: Chris Hooper
Account Mgt: Robert Riccardi
Account Planner: Kieran Darby
TV Producer: Ben Latimer
Director: Michael Bay
Talent: Chris Dollard (Father)/Abrams Artists, Doug Ely; Christopher
Loundsbury (Kid)/Helen Garrett Agency, Jim Garrett

Fig. 5.4 Title: "Grocery Carts"
Client: American Isuzu Motors, Inc.
VP, Marketing: Jerry O'Connor
Dir. of Marketing: Dick Gillmore
Natn'l Adver. Mgr.: Chris Perry
Agency: Goodby, Silverstein & Partners
Creative Directors: Jeff Goodby, Rich Silverstein
Copywriter: Scott Burns
Art Director: Erich Joiner
Account Mgt: Matt Seiler
Account Planner: Kieran Darby
Print Production: Suzee Barabee
Photographer: Duncan Sim
Represented by Michael Ash, CMP (212) 655-6500

Fig. 5.5 Title: "Dog"
Client: Polaroid Corporation
Dir. of Mktg. Comm.: Joanna Hughes-Brach
Grp. Mktg, Comm. Mgr.: Ken Mills
Agency: Goodby, Silverstein & Partners
Creative Directors: Jeff Goodby, Rich Silverstein
Copywriter: Bob Kerstetter
Art Director: Chris Hooper
Account Mgt: Robert Riccardi, Lisa Briggs
Account Planner: Kelly Evans-Pfeifer
Print Production: Suzee Barabee
Photographer: Hunter Freeman/San Francisco (415) 252-1910

Fig. 5.6   Title: "MOM/WOW"
            Client: Polaroid Corporation
                        Dir. of Mktg. Comm.: Joanna Hughes-Brach
                        Grp. Mktg, Comm. Mgr.: Ken Mills
            Agency: Goodby, Silverstein & Partners
                        Creative Directors: Jeff Goodby, Rich Silverstein
                        Copywriter: Al Kelly
                        Art Director: Mike Mazza
                        Account Mgt: Robert Riccardi, Lisa Briggs
                        Account Planner: Kelly Evans-Pfeifer
                        Print Production: Suzee Barabee
            Photographer: Hunter Freeman/San Francisco (415) 252-1910

Fig. 5.7   Title: "Architect"
            Client: Polaroid Corporation
                        Dir. of Mktg. Comm.: Joanna Hughes-Brach
                        Grp. Mktg. Comm. Mgr.: Ken Mills
            Agency: Goodby, Silverstein & Partners
                        Creative Directors: Jeff Goodby, Rich Silverstein
                        Copywriter: Harry Cocciolo
                        Art Director: Sean Ehringer
                        Account Mgt: Robert Riccardi, Lisa Briggs
                        Account Planner: Kelly Evans-Pfeifer
                        TV Producer: Jane Jacobsen
            Director: Kinka Usher
            Talent: Kenny Moscow (Architect)/Abrams Artists, Doug Ely; Taylor
                        Nichols (Architect)/Abrams Artists, Doug Ely

Fig. 5.8   Title: "Dog & Cat"
            Client: Polaroid Corporation
                        Dir. of Mktg. Comm.: Joanna Hughes-Brach
                        Grp. Mktg. Comm. Mgr.: Ken Mills
            Agency: Goodby, Silverstein & Partners
                        Creative Directors: Jeff Goodby, Rich Silverstein
                        Copywriter: Scott Aal
                        Art Director: Grant Richards
                        Account Mgt: Robert Riccardi, Lisa Briggs
                        Account Planner: Kelly Evans-Pfeifer
                        TV Producer: Jane Jacobsen
            Director: Kinka Usher

Fig. 5.9   Title: "Cop"
            Client: Foster Farms
                        President/CEO: Robert Fox
                        Dir. of Marketing: John Bartelme
                        Product Manager: Angel Ilagan
            Agency: Goodby, Silverstein & Partners
                        Creative Directors: Jeff Goodby, Rich Silverstein
                        Copywriter: Bob Kerstetter
                        Art Director: Tom Routson
                        Account Mgt: Greg Stern, Michelle Donald

Credits

Account Planner: Kieran Darby
TV Producer: Ed Galvez
Director: Marc Chiat

Fig. 6.1 Title: "Pilot"
          Client: Chevys Mexican Restaurants
                    President: Mike Hislop
                    Director of Marketing: Laura Brezner
                    Director of Marketing: Bruce MacDiarmid
          Agency: Goodby, Silverstein & Partners
                    Creative Directors: Jeff Goodby, Rich Silverstein
                    Copywriter: Steve Simpson
                    Art Director: Tracy Wong
                    Account Mgt: Marty Wenzell, Shannon Maher
                    Account Planner: Jon Steel
                    TV Producer: Betsy Flynn
                    Cameraman: Chris Routh

Fig. 6.2 Title: "Salsa"
          Client: Chevys Mexican Restaurants
                    President: Mike Hislop
                    Director of Marketing: Laura Brezner
                    Director of Marketing: Bruce MacDiarmid
          Agency: Goodby, Silverstein & Partners
                    Creative Directors: Jeff Goodby, Rich Silverstein
                    Copywriter: Steve Simpson
                    Art Director: Tracy Wong
                    Account Mgt: Marty Wenzell, Shannon Maher
                    Account Planner: Jon Steel
                    TV Producer: Betsy Flynn
                    Cameraman: Chris Routh
          Talent: Steve Simpson (Interviewer), Tracy Wong (Interviewer)

Fig. 6.3 Title: "Polygraph"
          Client: Chevys Mexican Restaurants
                    President: Mike Hislop
                    Director of Marketing: Laura Brezner
                    Director of Marketing: Bruce MacDiarmid
          Agency: Goodby, Silverstein & Partners
                    Creative Directors: Jeff Goodby, Rich Silverstein
                    Copywriter: Steve Simpson
                    Art Director: Tracy Wong
                    Account Mgt: Marty Wenzell, Shannon Maher
                    Account Planner: Jon Steel
                    TV Producer: Betsy Flynn
                    Cameraman: Chris Routh
          Talent: Steve Simpson (Interviewer), Dennis Flynn (Regular Guy)

Fig. 6.4 Title: "Fantasy"
          Client: Norwegian Cruise Line
                    President/CEO: Adam Aron

		VP, Marketing: Bruce Mainzer
		Dir. of Advertising: Signe Bjorndal
	Agency:	Goodby, Silverstein & Partners
		Creative Directors: Jeff Goodby, Rich Silverstein
		Copywriter: Steve Simpson
		Art Director: Steve Luker
		Account Mgt: Marty Wenzell
		Account Planner: Mary Stervinou
		TV Producer: Elizabeth O'Toole
	Director:	Carlton Chase
	Talent:	Britt Williams (Swimmer)/KSA, Michael Daly; William Burns (Cantina)/CED, Linda Jenkins; Lesley Baevis (Cantina)/CPC, Courtney Hanlon; Ron Kauk (Rock Climber)/Baldwin Talent, Lyn Baldwin.
Fig. 6.5	Title:	"There Is a Place"
	Client:	Norwegian Cruise Line
		President/CEO: Adam Aron
		VP, Marketing: Bruce Mainzer
		Dir. of Advertising: Signe Bjorndal
	Agency:	Goodby, Silverstein & Partners
		Creative Directors: Jeff Goodby, Rich Silverstein
		Copywriter: Steve Simpson
		Art Director: Steve Luker
		Account Mgt: Marty Wenzell
		Account Planner: Mary Stervinou
		Print Producer: Laurie Lambert
	Photographer: Herb Ritts	
Fig. 6.6	Title:	"Fantasy"
	Client:	Norwegian Cruise Line
		President/CEO: Adam Aron
		VP, Marketing: Bruce Mainzer
		Dir. of Advertising: Signe Bjorndal
	Agency:	Goodby, Silverstein & Partners
		Creative Directors: Jeff Goodby, Rich Silverstein
		Copywriter: Steve Simpson
		Art Director: Steve Luker
		Account Mgt: Marty Wenzell
		Account Planner: Mary Stervinou
		Print Producer: Laurie Lambert
	Photographer: Herb Ritts	
Fig. 7.1	Title:	"Chocolate Chip Cookie"
	Client:	California Fluid Milk Processors Advisory Board
		Chairman: Richard Walrack
		Executive Director: Jeff Manning
	Agency:	Goodby, Silverstein & Partners
		Creative Directors: Jeff Goodby, Rich Silverstein
		Copywriter: Jeff Goodby
		Art Director: Rich Silverstein
		Account Mgt: Tom Hollerbach, Michelle Donald

Credits

Account Planner: Jon Steel, Carole Rankin, Sue Smith
Print Producer: Michael Stock
Photographer: Terry Heffernan/San Francisco (415) 626-1999

Fig. 7.2 Title: "PB&J Sandwich"
          Client: California Fluid Milk Processors Advisory Board
                       Chairman: Richard Walrack
                       Executive Director: Jeff Manning
          Agency: Goodby, Silverstein & Partners
                       Creative Directors: Jeff Goodby, Rich Silverstein
                       Copywriter: Jeff Goodby
                       Art Director: Rich Silverstein
                       Account Mgt: Tom Hollerbach, Michelle Donald
                       Account Planner: Jon Steel, Carole Rankin, Sue Smith
                       Print Producer: Michael Stock
          Photographer: Terry Heffernan/San Francisco (415) 626-1999

Fig. 7.3 Title: "Cupcakes"
          Client: California Fluid Milk Processors Advisory Board
                       Chairman: Richard Walrack
                       Executive Director: Jeff Manning
          Agency: Goodby, Silverstein & Partners
                       Creative Directors: Jeff Goodby, Rich Silverstein
                       Copywriter: Harry Cocciolo
                       Art Director: Sean Ehringer
                       Account Mgt: Michelle Donald
                       Account Planner: Jon Steel, Carole Rankin, Sue Smith
                       Print Producer: Michael Stock
          Photographer: Dan Escobar/San Francisco (415) 777-0916

Fig. 7.5 Title: "Aaron Burr"
          Client: California Fluid Milk Processors Advisory Board
                       Chairman: Richard Walrack
                       Executive Director: Jeff Manning
          Agency: Goodby, Silverstein & Partners
                       Creative Directors: Jeff Goodby, Rich Silverstein
                       Copywriter: Scott Burns, Chuck McBride
                       Art Director: Erich Joiner
                       Account Mgt: Tom Hollerbach
                       Account Planner: Jon Steel, Carole Rankin, Sue Smith
                       TV Producer: Cindy Epps
          Director: Michael Bay
          Talent: Sean Whalen (Main Character)/Abrams Artists, Doug Ely

Fig. 7.6 Title: "Baby & Cat"
          Client: California Fluid Milk Processors Advisory Board
                       Chairman: Richard Walrack
                       Executive Director: Jeff Manning
          Agency: Goodby, Silverstein & Partners
                       Creative Directors: Jeff Goodby, Rich Silverstein
                       Copywriter: Chuck McBride

Art Director: Erich Joiner
Account Mgt: Tom Hollerbach
Account Planner: Jon Steel, Carole Rankin, Sue Smith
TV Producer: Cindy Epps

Director: Michael Bay
Talent: Jeff Austin (Dad)/Abrams Artists, Doug Ely, Amanda Elness (Baby)/Film Artists Associates, Ruth Devorin, Chelsea Elness (Baby)/Film Artists Associates, Ruth Devorin

Fig. 7.7   Title: "Trix"
Client: California Fluid Milk Processors Advisory Board
Chairman: Richard Walrack
Executive Director: Jeff Manning
Agency: Goodby, Silverstein & Partners
Creative Directors: Jeff Goodby, Rich Silverstein
Copywriter: Harry Cocciolo
Art Director: Sean Ehringer
Account Mgr: Michelle Donald
Account Planner: Linda Casey
TV Producer: Betsy Flynn, Cindy Epps
Director: Kinka Usher
Reproduced by kind permission of General Mills

Fig. 7.8   Title: "Oreo Kane"
Client: California Fluid Milk Processors Advisory Board
Chairman: Richard Walrack
Executive Director: Jeff Manning
Agency: Goodby, Silverstein & Partners
Creative Directors: Jeff Goodby, Rich Silverstein
Copywriter: Chuck McBride
Art Director: Todd Grant
Account Mgt: Suzanne Reeves
Account Planner: Sue Smith
TV Producer: Bob Wendt
Director: Kinka Usher

Fig. 7.9   Title: "Wheaties Box"
Client: California Fluid Milk Processors Advisory Board
Chairman: Richard Walrack
Executive Director: Jeff Manning
Agency: Goodby, Silverstein & Partners
Creative Directors: Jeff Goodby, Rich Silverstein
Copywriter: Harry Cocciolo
Art Director: Sean Ehringer
Account Mgt: Anne Salinas
Account Planner: Linda Casey
Print Producer: Michael Stock
Photographer: Dan Escobar/San Francisco (415) 777-0916
Reproduced by kind permission of General Mills

Fig. 7.13 Title: "Heaven"
          Client: California Fluid Milk Processors Advisory Board
                    Chairman: Richard Walrack
                    Executive Director: Jeff Manning
          Agency: Goodby, Silverstein & Partners
                    Creative Directors: Jeff Goodby, Rich Silverstein
                    Copywriter: Harry Cocciolo
                    Art Director: Sean Ehringer
                    Account Mgt: Tom Hollerbach, Michelle Donald
                    Account Planner: Linda Casey
                    TV Producer: Cindy Epps
          Director: Jeff Goodby
          Talent: Kenny Moscow (Man)/Abrams Artists, Doug Ely

I would also like to give special thanks to Stan Mack, for granting permission to reproduce the dialog of his "Out-Takes" cartoon featured at the end of chapter two. Stan Mack's graphic history book, "The Story of the Jews—The 4,000 Year Adventure," will be published by Villard (Random House) in 1998.

About the Author

Jon Steel graduated from Nottingham University in 1983 with a degree in geography, which still raises a laugh every time he admits it in public.

He applied to, and was rejected by, numerous London agencies before landing a job on Boase Massimi Pollitt's account management training program. (Actually, he was fourth on a list of three, but their first choice candidate took another job, and Jon was asked to make up the numbers.) After six months, much to his surprise, he was transferred to the planning department, where over the next five years he worked on advertising for Foster's Lager, Courage and John Smith's Ales, Sony, and the National Dairy Council. In 1988, at age 26, he was appointed to the BMP board of directors.

The following year, someone casually asked if he was interested in attending a meeting and talking about planning to "some hippies from San Francisco." Those "hippies" were Jeff Goodby, Rich Silverstein, and Andy Berlin, and that was the start of a relationship that led to Jon joining Goodby, Berlin & Silverstein as that agency's first Director of Account Planning in October 1989. He arrived to take up his new position two days after the October 17 earthquake, which is obviously why he's called a planner.

He has since built up the planning department to be one of the largest and most influential in American advertising, and the agency has grown from billings of $40 million in 1989 to $400 million today. Now a national force, the renamed Goodby, Silverstein & Partners handles clients as diverse as

Hewlett-Packard; the California Milk Processors ("got milk?"); Anheuser-Busch, Inc.; American Isuzu Motors, Inc.; Porsche Cars of North America, Inc.; DHL Worldwide Express; Foster Farms; Sutter Home Winery; Bell Sports, Inc.; SBC Communications; Nike; UNUM Insurance; Polaroid Corporation; and Pepsico.

In addition to his planning director responsibilities, Jon was named partner in 1994, and vice chairman in 1997. Outside the agency, he is a regular speaker at industry conferences and at Stanford University's School of Business, and is a board member of the advertising program at Virginia Commonwealth University. He also serves on the board of the Gorilla Foundation, helping with efforts to establish a permanent gorilla preserve on the island of Maui.

He has been profiled by *Adweek* as "West Coast Executive of the year," by *Advertising Age* as an "Agency Innovator," by *San Francisco Focus* as one of "the 100 smartest people in the Bay Area," and in 1995 was inducted by the American Advertising Federation into their Hall of Achievement for executives under 40 years of age. Clearly, none of them knew about his degree in geography.

Jon lives in Marin County, California, with his wife, two children, and too many cats.

Jon Steel
Goodby, Silverstein & Partners
720 California Street
San Francisco, CA 94108

Dear Jon Steel:

_____ I have read your book.

_____ It didn't suck.

_____ In the unlikely event that there is a second edi-

tion, here are some ideas for you to consider

including: _____

_____

_____

_____

_____

_____

_____ Here's a cool book you should read: _____

_____

_____ It sucked. There will be no second edition.

Don't give up the day job.

Name _____

Address _____

City _____State_____ Zip_____